University of
Chester CHESTER CAMPUS
LIBRARY
01244 513301

This book is to be returned on or before the last date stamped below. Overdue charges will be incurred by the late return of books.

RACE, CLASS AND EDUCATION

Race, Class and Education

Len Barton and Stephen Walker

CROOM HELM
London and Canberra

© 1983 L. Barton and S. Walker
Croom Helm Ltd; Provident House, Burrell Row,
Beckenham, Kent BR3 1AT

British Library Cataloguing in Publication Data

Race, class and education.
    1. Educational sociology—Great Britain
    2. Education and state—Great Britain
    I. Barton, Len   II. Walker, Stephen
    370.19'0941   LC191.8G7

ISBN 0-7099-0683-8
ISBN 0-7099-0684-6 Pbk

Printed and bound in Great Britain

CONTENTS

ACKNOWLEDGEMENTS

We are very grateful for the assistance given by Peter Sowden at Croom Helm and by Eileen Broughton in the preparation of the manuscript for publication.

The teaching bibliography included in section three of this volume has been compiled by Sally Tomlinson and we are grateful to her for undertaking this difficult but invaluable task.

Thanks also to Joan Barton and Sandra Walker for their criticisms and for their support.

LIST OF CONTRIBUTORS

Len Barton, Senior Lecturer, Education Department, Westhill College, Selly Oak, Birmingham, England.

Bruce Carrington, Lecturer, School of Education, University of Newcastle Upon Tyne, Newcastle Upon Tyne, England.

Jill Duggan, Research Assistant, Sociology Department, University of Liverpool, Liverpool, England.

Mary Fuller, Lecturer, Sociology Department, Bulmershe College of Higher Education, Earley, Reading, England.

Chris Mullard, Director of the Race Relations Policy and Practice Research Unit, University of London, Institute of Education, London, England.

Maria Noble, Research Assistant, Sociology Department, University of Liverpool, Liverpool, England.

Ken Roberts, Senior Lecturer, Sociology Department, University of Liverpool, Liverpool, England.

Sally Tomlinson, Senior Lecturer, Department of Educational Research, University of Lancaster, Lancaster, England.

Graham Vulliamy, Lecturer, Department of Education, University of York, York, England.

Stephen Walker, Principal Lecturer, Education Department, Newman College, Bartley Green, Birmingham, England.

Philip Wexler, Associate Professor, Graduate School of Education, Univeristy of Rochester, Rochester, New York, U.S.A.

Paul Willis, Research Fellow, Centre for Contemporary Cultural Studies, University of Birmingham, Birmingham, England.

RACE, CLASS AND EDUCATION

INTRODUCTION

Len Barton and Stephen Walker

The papers collected in this volume emanate from the
fifth Westhill Sociology of Education Conference
held at Westhill College, Birmingham in January,
1982.   The theme of this conference was 'Class,
Race and Gender', a theme selected because of its
obvious topical relevance for educationalists and
teachers.   Topicality, however, was not the only
factor which influenced the eventual selection of
this title.   More important was a feeling that
analyses of race relations in schools, of gender
relations and of class relations, though differing
in focus, make use of similar theories, descriptions
and approaches and that, consequently, there would
be great benefit in providing a forum within which
individuals interested in any of these areas could
exchange ideas.   In many ways, therefore, it is
unfortunate that, for publishing convenience, we
found it necessary to produce two separate
collections of conference papers, this volume and
the collection published by Falmer Press, 'Gender,
Class and Education'.   Papers in both volumes
explore concepts and raise issues which are equally
applicable to the analysis of both race and gender
relations and for this reason we recommend that
readers treat the Falmer collection as a companion
volume to this one.
     The Westhill Conference was formed with the
intention of providing people working in education
with different theoretical perspectives the
opportunity to enter into dialogue and critical
challenge.   It is not surprising, therefore, that
the papers in this collection are characterised by
attempts to develop theory, to critically examine
competing explanations and, sometimes, to refute
established beliefs about race and class relations
in education.   We do not apologise for this.

However, because a second intention behind the
Westhill Conference has been the establishment of
closer links between theory and practice in
education, we would like to devote this introduction
to an identification of some of the major issues
raised in the theoretical discussions in this book
and what we take to be the practical relevances of
these issues.

In terms of the development of our awareness
and understanding of racism and race relations in
Britain, the 1982 Conference took place at a
significant time.   It followed the publication of
the Rampton Report on the educational experience of
West Indian children, the riots which had broken out
in places like Brixton, Toxteth and Moss Side, and
the presentation to Parliament in November, 1981 of
the Scarman Report.   Thus, the Conference took
place against a background in which public attention
was being focussed in a particular way.   Both the
public events and the parliamentary reports had
served to inject a new urgency in discussions about
race and community relations in terms of the need
for a re-consideration of the nature of the struggles
which were emerging between different ethnic groups
and between certain members of the community and the
established order.   These struggles were depicted
in various ways.   On the one hand, descriptions in
some tabloid newspapers made use of terminology and
analysis (sic) through which the conflicts were
portrayed as mere expressions of lawlessness and
mindless urban violence, as products of the feckless-
ness and low social conscience of certain groups of
young people.   On the other hand, more sensitive
commentators, like Scarman, were at pains to build
a description of the struggles which incorporated
reference to the social context in which these
tensions had developed.

In the more developed portrayals of the
conflicts and tensions being expressed in multi-
racial Britain, the number of factors being used
to explain these struggles was increased.   Scarman,
for example, insisted that the Brixton disorders
could not be adequately understood solely through
reference to isolated factors like local unemployment, poor environmental conditions, misguided local
policing policy, police racism and moments of police
harassment, and the frustrations experienced by both
members and leaders of local communities when it
comes to seeking legitimate means for the resolution
of particular grievances - significant though each
one of these may be.   More importantly, Scarman

stressed the need to see these in complex interrelationship, an interrelationship shaped by more
general social conditions, and it was this emphasis
which led him to conclude that

> "The disorders were communal
> disturbances arising from a
> complex political, social and
> economic situation, which is
> not special to Brixton."

But how are we to understand this 'situation'?
What are the particular ways in which specific
instances of unrest, of struggle, of racism, can be
related to this understanding?   In our readings of
reports and commentaries about race relations we
keep getting forced back to these questions - and
these questions are not trivial.   It seems to us
that if we are to speak with assurance about issues
like the origins of community conflict, the nature
of racism, the constraints upon the conditions of
schooling, social policy and community care provided
for a multi-racial society, then we need a more
developed exploration of 'the political, social and
economic situation' in Britain and of the ways in
which this relates to race relations and to
institutional provision and practices.
     It would be naive to imagine that the kinds of
explanations we are calling for here are easy to
develop.   In the academic community of social
science alone, disagreement about ways of concept-
ualising politico-economic and social formations
and about the impact these formations have upon
day-to-day experience is fierce.   Nevertheless, in
this book several of the contributors make use of an
approach which seems to us to have considerable
strength in terms of the possibilities it provides
for clarification of the nature of the interplay
between social formations and individual behaviour,
or, more specifically, between the 'situation' in
which race relations in Britain are constructed and
enacted and individual's perceptions and practices.
     Summarised in a somewhat over-simplified way,
this approach involves an insistence that educational processes, (be they itemised as race and education, or gender and education or school and community
relations of a less specific nature), are
inextricably related to the conflicts in society
which arise through class struggle, through contests
between groups of people who occupy different
positions in the economic order.   Thus, the nature
of the 'situation' against which many writers would

set the acting-out of race relations in schools and the community, is given a particular edge. The 'situation' is inherently conflictual. One of the basic tasks, therefore, for analysts of social and educational processes becomes to delineate the links between the contest amongst class groups which is endemic in society and specific instances of cultural struggle. Of course, such a linkage is not a simple matter. It would be ludicrous, for example, to propose that the disaffection of certain black pupils in schools can be explained by drawing an easy parallel between this reaction and the frustrations and alienation of particular working-class children. The notion of 'struggle' is more sophisticated than to allow this kind of simple equation. Indeed, it incorporates the idea that although the class location of a particular group of people will condition the kinds of struggles in which they are involved, i.e., to conserve power or to challenge it, the outcomes of these struggles in terms of the cultural practices and preception they produce, are neither completely predictable nor wholly homogeneous. 'Struggle' is a dynamic concept and implies variation in the responses and reactions individuals construct, albeit variations contained within certain, crucial, class-specific boundaries.

The question arises, however, as to the particular benefits and applications which can be derived from the use of this approach. How might the employment of a conceptual framework which draws together class struggle and cultural practice serve to extend of understanding of issues to do with race and education and to promote various forms of action within this domain? It seems to us that the following points might be considered as an initial response to this question.

(1) One of the difficulties facing those concerned with race and education and with the development of educational policy for a multi-racial society is the formulation of what should be identified as the significant problem areas, the focal issues which arise in the field. At first glance this might seem a strange statement. Surely, there is no shortage of problems here - the problem of integrating pupils from different cultural back-grounds into schools, the problem of developing a curriculum which reflects cultural pluralism, the problem of the educational under-achievement of some ethnic groups and the problem of combating racism in schools and classrooms. However, careful inspection

4

of the way these concerns are expressed reveals a crucial weakness. This is that certain fundamental assumptions which have a bearing on how one perceives and responds to the problems are set aside in the very manner in which the problems are articulated. As expressed above, each problem leads to another. Integration to what purpose? A multi-cultural curriculum designed by which group? Improved educational achievement according to whose criteria? The elimination of expressions of racism as identified from whose vantage point? Essentially, then, the problems listed above would seem to be formulated in a manner in which it is taken for granted that we know and accept certain, basic, educational purposes and that the main difficulty in the area is to do with matching practice to purpose. But is it not the case that this taken-for-grantedness exacerbates the problems? The refusal to subject the prevailing assumptions about the nature and aims of education to critical scrutiny produces a built-in conservatism in debate in the sense that the problems are eventually seen as solvable within existing structures and frameworks through a process of accommodation or assimilation. Furthermore, once certain a priori assumptions about education have been accepted the problems are seen as temporary and isolated difficulties which emerge as a result of episodic dysfunctions, thus requiring piecemeal treatment for their solution.

The approach we have been discussing in this introduction has direct relevance here.
(a) Because the approach has a particular basis from which institutional life is seen as being conditioned by social conflict and this conflict is seen as having its roots in contests in and around production, the practices, the definitions and the policies manifest in contemporary institutional settings like the education system demand careful scrutiny and evaluation. Even if it is sometimes difficult to trace the particular origins of meanings and processes in education which have become routinised, the fact that these are recognised as the outcomes of certain moments of struggle in the past makes them open to re-examination of a particular kind. Whose interests do such interpretations serve? On what assumptions might such routinisations be based? Do existing patterns contradict the circumstances of contemporary educational ideologies and goals? And, quite crucially, what relationship do the interpretations,

routines and patterns of education have with the
established conditions of economic life? In short,
the emphasis is upon the relation between competing
interests and the conditions of social life. It is
important to stress, though, that we are not saying
that the use of an approach which gives prominence
to a consideration of the interests being served
through certain educational ideologies and practices
makes problems like cultural integration or fighting
racism in schools disappear. What it does do is to
add another dimension to the way these problems are
conceptualised. It brings to the fore a concern
to scrutinise the interests which are reflected in
definitions as well as within practices.
(b) The conceptual framework also has a bearing on
the consideration of policy-making in the field of
race and education. If, by using a conflict model,
it is argued that key social definitions will in
some way reflect the interests of dominant groups,
we must also inspect the ideologies embedded within
official policy proposals, government legislation
and educational prescription. Again, the question
of interest arises. Whose interests are reflected
in the definitions and interpretations on which
policy is based and whose wishes are served in the
details of particular programmes? This question
has implications at both a general and a particular
level. What is at issue here is not just the
question of how, say, the intentions of an
individual teacher developing literacy programmes
for black pupils relates to a wider educational
purpose. More significantly, perhaps, the whole
overall design behind multi-racial education is
brought back into debate. Here too, the issue
does beyond consideration of definitions and embraces
a concern to question the whole purpose of multi-
racial education — is it designed to realise democratic ideals or is it a more insidious form of
social control?

(2) The usefulness of the approach is not
confined to an inspection of current problems and
present policy. Indeed, perhaps the most
significant contribution it can make lies in the
insights it offers for our understanding of the
possibilities and mechanisms of change and it is
this application which is explored most fully in
this book.
The value of the approach in this respect works
at least two levels. Firstly, it provides a
corrective to certain forms of explanation in which

the impact of economic and cultural factors upon race relations in education has been depicted in an ultra-deterministic fashion. Though it is important to recognise that the approach is concerned with having the structural limitations on social relations carefully marked-out, it is equally concerned with an exploration of the ways in which individuals react to these conditioning parameters in creative, reflective response. Moreover, in emphasising the notion of struggle as a vital element in the construction of this response, attention is focussed upon an examination of the ways in which economic and cultural pressures are resisted and transformed at the level of individual and group interaction. What is needed now is careful documentation of the forms these challenges take so that those concerned with the vital task of intervening in educational processes can use such data to relate proposed interventions with challenges already being attempted. Secondly, the approach reminds us of the contradictory nature of social life. Resistance is not always successful. The possibilities people have to change the world are not limitless and the power dominant groups have to prevent change should never be underestimated. However, it may well be that by inspecting empirical instances of where cultural groups have both succeeded and failed in their efforts to construct a set of alternative interpretations and practices we can increase our understanding of the way power is both exercised and dealt with, an understanding which can be used in the evaluation and assessment of intervention programmes.

This last point is important. We are very conscious of the fact that, at present, many teachers are being subjected to a variety of contradictory pressures. On the one hand, it is being demanded that they do not shirk a responsibility to combat racism in schools. On the other, they are being asked to respond to this demand at the same time as they are being required to deal with cut-backs, higher teacher-pupil ratios, lack of equipment and an extension in their teaching role. In effect, then, their position as what Grace (1978) has called 'the mediators of contradictory expectations' is being made more apparent and less secure and it seems to us that unless this position is appreciated by those calling for educational change and unless assistance is given to teachers on ways of identifying and resisting the challenges of powerful, conservative pressure-groups, then the future is bleak.

(3) The caution voiced above is not unrelated to what can be described as a third benefit to be derived from the approach we have identified in this introduction. This is that it places an emphasis on the importance of the interrelationship between group life and individual action and thus reminds us that collective effort is essential if real transformations are to be achieved.

One of the perspectives embedded within the approach is that not only are social relations constructed out of the conditions which surround struggles over production but that such struggles are unequivocally contests between groups, between collectivities. The complex nature of production, the enormous problems associated with winning and holding control of this complex enterprise, the immense difficulties involved in managing and monitoring the ideologies which legitimate this control and, crucially, the fact that social production only takes place in association with others, combine to support this contention.

For us, this perspective has profound, practical implications. Individuals involved in combating racism in schools or society will need to relate their present efforts to an understanding of the historical processes of dominances, resistance and collective struggles which produced the very conditions in which they now operate. From such an historical perspective, especially when this is used alongside an appreciation of the nature of contemporary forms of collective assertion like the riots and conflicts in schools, these individuals must develop an understanding of both the power of collective action and of the strategies groups engaged in contest have adopted. But, most important for us, is the fact that the perspective serves to remind us that both racism in schools and conflict in the community are not simple products of isolated episodes or of individual interpretations and whims; rather, they are rooted in the well-established and deeply-entrenched institutional routines of group life. Strategies for change, therefore, must aim beyond the particular and the superficial and identify the fundamental bases of these routines as the essential target. It is the spirit of this last assertion which unites the writers of the papers in this book and although they do not always share the same interpretation of the general perspective they, nevertheless, have as a common concern a desire for radical reform.

INTRODUCTION

REFERENCES

Grace, G. (1978) Teachers, Ideology and   R.K.P.
The Scarman Report.   'The Brixton Disorders 10-12 April, 1981.
    Penguin Edition, 1982.
Walker, S. and Barton, L. (Eds.) (1982)   Gender, Class and
    Education, Falmer Press.

PART ONE

RACE, RESISTANCE AND COLLECTIVE IDENTITIES

INTRODUCTION

The writers of all the papers which appear in this
collection are strongly commited to linking analysis
of race relations and education with an exploration
of the possibilities and mechanisms of social change.
Such a linkage might be established in a variety of
ways.   However, as was noted in the editorial
introduction, a major concern in this book is with
how we might move from an analysis of the moments of
cultural resistance and collective struggle developed by different individuals and groups who live in
multi-racial educational and community settings
towards the construction of policies and strategies
aimed at reform.   Two particular aspects of this
question emerge as focal points of debate - discussion about how individuals struggling with established routines and structures identify with others who
are similarly motivated, and discussion about how
such groups develop a basis and a strategy for
resistance.   Clearly, both these discussions will
involve a consideration of other important issues
and questions.   It is important to recognise, for
example, that in both debates, processes of
identification and of resistance are recognised as
problematic and this recognition is developed in
many of the papers collected here.   However, we
have arranged the papers in this book in a framework
built around these two main focal concerns, not
because we think that they represent the only issues
of importance in an analysis of race and education
but because of the enormous significance they have
for the major theme of this volume - the accomplishment of effective social change.   The book, then,
is divided into two main sections, each of which
contain papers which reflect this separation in
analytical interest.   Each section begins with a
major theoretical paper in which the current state

of sociological debate about education and cultural
reproduction is reviewed. Whilst these reviews
encompass considerations which have relevance beyond
analysis specifically to do with race and education,
by extending our understanding of how cultural
reproduction through education is both achieved and
resisted, they provide a framework within which the
exploration of particular issues like racism and
race relations in education can be set in a location
which permits one to see how these concerns relate
to wider public and private·social problems.

      In this first section of the book a number of
interrelated themes are introduced. Perhaps the
most important one is the idea that adequate analysis
of the conditions which lead to problems like racism
in schools, unequal educational opportunity for
various ethnic groups and the alienation of pupils
who are constantly being reminded of their relative
educational failure, is unlikely to be achieved
unless more careful attention is paid to a consideration of the two points at which collective
struggles have impact upon schooling. Educational
systems and practices are not seen here as free-
floating, neutral phenomena but as taking their
major characteristics from the conditions which
emerge through collective struggle. These
conditions influence both the forms such systems
and practices take and the nature of the responses
individuals make to these forms. The idea, then,
involves a chaining in analysis; a linking of issues
concerning race and racism in school with the
cultural conditions of education which are themselves inextricably related to contests between
social groups and the outcomes of such struggles.
      One of the advantages of this basic approach to
analysis is that, by relating cultural <u>response</u> to
cultural <u>conditions</u>, the opportunity is created for
the development of a less deterministic view of the
impact of educational ideologies and processes.
This section contains three case studies by
Carrington, Tomlinson and Vulliamy, of ways in which
cultural responses to different aspects and forms of
schooling are made by individuals and groups in such
a way as to create observable social circumstances
which can not be accounted for through reference to
simple reproductionist or determinist theory. This
work stands in direct opposition to explanations of
the oppression of minority groups which uses a crude
<u>control model</u> and it provides evidence of the ways

in which subordinate race, class and gender groups
in educational contexts can construct sets of
practices which in some ways challenge the dominant
ideologies of the context and the established
routines.

Of course, to challenge over-deterministic
theory is not to suggest that schools are not
influential in the maintenance and transmission of
racist and oppressive ideologies.   Rather, it is
to argue that how these ideologies are interpreted
in the moments they are re-constituted and how they
are used by those individuals and groups to whom
they are being made available will vary according
to the cultural milieu drawn upon by the people
involved in this construction and usage.   As both
Carrington and Tomlinson observe, this will sometimes involve challenges of operational ideologies
being made by minority groups in education and it
will sometimes involve a process of accommodation
by such people.   The extent to which influential
ideologies constrain action or promote resistance
cannot be determined in advance of scrutiny of the
empirical conditions of such action and resistance.

This kind of scrutiny will need to be broad in
both scope and method.   There has been a tendency
in past investigations of issues relating to race
and education to focus upon isolatable ideological
mechanisms of schooling, like the curriculum, the
nature of social relations in school or the
pedagogical codes found in classrooms, and to
concentrate upon the impact of this single variable
upon the formation of cultural identities and of
attitudes to race and race relations.   These
mechanisms exert different kinds of influence but
are themselves underrelated - and as Carrington and
Tomlinson both show, the development of specific
collective identities is an intricate process
subject to the impact of a delicate network of
different ideological inputs and cultural responses
in complex combination.

A careful re-examination of the ways in which
messages about race and race relations carried
through the process of schooling shape group
identity and practice has a further advantage.
It allows for a critical comparison to be made
between the rhetoric used to support and justify
educational and community programmes designed to
democratise the form and content of these message
systems and the practical effects of such
programmes.   Tomlinson, for example, in her paper,
suggests that whilst rhetoric might suggest that

appeal is being made to meritocratic ideals in the educational and career-selection assessment of individuals from different racial groups, nevertheless, the impact of structural inequalities in the educational provision made for these groups (and on, therefore, their collective educational experience), means that, for many, the ideal cannot apply.

Being sensitive to the way in which minority groups form cultural associations around the resistances to educational processes individual members construct forces us beyond mere theoretical speculation about how educational systems work. An awareness of the existence of groups contesting, challenging and transforming prevailing practices inevitably means that, in reflecting upon how we might respond to such social movements, we are compelled to re-examine essential questions about the kind of educational system we want and the kind of society we wish to prepare children for through education. It is out contention that all four papers in this section explore issues of deep significance to such a re-examination.

MOVEMENT, CLASS AND EDUCATION

Philip Wexler

INTRODUCTION

My intention is to understand the relation
between movements of oppressed people, class
formation and education.   Education can work to
block the development of collective action.   Historically, its effects often have often been quite
the opposite;   education contributed to the development of collective action and revolt.   Despite this
history, we are now accustomed to thinking of
education in the post-industrial capitalist
societies as part of an established order, and
particularly as a social institution charged with
helping to sustain it.   In America, this has been
the prevailing view among revisionist historians,
radical economists of education, and of a vocal
liberal wing of the younger generation of curricularists.   The sociologists of education have, of
course, had their heads stuck in the mud as usual.
They continue their research business of individual
status attainment, despite declining rates of
academic return.
There are small signs that we are moving away
from a preoccupation with the documentation of
domination, in and through education.   The
discourse of liberal curriculum now labels 'vulgar',
'mechanical', or 'crude' any writing on educational,
social and cultural reproduction that does not
declare such processes contradictory, contested,
and even potentially transformative.   The
discourse follows liberalism also in its
participatory extensions;   it offers formal
equality to the reproduction of gender and less
often, of race.   The reproduction discourse has
its own coterie of critics. ` Their job is to
insist on the importance of the subject, conscious-

ness, and critical thinking.

In a series of recent papers (1981a, 1981b, 1981c) I have specified what I see as limitations of the language and imagery of reproduction. Perhaps this criticism remains unheard because it is stated too obliquely. I am now going to say it more directly and to also indicate why I think it needs to be said.

CRITICAL OVERVIEW

Much of the current thinking about social relations, as part of the effort to understand education socially, uses a surface language of Marxism but expresses a static organicist mentality. This organicism is an ideological aspect of the ruling group's own self-understanding. Conflict is tacked on to a static essentialist core. The conservative implications of this mentality are not vitiated by writing the phrase "class struggle" on it. The problem is that as the liberal curricularists introduce the language of Marxism into wider educational discourse, they are carrying with it an organicist baggage of a backward looking bourgeoisie. This baggage is revealed even in so-called "class analysis". The language and study of class is undertaken from within a social theory which misrepresents an historical production of social relations as fixed places within an order. No wonder it takes so long and seems so hard to reintroduce social dynamism - with props like "contestation" and "transformation".

There is the same problem in research: a conservative ideology works beneath the surface of a derived Marxism. Empirical educational studies are now encouraged to support the putatively critical paradigm and to cash in on empiricist academic currency. But the way in which faddish qualitative and ethnographic research is actually performed displays nothing practically critical - only the same abstracted fragmentation and ahistoricism as conventional technicist empiricism.

The theories of educational practice, pedagogy, which grow out of this work, are, beneath their radical veneer, fundamentally opposed to historical materialism. Transformative pedagogies are advocated. But they are abstracted from history, from place, and from the needs and purposes of concrete social groups.

In every domain - theory, research and practice - liberal curricularists unintentionally display the powerful hold of prevailing ways of thinking and the mixed ideological forms in which efforts at making change are represented. This transmission of prevailing modes of thought is not the result of the operation of some abstracted hegemony. Rather, it indicates the critics own lack of social self-understanding. I believe that it is the result of a failure to understand that the current critical discourse in education developed only in relation to successful collective action. The historic cultural basis of a critical approach to education in the United States is in the Black movement, in the Student movement, and increasingly, in the Women's movement, the Gay movement, the ecology, anti-nuclear and consumer movements. Liberal and critical work in American education that was made possible by historical, collective social action now develops a mode of analysis that does not place collective action at its center.

It is necessary to criticize the organicist structuralism - which alternatively calls itself reproduction theory, contested reproduction, and even simply the new sociology of education - because it moves understanding ever further from analysis of the social present and its possibilities. We will not be able to grasp the meaning of this present if we allow ourselves to be incapacitated by structuralist homilies, decontextualized ethnographies, and so-called liberating pedagogies.

The alternative is to understand how collective historical actors produce social life, and to specify the conditions under which the movements of some of these actors enable the formation of a class. I want to suggest what some of these collective movements are, what they are now doing in the United States, and whether there is some path of development occurring which indicates the possibility of class action capable of forming a central post-industrial class actor. I want to look at the present conjuncture in the United States from the point of view of collective action and to ask what the relation is of education to such action. The theoretical position which makes these questions possible is a general one. The questions themselves are conjucturally specific, as is my brief discussion of educational practice and of the research on high schools which students and I are now doing. But first we need to clear a little ground.

THEORY

REPRODUCTION, CLASS AND CRITICAL THINKING

Recent critiques of reproduction imagery in
education (Apple, 1981; Giroux, 1981) are
accomplishing what Merton (1957) did for functionalism; shedding its fundamentalism in order to
preserve its basic logic of analysis. Adding
terms like 'contested reproduction' or 'structural
autonomy' doesn't displace an organicist inte-
grationism that reifies historical action, and
enables social analysis to be formulated in a way
that naturalizes, as systemically necessary, the
practices of ruling groups. Reproduction theory
naturalizes the present. It wrongly accepts the
ruling groups' false claims that their practices
constitute a natural order. It disprivileges
the alternative view of social life as a collective,
conflictual, historical accomplishment. Reproductionism makes it appear as if social action takes
place only within some pre-existing order. For
Apple (1981; 36) for example, contestation and
resistance "occur on the terrain established by
capital". This reification of an historic social
accomplishment - the collective production of
social relations - is one of the ways that
reproduction theory redeems a naturalistic
organicist logic. Functionalist organicism merely
translated the earlier sacred justifications for
feudalism into the newer secularized language of
society. Reproduction theory translates this
social naturalisation into the language of Marxism,
maintaining the same social logic ("... a mode of
production", "attempts to reproduce the conditions
of its own existence...". Apple (1981: 27)).
    Apple following Hall, claims that reproduction
theory is not functionalist because reproduction
occurs, in part, through contestation and because
the society which is reproduced contains hierarchy.
What they both miss is that functionalism is a way
of thinking that accepts the ruling groups' social
victories and pronouncements of its hegemony as
social order. It accomplishes that acceptance by
reifying and naturalizing collective history as
systems operations. The way that this reification
works theoretically can be seen in the analysis of
social change.
    The possibilities of social change are thought
of as occurring against a given social order ("on
the terrain of capital"). Social change is not

understood as a path of development, as a goal-oriented collective process of realization in which the appearance of order is only the result of class conflict on the field of historical action. The theoretical result of the reduction of historic class conflict to contestation on the grounds of an evolutionary pre-existing social order is further revealed by the way in which the ensuing conflict is then understood. Class conflict is not theorizied and studied as a struggle over the forces of societal self-production, of all the social apparatus on the battlefield of recognizably shared cultural orientations. Conflict, in the logic of reproductionism, is reduced to "resistances".

The theoretical, empirical and practical reduction of class conflict to resistances has several effects. Conflict is limited to opposition as defined by the superordinate group, rather than as an expression of a group's struggle to realize its goals and identities. (For a parallel analysis, in the language of psychoanalysis, see Pinar, 1981). Opposing collective actions are reified as if "resistances" were things that could be easily identified, picked up, as it were, out of the conflict of historical groups. But, as E.P. Thompson (1978) has argued, so-called resistances need to be decoded, which means that they must be placed within an historically specific context of symbolic struggle. But the emblematic theoretical practice of organicism is not historical, but classificatory. Instead of decoding opposition by contextualizing it as an aspect of collective conflictual action, educationists do exactly the opposite. They substitute a fragmenting de-contextualized labelling for historic cultural analysis. They want to know which resistances are "reproductive" and which ones are "transformative" (Anyon, 1981b). In the absence of an historical cultural contextualization, a "de-coding", the analysis of resistances can become a naive imposition of naturalised definitions. Without symbolic contextualisation in collective struggles, resistance comes to be defined from the point of view of dominant groups. Resistance has, on the contrary, to be interpreted from the point of view of the formation and struggle of a subordinate group for ascendance; otherwise, it becomes a naturalised and reified label, unreflexively appropriated by educational researchers and complementary to a naive social organicism.

21

A second major theoretical assertion common among liberal curricularists is that, unlike the conservatives, they are performing a class analysis of education. In addition to the metaphors of resistances that occur on the contested terrain of an order, and the reproduction imagery that occludes the collective historical action of groups in conflict, they proffer a type of class analysis that first, reduces the meaning of class from that of a collective, historical actor to a location or place in an order, and then to that of a salient, static attribute describing group differences. Anyon's class analysis (1981b) is a good example. In relating class distinctions to school knowledge she not only reduces class to a location, but even further to a multidimensional set of attributes. The result is that class becomes an attribute which can be correlated with other attributes in a thoroughly cross-sectional way and in separation from other aspects of social relations. This is the customary practice by which conventional sociology removes the political meaning from the term "class". It eliminates from usage the meaning of class as an historical process of group formation in social antagonism. E.P. Thompson wrote of this practice: (1978: 147):

> From this (false) reasoning there arises the alternative knowledge of class as a <u>static</u>, either sociological or heuristic, category. The two are different, but both employ categories of stasis. In one very popular (usually positivistic) sociological tradition, class can then be reduced to literal quantitative measurement: so many people in this or that relation to the means of production....

This understanding of class as static relational attribute then becomes the basis upon which different attitudes and resistances develop. Like reproductionism, the discourse of static class analysis relegates collective action to an arti-factual product of society, denying that it is its dynamic constituent and formative process. It speaks of distinctions and resistances, but not of historical collective social action. Still, it scribbles "class struggle" across its covers.
Reproductionism is not without its critics. Giroux (1981) criticizes, without directly naming, the work of Michael Apple because he claims that it

pays insufficient attention to human agents,
consciousness, and critical thinking. He argues
against reproductionism for being "too passive",
and for neglecting the human capacity for reflex-
ivity, consciousness, dialectical reasoning,
emancipation and liberation. The irony of Giroux's
critique is that it too speaks the language of
Marxism (albeit the critical Marxism of the Frank-
fort school), while replicating the very discourse
which justified structuralist critiques of empty
humanism in the first place. What appears to be
an alternative to the natural order of feudalism,
an opposition to its reproductive static class
surface, belongs to the same mentality. It is
feudalism's transcendent face, its natural historic
partner, organicism's old friend - essentialist
spiritualism. Naturalism and spiritualism are
only an apparent difference within an ideological
sameness. They keep occluded an alternative
understanding of society: <u>society as the practial
material accomplishment of conflicting groups of
collective actors struggling for control of the
field of historic cultural action</u>.
     Giroux's alternative poses an opposition to
structuralist organicism, an individualistic
idealism which is really its historic complement.
Instead of static reproductionism, we are offered
subjectivity and human consciousness, but always
abstracted from any really human, concrete,
historical, class specificity. Isn't this the
same kind of talk as that of the Young Hegelians,
whom Marx ridicules in the <u>Germany Ideology</u>
(Giroux, 1981: 114)?

> It is my belief that the <u>notion of</u> the
> dialectic becomes important only with a
> commitment to the <u>notion</u> of emancipation,
> one that seeks to <u>liberate human beings</u> in
> both subjective and objective terms
> (emphasis added).

Borrowing consciousness from Gramsci, dialectic
from Kosik and pedagogy from Freire, Giroux manages
to reconstitute Marxism as individualistic
essentialism, by downplaying, in turn, class,
concreteness, and the cultural historical
specificity of practice. An alternative tradition
begins with the concrete historical struggles of
real groups of people through which society is
produced.

SOCIAL ACTION, SOCIAL MOVEMENT, CLASS

Preface

There are at least two general types of collective
action occurring in the U.S.   One is the
continuation of struggles recognizable from the
sixties and seventies - struggles of class, race
and gender which unfortunately are now more
familiar to us not as real movements of collective
action, but as static categories used in the
documentation of domination. The collective
struggles, particularly the Black and Women's movements, have, I suggest, now entered new and parallel
stages.   While displaying important general social
dynamics of collective life, the movements also
indicate possibilities of class formation, and of a
further possibility that a movement is now emerging
which can turn the prevailing social apparatuses of
management toward mass social self-production.   I
doubt that this last stage is imminent, but we may
at least wish to turn some of our scientific
energies toward its analysis.

A second type of social movement ordinarily
considered less progressive by radicals in the
Anglo-Saxon capitalist countries is the mass
religious movement that is a central fact of
contemporary American social life.   Movements of
so-called fundamentalist Christians are generally
conservative and may move further toward the right,
perhaps eventually even so far as supporting a
corporatist, fascist regime.   These movements,
perhaps not unlike the Christian sects of the
seventeenth century described by Christopher Hill
(1972), may yet have a role to play as historic
actors in social upheaval.   Religious movements
have been historically important in American social
ruptures, and more generally have played significant
roles in pre-industrial revolts and revolution
(Rude, 1980).   The first level of my inquiry then
is to develop an analysis which takes account of
these social realities, and, from an interested
point of view, interrogates their actual and
potential relation to education.

The second level of my inquiry is microscopic -
field analyses that I have been doing for the past
several months.   In our first work, we are trying
to use, as a guide to observation, the point of view
of historical collective movements.   We do not
simply look for expressions of these movements in
the schools (although they are there), but rather
we take the movement point of view practically.

That means that we are beginning to understand the lives of students as a set of paths of collective development and group formation. We see the operation of the repressive apparatus of the school as blockages to the paths of collective identity formation (Weiner, 1982). In its most developed expression this means class action. These sense-making activities, in society and school, are guided by a theoretical position.

Theory

I want to make three theoretical points to indicate the outlines of that position. The first point in this position is that in opposition to the model of a natural, hierarchical, evolutionary order (one qualified by categories like relatively autonomous structures and resistances), we propose a model of society as the product of social action. The social action perspective is particularly developed in the work of Alain Touraine. For Touraine, society is produced through social action. He writes (1981: 50, 25):

> ...nothing can be further removed from this self-production of society than the image of reproduction.... A society has neither nature nor foundations; it is neither a machine nor an organization; it is action and social relations. This idea sets a sociology of action against all the variants of functionalism and structuralism.

The second point is that social movements are quintessential representations of social action. Understanding social life depends less on mapping structural locations and more on grasping social dynamics of the historic movements which produce the relational patterns that ideology stabilizes for us as "order". Touraine writes (1981: 29):

> Social movements are not a marginal rejection of order, they are central forces fighting one against the other to control the production of society by itself and the action of classes for the shaping of historicity.

In developing the point that social movements are central, Alberto Melucci (1980: 199) contrasts the social action approach with traditional Marxism and functionalist sociology. Melucci (1980: 199):

Centering its investigations on the logic of
the system, it has underestimated the
processes by which collective action emerges,
as well as the internal articulation of social
movements (mobilization, organization,
leadership, ideology) and the forms through
which revolt passes in becoming a class
movement.

Like Touraine, Melucci highlights the importance of
analysing the path from one to another type of
collective action (Melucci, 1980: 200):

In order to extricate itself from this
theoretical impasse, the Marxist tradition
must, therefore, move from a structural analysis
of class relations and the logic of the
capitalist system towards a definition,
first, of class action, and then, of political
action. Reflection on social movements is a
crucial theoretical issue that cannot be
avoided.

The third point, following social action and
social movements, is class analysis. Adam
Przeworski (1977: 343) defines class analysis as:
"...a form of analysis that links social development to struggles among concrete historical actors."
Przeworski states the dynamic class movement
position quite plainly. (1977: 363; 377):

Classes are not given uniquely by any
objective positions because they constitute
effects of struggles (emphasis added) and
these struggles are not determined uniquely
by the relations of production. (emphasis
added)

Social relations are objective with regard to
processes of class formation only in the sense
that they structure the struggles that have
the formation of classes as their potential
effect.

Edward Thompson also argues against the
organicist view of class analysis, even more
strongly. For Thompson, classes are constituted
in the processes of movements of collective action,
conflict and struggle, and not as positions in a
grid, markers in the logic of natural evolution
(1978: 149):

26

...to put it bluntly: classes do not exist as separate entities, look around, find an enemy class and then start to struggle. On the contrary, people find themselves in a society structured in determined ways...they experience exploitation... they identify points of antagonistic interest, they commence to struggle around these issues and in the process of struggling they discover themselves as classes, they come to know this discovery as class-consciousness. <u>Class and class-consciousness are always the last, not the first, stage in the real historic process</u>. (emphasis added)

The point that class is an historically formed product of collective action and not a location in a grid of places, represents a disagreement about the character of social life and about the course of practical action. To take just a brief example, I see the analysis of social action in school as resistance which parallels a contested labor process as an <u>economism</u> of educational action. It represents an economist argument for class formation from the shop floor of the school. If it is then argued in reply that qualified reproductionism does not display a new economism of the school because it relates education not only to the labor process, but also to the state, it becomes even more evident how much reproductionism misses the point: <u>class formation is an historical process of collective movement in which education plays a role.</u>

Social structure is not assembled from bits and pieces of structuralist discourse about labor process and state. It is the real movement, constituent and resultant, of concrete historical collective action. The collective social movement cannot be made economic by talking about the labor process or made political by talking about state, and then made social by gluing these pieces together. On the contrary, in the earliest phases of the movement, class action, as Melucci writes (1980: 203): "...goes beyond the institutional limits of the system and challenges its fundamental relationships."

EDUCATION AND COLLECTIVE ACTION

From this point of view, the analytical task then becomes to understand education in relation to collective action. It is difficult to understand education as an aspect of the formation of a class

through historical collective action in part
because we are accustomed to theory as an ahistor-
ical formalism. For example, when I first began
this inquiry, I borrowed a general model of
collective action and proposed it as a model for
pedagogy (Wexler, 1981a). The paths beyond
abstracted formalism are an historical study of
collective action, describing conjunctural
specificity, and understanding the important role
which different kinds of educations have played in
the process of struggle, collective action, class
formation and social revolution.

I am not going to review here the relevant
historical work on collective action of Rude (1980),
Talmon (1969), Hill (1970), Gwynn Williams (1969)
and others except to say that if we are looking for
historical antecedents of collective action, we must
acknowledge first, that pre-industrial protest is
often stated in the language of custom, in the call
to restoration, and in the hope of millenial
upheaval - not within a liberal discourse. The
development of the discourses of protest has not been
historically limited to the mediation of liberalism.
In these historic collective struggles, education
has often played a central, and self-conscious role.

Again, I am going to scant description of the
relevant historical work, except to offer an
example from the American context about the
relation between education and collective action.
Revisionist description of American educational
history, which has provided an empirical justification of reproductionism and its continuing
documentation of domination, is itself now being
revised from the left. Julia Wrigley (1980) in
her history of public education in Chicago, shows
how educational policy, even in that highly
organized bureaucratic context, was the result of a
series of concrete historical struggles between
labor and business groups; not as revisionists
have argued an "imposition of reform" from above.
The unions, for example, while they may have lost
the major educational battle of Chicago, fought
for public schooling, held an educational ideology
quite different from the business view of education,
and one articulated to a wider process of class
struggle. Wrigley summarizes her detailed
empirical documentation (1980: 167):

> The image of a disordered mass of people on
> the bottom rungs of the society who were
> basically confused and uncomprehending and

lacked any sense of collective consciousness
or clarity about their political strategies,
is not borne out by the record of
educational controversies in Chicago.

The role of the popular societies in the
French Revolution, the Corresponding Society in the
making of the English working class, the labor
victories against the platoon school in Chicago,
provide no formula for the relation between
education and class formation.   But we may not
even be able to begin thinking about education as
an aspect of class formation unless we move away
from an abstracted imagery of educational
reproduction with, as I shall argue, its complementary quick ethnographies and dehistoricized
pedagogies - toward conjunctural analyses of social
movements.

A MOVEMENT PATH IN THE UNITED STATES?

Social movements can begin their development far
from the site of anything that is traditionally
recognized as "economic" or "political".   The
question of class formation and educational intervention is what will enable realization of a path
from cultural expression, in the domain of
consumption, for example, back toward questioning
a society's institutional apparatus of social
production?   The "new" social movements are
movements of identity, and not traditional economic
or political movements.   The "new movements", as
Melucci calls them, are not fighting directly
against the state.   Rather, they are attempting to
reappropriate identity from an encroaching apparatus.
They are the movements of the body, of personal
freedom in daily life, and integralist utopian
movements which aim to provide meaningful bases for
personal identity, often expressed in religious
languages.   These movements contain the possibility
of degeneracy to immediacy and terrorism.   But
they also provide a basis for developing a more
articulated sense of how and why it is worth
struggling on the social field for the stakes of
control of the resources of societal and self
production.   The path from that initial identity
politics to the struggle over society's stakes is
precisely the path of class formation.   What at its
present prospects in the U.S.?
     In the restorationist moment of the crisis,
there are indications of a common path of develop-

ment, for example, from within the Black and
Women's movements. Manning Marable (1980) traces
the recent path of the Black movement from a
liberal integrationist course of demands for equal
participation, through the appearance of various
expressions of the identity politics of Black
nationalism, to the current period of political
reaction and the ascendence of the "pro-capitalist"
politics of the Black elite (1980: 98).   What is
particularly significant about Marable's analysis
is the extent to which the failures of the movement
are not simply attributed to "hegemony", the "inner
logic of capital" or the "reproduction of racial
distinctions".   This imagery and language is
totally absent from Marable's view.   Instead, the
analysis depends on the actions of the movement
(1981: 176; 178):

> Each little formation was so concerned and
> involved with meeting the reformist needs of
> its primary constituency that most neglected
> to raise issues that transcended the narrow
> boundaries of ethnicity, sexual preference,
> neighbourhood control, etc.   Thus, the
> politics of particularism and self interest
> in the 1970s inevitably became the politics
> of chaos in the 1980s.

> What we must do in the 1980s is struggle
> together, along parallel lines of development,
> finding those points within our own agendas
> that promote common work...

While Marable now speaks of a "Common Program",
Betty Friedan writes of a "second stage" (1981).
Friedan describes an historically parallel development from the politics of equal participation,
through the politics of identity and separatism
through the present reaction, to a "second stage".
This stage, may involve men and will "...transcend
the battle for equal power in institutions..." and
"...will restructure institutions and transform
the nature of power."   Insisting on women's
fight in both the family, broadly defined, and
workplace, Friedan, argues for the convergence of
gender needs, and urges a consequent struggle
against a common enemy.   Obviously, neither
Marable nor Friedan speaks for a unified movement.
But they do speak from a history of identity
politics, for a common program, which, I believe,
is a step toward the movement of the whole.

I am not going to offer here an analysis of the
new American religions (Robbins and Anthony, 1980),
any more than of the Black, Women's, Gay, ecology,
anti-nuclear and consumer movements in the United
States.   But I do wish to draw attention to these
movements, and to urge an analysis of their developmental paths from the standpoint of class formation
and educational intervention.   Rather, I want to
describe the second level of my inquiry, one that
is framed by a critical sociology of action.

RESEARCH

Marxist Ethnography
The scientific value of traditional fieldwork is
that in the activity of reflexive immersion, the
fieldworker can interpretively re-present or read
the discourse of a culture in a way that is an
advance beyond the members' own meanings (Geertz,
1973).   It is a reading which does not partial the
cultural gestalt into a series of variables, nor
scant the integrity of the cultural formation.
    The irony of current so-called Marxist ethno-
graphies and qualitative researches is that they
abandon this traditional methodological organicism
in favor of an imitative display of unquantified
positivist variable analysis.   While the language
of the analysis is vaguely anthropological, its
logic is that of the ordinary quantitative
correlational study typical of bourgeois sociology.
This logic is simply the selection of an independent
variable, for example, in Anyon's recent study,
class, which is then plotted against a series of
differences in school knowledges.
    Interrelation of events within the setting,
description of the interpretative work of the
researcher in making sense of the structure and
her/his own relation to it, and to the categories
of the members, becomes totally unproblematic in
this type of abstracted correlational approach to
fieldwork.   Its real political and scientific
effectivity is the work of naturalisation.   The
interpretive practices and methods of making sense
used both by the members and the observers are
described rather than de-constructed.
    The micro-naturalisation which is performed
by combining structural abstraction and interpretive agnosticism, negates the potential value
of ethnography as a de-reifying interpretive
practice.   A field study which does not examine -
not for a single moment - the external and internal

31

general conditions of its own production, and the
methods by which it actually accomplishes the
production of an account, does something. What it
does is to diminish the capacity for interpretation,
which is the "subjective" aspect of the work of
de-commodification.

TOWARD AN ALTERNATIVE RESEARCH PRACTICE

I think that, even within the academy, some research
is still possible. Despite the market pressure for
the intensification of the rate of academic production, the advantages of the traditional field
study can perhaps still be redeemed. Its virtues
are that it is an occasion for both the contextualization of observed relations, and for the
reflexive articulation of the interpretive
practices both of members and researchers. The
ethnographic study can be a way to avoid the fragmenting consequences of variable analysis, enabling
the developing of an interpretive cultural, rather
than naturalised, understanding of social interaction. It affords the opportunity for complex
and nuanced interpretation.

In our current analysis of schools, we are
just in the process of discovering the structure
that enables us to understand as we say colloquially,
"what is happening here?"; to answer the question
which we ask people, "what are you doing?"; and,
particularly, to then pursue our theoretical
interest - which is in the methods of collective
identity formation and the processes of structurally
conditioned methods of patterned social withdrawal
and disaffection. Just in doing that, we have
come to appreciate the complexity of the school.
We are struck by the patterned mixture of social
forms borrowed and blended from other domains of
social action, and the complexity and range of the
discourses through which the antagonistic and
complementary groups struggle over the realization
of their cultural orientations during the practice
of the accomplishment of the order of the school.
We are discovering the struggle over the social
resources of interaction, in which the power of
identity formation through language, esteem and
approval is itself being fought over - and the
interactional methods through which the production
of a valued social identity is collectively
accomplished.

We are beginning to understand the political
systems of school, by which I mean at least to know

how the administrative mediation of collective
cultural action occurs; to recognize what are its
stratifying and controlling practices; and to see
how groups build their collective insurrections for
purposes of self-management. We are trying to
understand how they are thwarted, blocked in their
collective efforts at self realization, by those
who control the resources and social means of
realization. We are not studying the students'
behaviors as abstracted resistances, and then
putting them on the old punch cards of our minds to
later sort them into reproductive or non-reproduct-
ive ones. We are studying their collective struggle
for the social and cultural stakes through which they
product their lives, in their historically unique
specificity.
We are studying the school economically. This
does not mean that we are trying to count up points
in favor or against so-called correspondences with
alienated workplaces, although we are certainly
aware of the world of adult work since so many of
the young people we are studying split their time
between the school and work settings. Rather,
studying the school economically means we are trying
to understand the social organization of production
in the school itself; to understand how the work
of the school is accomplished, collectively by the
different groups; and to discover what the
relations are between their accomplishments.
All this takes some time and cautions us
against advertising quick findings. Our work makes
us wary of reports about correlations between knowledges or about types of youth subcultures,
particularly when they are abstracted from the
conflictual socially organized production of the
school as a whole. We accept with Hebdige (1979)
and Willis (1977) the importance of subcultural
styles and the importance of the visual codes. But
we are no more willing to acknowledge the unified
signifier for the individual than we are to
substitute the system of reproduction for collective
action, or fragmenting correlations for the con-
textual meaning of the social totality. In time
we shall have more to say about "what is happening"
in some American high schools.
Yet, this is still far from a research
alternative because it is not a fully articulated
intervention. We are not self-consciously helping
the blocked groups to mobilize their cultural
resources for the purposes of collective self-
realization. While we give off sparks of any

33

strangers' awareness to be shared by the participants, we stand, fundamentally, in a relation of
spectatorship to them, and not as committed inter-
locutors of their collectively evolving practice.
We are not representing to the groups the nature of
their struggles (Touraine, 1981: 142). The more
we stand in this relation of spectatorship to these
groups, the longer we refuse their demands for
reciprocity under the guise of "objectivity", the
more we model for them, in our practice, the social
form of the spectator as the exemplar of bourgeois
science. Yet the possibility of representation for
the purposes of realizing collective action is no
fantasy. Our "subjects" are asking for our help
in the process of their own identity formation and
collective mobilization. "We really want to have
your feedback," they say, in a currently administrative language. "How you doing? Find out
anything yet?" "I'll be interested to know what
you think of this...sometime." The request for
reflexive knowledge comes from those furthest
articulated in their struggle for self-determination
against the apparatus controlled by the dominating
groups. For the time being though, our research
group avoids the intervention. Perhaps we can
partial out the demand for everyday practice into
the compartment of pedagogy.

PRACTICE AND PEDAGOGY

So great is the experienced need for conscious
collective action and the formation of social movements from cultural movements and of classes from
social movements, that well-meaning liberal
educators, myself included, rush to market with
packaged and dehistoricized plans for educational
interventions into class formation, which we then
call pedagogy.
    One educator (Anyon, 1981: 131) writes,
without a hint of hesitation: "...the theoretical
model of transformative pedagogy developed here is
one that is equally applicable to all such
settings." Another (Giroux, 1981: 81) reiterates
the importance of "a pedagogy of critical thinking",
and "radical pedagogy". This attempt to discover
the "transformative pedagogy" in general, without
regard to the specific historical conjuncture, the
level of collective development, or the specific
needs of a particular group, completes the dis-
placement of historical collective practice. It
finally and ironically removed education from the

34

specific collective historical process of class formation, by making it a _universal_ "radical" pedagogy.

I am not going to add to this current compilation of pedagogical formulae. But I do want to indicate one front of the educational struggle in the United States - the very existence of public schools. Everyday newspapers report more school closings, under the pretext of demographic decline, a pretext revealed by the parallel decline in educational services within schools and the intensification of the workloads of teachers. These school closings are related to other developments, including the return of more extensive corporate involvement in education, as well as an increasingly developed private, corporate educational apparatus. In recent work (Wexler, Whitson and Moskowitz, 1981) we tried to interpret some of these tendencies, as a corporately supported solution to the contradictory demands placed upon the production of labor-power. But, I now think that the deschooling possibility has to be analyzed more squarely within the general shrinkage of the social service and public sector, in the United States. One effect of this is that the possibilities for the communicative development of an awareness of a common plight among these groups is being reduced with the reduction of the public and social, to the subjective formation of private life and the objective destruction of whatever existed of the bourgeois public sphere. Under these conditions, both the skills which the school has still to offer and its very publicness as a site for collective communication are being destroyed. The specific conjunctural polarization and the possibilities of class formation suggest, as a basic educational politics, the need to defend the very existence of public education.

The current relation between education and collective action is a contradictory one: educational fragmentation and splintering of social groups portended by such possibilities as the voucher system, precisely contradicts the development of unifying tendencies that are indicated by political expressions such as Marable's "common program" or Friedan's "second stage". The fragmentation which counteracts unifying possibil-ities of collective action (such as the Solidarity march of this fall, led by the labor establishment, and the resurgence of anti-nuclear demonstrations within the United States, as well as in Europe) is

also occurring within the school, with an intensification of tracking, sorting, and procedures of
collective social segregation.   We are trying to
understand these educational practices of fragmentation that occur, while the most articulated social
movements move again toward unity and solidarity.
We are studying the meaning of the new "minimum
competency tests" (Whitson, 1982) the medicalization
of differences as learning disorders (Bart, 1982)
and the continuing language of sexism in children's
textbooks (Moskowitz, 1982).   We are not denying
the sorting, tracking and dominating procedures that
are used in the schools, but we are trying to
understand them in relation to the historical context
and the developmental paths and needs of contending
groups.   I think that we are going to be forced to
pay increasing attention to educational practices
that more directly articulate with the needs of
particular collective movements.

Postscript

We are not now, nor ever should have been,
surprised when ruling groups represent their
interests and activities as general and as natural.
That is one of the oldest weapons in the struggle
for power.   But when people who say they are
Marxists, or liberals, unwittingly begin to
introduce naturalising and generalising languages
and practices which cover over the specifying and
collectivising intellectual work which we have been
doing, it is necessary to criticize their actions.
The path of class development requires a rejection
of reification and naturalisation at every turn.
     We are not going to realize ourselves, to
deeply increase our self-capacities by shouting
for "optimism", but only by engaging in practices
which affirm our own self-management and self-
production.   It is in the combination of the
struggle toward class and the everyday development
of self-determinative power in relation to
collective life that we are going to become who
we are.   For the time being, we might begin by
not advertising ourselves as the organic intellectuals of the working class and to better wonder how
we can cease operating as the labor aristocracy of
the academies.

REFERENCES

Anyon, J. (1981a) 'Schools as Agencies of Social Legitimation', in *Journal of Curriculum Theorizing*, 3:2, Summer, pp. 86-103.

Anyon, J. (1981b) 'Social Class and School Knowledge', in *Curriculum Inquiry*, Eleven, 1, pp. 3-41.

Anyon, J. (1981c) 'Elementary Schooling and Distinctions of Social Class', *Interchange*, Volume 12, No. 2-3, pp. 118-132.

Apple, M.W. (1981) 'Reproduction, Contestation and Curriculum: An Essay in Self-Criticism', in *Interchange*, Volume 12, Nos. 2-3, pp. 27-47.

Arnot, M. and Whitty, G. (1981) From Reproduction To Transformation: A British View of Recent American Work, May, unpublished manuscript.

Bart, D. (1982) The Differential Diagnosis of Special Education: Managing Social Pathology as Individual Disability, unpublished manuscript.

Fitzgerald, F. (1979) *America Revised: History Schoolbooks in the Twentieth Century*, Boston, Toronto: Little, Brown and Company.

Friedan, B. (1981) *The Second Stage*, New York: Summit.

Geertz, C. (1973) *The Interpretation of Cultures*, New York: Basic.

Gintis, H. (1980) 'Communication and Politics: Marxism and the "Problem" of Liberal Democracy', in *Socialist Review*, No. 50-51, Summer, pp. 189-232.

Giroux, H. (1981) *Ideology, Culture and the Process of Schooling*, Philadelphia: Temple University Press.

Hebdige, D. (1979) *Subcultures: The Meaning of Style.* London: Methuen.

Hill, C. (1972) *The World Turned Upside Down: Radical Ideas During the English Revolution*, New York: Viking.

Marable, M. (1981) *Blackwater: Historical Studies in Race, Class Consciousness and Revolution*, Dayton, Ohio: Black Praxis Press.

Marable, M. (1980) 'Black Nationalism in the 1970s: Through the Prism of Race and Class', in *Socialist Review*, No. 50-51, Summer, pp. 57-108.

Melucci, A. 'The New Social Movements: A Theoretical Approach', in *Social Science Information*, 19, 2, pp. 199-226.

Merton, R. (1957) *Social Theory and Social Structure*, Glencoe: Free Press.

Moskowitz, E. (1982) "Why Did the Little Girls Grow Crooked?', Images of Females in Elementary School Reading Texts, unpublished doctoral dissertation, University of Rochester, New York.

Nisbet, R.A. (1965) *Emile Durkheim*, Englewood, New Jersey: Prentice-Hall.

Pinar, W.F. (1981) 'Gender as Curriculum Text: Notes on Reproduction, Resistance, and Male-Male Relations', unpublished manuscript, University of Rochester, New York.

Przeworski, A. (1977) 'Proletariat into a Class: The Process of Class Formation from Karl Kautsky's *The Class Struggle* to Recent Controversies', *Politics and Society*, u, No. 4, pp. 343-401.

Rifkin, J. and Howard, T. (1979) *The Emerging Order: God in the Age of Scarcity*, New York: C.P. Putnam and Sons.

Robbins, T. and Anthony, D. (eds.) (1981) *In Gods We Trust: New Patterns of Religious Pluralism in America*. New Brunswick: Transaction.

Rude, G. (1980) *Ideology and Popular Protest*, New York: Pantheon.

Talmon, Y. (1969) 'Pursuit of the Millenium: The Relation between Religious and Social Change', in McLaughlin, B. (ed.) *Studies in Social Movements: A Social Psychological Perspective*, New York: Free Press.

Thompson, E.P. (1978) 'Eighteenth-Century English Society: Class Struggle Without Class?', in *Social History*, Volume 3, No. 2, May, pp. 133-165.

Thompson, E.P. (1966) *The Making of the English Working Class*, New York: Vintage.

Touraine, A. (1981) *The Voice and the Eye: An Analysis of Social Movements*, Cambridge: Cambridge University Press.

Weiner, Richard R. (1982) 'Collective Identity-Formation and Social Movements', *Psychology and Social Theory*, No. 3 (in press).

Wexler, P. (1981a) 'Structure, Text and Subject: A Critical Sociology of School Knowledge', in Apple, M.W. (ed.) *Cultural and Economic Reproduction in Education: Essays on Class, Ideology and the State*. London: Routledge and Kegan Paul.

Wexler, P. (1981b) 'Body and Soul: Sources of Social Change and Strategies of Education', in *British Journal of Sociology of Education*, Volume 2, No. 3, September, pp. 247-263.

Wexler, P., Whitson, T. and Moskowitz, E. (1981) 'Deschooling by Default: The Changing Social Functions of Public Schooling', in *Interchange*, Volume 12, Nos. 2-3, pp. 133-150.

Whitson, T. (1982) 'Validity and Due Process in Political Uses of Testing', unpublished paper, University of Rochester, New York.

Wilkinson, P. (1971) *Social Movements*, New York: Praeger.

Williams, G.A. (1969) *Artisans and Sans-Culottes: Popular Movements in France and Britain During the French Revolution*, New York: W.W. Norton.

MOVEMENT, CLASS AND EDUCATION

Wrigley, J. 'Class Politics and School Reform in Chicago',
    in Zeitlin, M. (ed.) *Classes, Class Conflict, and The
    State: Empirical Studies in Class Analysis*. Cambridge,
    Mass.: Winthrop, pp. 153-171.

SPORT AS A SIDE-TRACK. AN ANALYSIS OF WEST INDIAN
INVOLVEMENT IN EXTRA-CURRICULAR SPORT

Bruce Carrington

Nine years ago Harry Edwards made the poignant
reference to black athletes as 'the twentieth
century gladiators for white America', in a
critical commentary upon the overrepresentation of
blacks in American sport (1).   There are signs of
a similar development occurring in contemporary
Britain where, during the past decade, there has
been an upsurge of black involvement in sport at
every level.   Much prominence has been given by
the mass media to the achievements of athletes of
Caribbean descent - such as Daley Thompson, Sonia
Lannaman, Justin Fashanu, Garth Crooks, Viv
Richards, Maurice Hope and many others - who have
made considerable inroads into several amateur and
professional sports, in particular, track and field
events, soccer, boxing and cricket.
    It is not surprising, therefore, that a number
of studies undertaken in British Secondary Schools,
have revealed that West Indians are more likely to
participate in extra-curricular sport and to play
in school sports teams than pupils of other ethnic
groups (2).   From the evidence available, it would
seem that West Indians are set to become 'the
twentieth century gladiators' for white Britain!
    This paper is primarily concerned to analyse
West Indian involvement in school sports teams.
From the standpoint that this phenomenon cannot be
'read' simply in biologistic or naturalistic
terms (3), Section I of the paper attempts to explore
the interrelationships between West Indian school
failure, the apparent success of this group in
school sport and their structural position in the
social formation.   In Section II, the preliminary
findings of an ethnographic study undertaken in a
multi-racial, urban comprehensive school, are
presented.   The paper concludes by addressing some

40

of the policy implications raised by the research.

I - RACE, SCHOOLING AND SOCIAL REPRODUCTION

Despite various state interventions to curb
racism and offset racial disadvantage, the
structural position of West Indians in Britain has
barely altered since the initial phases of
immigration.   If anything, it has deteriorated.
The bulk of the West Indian population - along with
a substantial part of the Asian population - entered
this country during the '50s and early '60s as a
'reserve army of labour' to fill the low status,
often menial occupations, formerly spurned by the
indigenous workforce during a period of full
employment and economic expansion.   The subsequent
recession and crisis of capital accumulation in the
'70s and '80s have served to consolidate their
largely secondary position within a segmented
labour market.   Black workers, especially the
young have continued to face higher levels of
unemployment than their white counterparts.   Furthermore, widespread discrimination in the labour
market has also ensured that those West Indians who
are 'waged' have remained concentrated in the
unskilled and semi-skilled strata of the working
class (4).   In Britain, as in the United States,
sport would appear to be <u>one</u> of the few spheres
where blacks (albeit a tiny minority) have been
able to gain legitimate success.
        The education system has played a major part
in maintaining the apparently immutable position of
black workers in the class structure and labour
market.   Whilst it is acknowledged that credentials
per se neither guarantee entry to the labour market
nor access to positions within the occupational
structure, they nevertheless function as a 'screening
device' and as such may be regarded as an essential
pre-condition of entry to certain forms of work.
In view of this, therefore, it can be argued that
the education system, by facilitating West Indian
academic failure, has not only legitimated the
exclusion of this ethnic group from all but the more
menial forms of wage labour, but during a period of
mass unemployment, has legitimated their exclusion
from the labour market altogether.
        The massive underachievement of West Indian
pupils, from primary through to tertiary stage, has
been well documented and needs little elaboration
here.   West Indians tend to be overrepresented
among the poorer readers in primary schools, fare

much less well than their Asian and white peers in
'C.S.E.' 'O' and 'A' level examinations, and are
markedly underrepresented on full time degree
courses.   Several policies and practices within
education have been identified as variously contributing to the educational disadvantage of this
ethnic group.   These include:- the reluctance of
the D.E.S. (until recently) to acknowledge fully
'racially-specific' forms of educational disadvantage or to pursue 'racially-explicit' policies;
the non-representation, misrepresentation or
devaluation of black culture, history and language
through ethnocentric and/or racist curricula,
school tests and pedagogy;   the use of culturally-
biased and inaccurate assessment and selection
procedures resulting in the placement (and mis-
placement) of West Indian pupils in non-academic
streams and Special Schools;   racism within the
teaching force itself (5).   It is proposed to
focus upon this latter 'determinant' of West Indian
academic failure, because it is hoped to show it is
also a critical causal factor in the apparent
success of this ethnic group in extra-curricular
school sport.
     It is not surprising, given the history and
structure of British society that many teachers
should operate with - either wittingly or
unwittingly - racist frames of reference, or act
and behave in a manner which could be judged as
racist in terms of its consequences and effects.
In this paper, racism is viewed as a body of ideas
rationalising and legitimating social practices
which reinforce an unequal distribution of power
between groups usually (but not always) distinguished in terms of physical criteria.   Notwithstanding this, however, it should be noted that it
is not strictly possible to talk of racism in the
singular, or to abstract if from its social and
material context.   The forms taken by racism vary
considerably.   Whereas, on most occasions, it
surfaces at the level of commonsense;   on others,
it surfaces in the form of a 'worked-out' ideology,
such as biologism (6).   Racism is variously pre-
missed upon beliefs, presuppositions, preconceptions
and misconceptions, forms of augumentation and
'theories' about the biological and/or cultural
superiority of one racial group and the concomitant
inferiority of others.   In general terms, I endorse
the characterisation of racism outlined by David
Wellman in <u>Portraits of White Racism</u>.   Emphasising
racism's materiality, that is its social dimension,

he states:-

> Racism has various faces; it manifests itself
> to the world in different guises. Sometimes
> it appears as "personal prejudice" which, it
> is argued here, is really a disguised way to
> defend privilege. Other times racism is
> manifested ideologically. Cultural and
> biological reasons are used as rationalizations
> and justifications for the superior position
> of whites. Racism is also expressed
> institutionally in the form of systematic
> practices that deny and exclude blacks from
> access to social resources (7).

Later in the same account Wellman stresses that
racism is expressed in both subtle and crude terms,
and that racism may be regarded as having both
intentional and unintentional forms. He notes:-

> The essential feature of racism is not host-
> ility or misperception, but rather the
> defence of a system from which advantage is
> derived on the basis of race. The manner in
> which the defence is articulated - either with
> hostility or subtlety - is not nearly as
> important as the fact that it insures the
> continuation of a privileged relationship.
> Thus it is necessary to broaden the
> definition of racism beyond prejudice to
> include sentiments that in their consequence,
> if not their intent, support the racial
> status quo (8).

As Rampton and others have indicated, whilst
few teachers are consciously or deliberately racist,
there are many who are sub-consciously or unintentionally racist in outlook and behaviour. It is
well known that teachers generally operate with
preconceived notions about the patterns of
behaviour and levels of ability of different
categories of pupil, and these stereotypes (which
may relate to race, class or sex) not only influence
teachers' attitudes and behaviour towards the
category in question, but also the curriculum
content and teaching style selected. In the case
of racial stereotyping, there are indications that
teachers are more likely to view West Indian pupils
in prejorative terms and compare them unfavourably
with their Asian or white peers. Teachers, it
would seem tend to regard West Indians as a problem-

atic group - disruptive, aggressive, unable to concentrate, poorly motivated and with low academic potential. Moreover, whilst teachers often underrate West Indian academic potential, they are more likely to stereotype this group as having superior physical and practical capabilities and have higher expectations of their potential in areas such as sport, drama, dance and art (9). The submission of the National Association of Headteachers to the Rampton Committee in April 1980 gave explicit articulation to the stereotype, sparking off a furore among sections of the West Indian Community, who were reported as being 'horrified' and 'appalled' by the nature of Heads' evidence. The Association claimed:-

> If there is a difficulty of cultural identity among second generation West Indians, there is also much to counterbalance that deficiency including their natural sense of rhythm, colour and athletic prowess (10).

What effect do such stereotypes have upon pedagogical practice? As Maureen Stone has argued in The Education of the Black Child in Britain, they not only prompt teachers 'to cool out' black pupils and divert them away from the pursuit of credentials but may also provide a rationalisation for West Indian pupils in the non-academic bands receiving 'a watered down curriculum'. Her research suggests that in some schools black pupils are being encouraged to devote time and energy to ethnically specific cultural pursuits, such as steel bands, during the normal timetable, when they already have very heavy commitments in extracurricular sport. She notes, referring to the Head and many of the white teachers in a London comprehensive school:

> They were, as far as they were concerned, doing their best to encourage West Indian cultural forms in school; since West Indians performed best in sport it made sense to encourage them to succeed in an area where they were competent. To the black teachers it was simply the school confirming the old racial stereotype: 'Music and Sports that's all we're good at' was the way one of them put it to me. They saw black children being seduced into activities which were

immediately rewarding but carried no prospect of future advancement, and to them it was ironic that this was done in order to give the black children identity and improve their self esteem through their own cultural forms (11).

The growing involvement and apparent over-representation of West Indian pupils in school sports teams, as indicated by the research of Sargeant, Wood, Beswick and Jones (12), not only lend support to Stone's argument, but also, appear to confirm the anxieties of many West Indian parents and community leaders that schools are sponsoring black academic failure by channelling black pupils away from the academic mainstream and into sport.
Whilst stereotypes held by teachers of West Indian pupils undoubtedly perform a critical function in facilitating this channelling, account must also be taken of other related factors when analysing black involvement in school sport.
In common with certain other curricular and extra-curricular activities (e.g. Steel Bands, Black Studies, drama, etc.) sport may provide the school with a convenient and legitimate side-track for its disillusioned black low achievers, for whom schooling may have little or no relevance. In this sense, the school may utilise black sports involvement as a social control mechanism; a means of 'gentling the masses' and curbing, containing or neutralising pupil disaffection and resistance to schooling. Black pupils, therefore, may be encouraged by teachers to promote their sporting abilities in the earnest hope that success in one sphere of school activity will compensate for failure in most others. Hal Lawson's observations about the role of physical activities in American ghetto schools would appear apposite to the situation in Britain. He notes:-

> Commonly, they are employed as devices to compensate for academic tasks and as an arena in which 'motor minded' students may enjoy some success. In either instance, social control, not education, appears to be the concern (13).

Whilst there is probably a growing number of disaffected black youth in British schools who recognise that they are being processed for marginal positions in society and the labour market

45

and who reject all aspects of schooling, including
extra-curricular sport, there are, nevertheless,
many others who are prepared to co-operate with
channelling.   Their reasons for doing so will vary.
Some, like the 'Mainstreamers' studied by Barry
Troyna, may underplay their ethnicity, reject the
oppositional features of black culture, and seek to
gain social acceptability by promoting their
academic or athletic abilities at school (14).   In
contrast, it is likely that other West Indian pupils
will look upon sport as providing an opportunity to
'colonise' one major area of school activity and
make it their own.   Undoubtedly, there will be some
who will have internalised the stereotype of black
physical prowess and athletic superiority, or who
identify with (and in certain cases seek to emulate)
the achievements of prominent black sports personal-
ities such as Fashanu, Hope et al.   As Kew has
argued, these athletes, as symbols of black success,
now constitute 'significant others' for many black
youth in Britain (15).   Furthermore, with conventional routes to status blocked, some young blacks
(in common with some of their white working class
peers) may hold unrealistic aspirations of a career
in professional sport and look upon it as providing
an alternative to menial wage-labour or the dole
queue, and a means of escape from the 'ghetto'.
Insofar as opportunities for social mobility via
sport are extremely limited and, as Cashmore,
Gallop and Dolan and others have argued, only a tiny
minority of the most able and talented youngsters
ever gain a place in the sporting elite (16).
Sport can be regarded as providing this section of
youth with little more than an 'imaginary solution'
to problems which at the concrete level remain
unresolved.

II - HILLSVIEW COMPREHENSIVE SCHOOL - A CASE
STUDY (17)

Edward Wood and I have explored these and related
issues for a period of sixteen months at Hillsview,
an 11-16, mixed comprehensive school, located in a
declining inner urban area in Yorkshire.
      Hillsview was selected for investigation
primarily because of its ethnic composition.   We
felt that since the Asian population of the school
was relatively small, it would be easier to make
direct comparisons between West Indian and white
pupils.   There are nearly one thousand pupils at
Hillsview (4% Asian, 32 West Indian, 64% white).

SPORT AS A SIDE-TRACK

The School has a teaching staff of 55. Of these
is one Asian teacher; the remainder are white.
     Formerly a secondary modern, built in the
1950s, Hillsview has an S.P.S. designation and
many of the characteristics associated with that
status. The School serves a 'rough' working class
neighbourhood. Its catchment area comprises of a
run-down interwar council estate and several streets
of decaying 'two up, two down' Victorian terraces.
Most of the men in the locality are employed as manual workers in the textile, chemical and engineering
industries. With opportunities for female employment in the area restricted, few of the women, with
children at the School, are waged. In April 1981,
it was estimated that about 22% of the white pupils
and 35% of the black had fathers who were out of
work. Hillsview's pupils have a grim present and
face the prospect of an even grimmer future as
youth unemployment mounts, and as opportunities for
apprenticeships and unskilled work in the locality
steadily diminish. The School has a reputation
for being 'rough' and 'tough' which extends far
beyond its immediate catchment area. Teachers in
adjacent schools appeared to view their Hillsview
colleagues with disdain. Many parents too - even
those with modest aspirations for their children -
were highly critical of the School. As Donalyn,
an Easter leaver remarked:

> My mum thinks this school is rubbish. She
> wanted me to go to Brampton cos it's not
> so rough and has a better reputation for
> work and behaviour.

     Hillsview School does not have a distinguished
academic record and, as a whole, could be
considered to be underachieving for West Indian and
white pupils alike. The overall attainment levels
for West Indian pupils were nevertheless found to
be depressed in relation to those of their white
peers. Of the 1980 school leavers, for example,
only 2% of West Indians and 4% of whites obtained
five or more 'O' level passes or their C.S.E.
equivalent. Moreover, the proportion of each
ethnic group achieving less than five but more than
one 'O' level pass (or C.S.E. grade one) was 21% in
the case of West Indian pupils and 35% in that of
whites. These ethnic differences in attainment
were especially pronounced amongst male pupils.
     The aim of the research was to capture some-
thing of the 'lived experiences' of pupils and

teachers in an institutional setting and to
describe, analyse and assess the reponses of each
to channelling.   To this end, a variety of research
techniques were employed.   We began by conducting
informal group discussions with the pupils.
Initially, these took place during school time but
on fairly neutral territory - a local sports centre
used by the School for some of its P.E. lessons.
Later in the research, having established a rapport
with a large cross-section of pupils, further
discussions were arranged on the school premises
with various groups.
      Similar discussions were conducted with groups
of teachers.   Questionnaires were administered to
the entire teaching staff and to each pupil in the
fourth and fifth years.   In-depth, semi-structured,
follow-up interviews were undertaken with 46 teacher
respondents and a heterogeneous sample of 50 pupils.
The latter group comprised boys and girls, blacks
and whites, drawn from both the upper and lower
bands.   These pupils showed some variation in
their respective commitments to the school, the
pursuit of credentials and sport.   Data were also
gathered from other sources, namely:- lesson
observation and consultations with local authority
advisory staff, careers officers, and teachers in
adjacent schools.

Indications of Channelling
Although there is a tendency for pupils of West
Indian origins to be clustered in the lower bands
or streams in schools (18), there was little
evidence of this at Hillsview.   Whilst West Indian
and white pupils were found to be proportionally
represented in both the upper and lower bands, the
relatively small Asian population was concentrated
in the upper band.
      An analysis of the ethnic composition of the
school sports teams, however, revealed an altogether different picture.   Leaving aside the
question of Asian participation (only two or three
Asian pupils played regularly in school teams) it
was found that whereas West Indian pupils accounted
for 32% of the school population, they nevertheless
occupied 63% of the team places.   (N.B. The analysis
covered all of the teams regularly fielded by the
School, from first to fifth years, viz. soccer,
rugby, basketball, netball, hockey and athletics.
Despite the strong tradition and passion for
cricket in Yorkshire, the School no longer has a
cricket team!)

Most of the white male team members (67%)
and almost all of the female team members (93%
white and 92% West Indian) came from the upper band.
This finding it not unusual for, as the work of
Hendry and Thorpe, Hargreaves, Corrigan and others
has suggested, extra-curricular activities,
including physical activities, tend to attract more
conformist pupils; viz. pupils, often with
academic inclinations, who are more readily able to
identify with the school as an institution (19).
Many of the West Indian male team members, however,
did not fulfil these criteria, for 68% came from the
lower band and, of these, there was a substantial
proportion of disaffected pupils who appeared to
reject most aspects of schooling except for sport,
or in some cases, other practical curricular and
extra-curricular activities such as metal work,
woodwork, drama etc. The following question
immediately arises - Why were these black boys
willing to take part in school teams when most of
their disaffected white peers simply rejected extra-
curricular sport as 'just another school subject
outside school hours'?
Very few teachers at Hillsview appeared to be
overtly hostile to ethnic minorities or gave the
impression of being 'consciously racist' in outlook.
Many, in fact came across as 'liberal minded' and
genuinely concerned with the well-being of pupils,
irrespective of their colour or ethnic background.
Notwithstanding this, however, often there appeared
to be a disjunction between the attitudes and
values held by some teachers and their behaviour
and practices in the classroom. Some, including
those who regarded themselves as non-racist or even
anti-racist, behaved in manner which, in Wellman's
terms, could be described as 'racist in consequence,
rather than intent'. Several indicated that they
held lower expectations of West Indian pupils and
were prepared to tolerate poorer standards of
academic work and behaviour from this group. One,
concerned to make education a less alienating
experience for his black pupils and anxious to
establish a good relationship with them, when asked
if he varied his approach in the classroom to suit
pupils of different ethnic backgrounds, replied:-

I'm reluctant to push black kids too hard...
I frequently indulge them - and myself - in
informal conversations relating to music,
home life etc.

Others, who regarded West Indian pupils as posing a particular control problem, recounted the strategies they employed in the classroom to assuage this group, e.g.

> I tend to give West Indians as much oral work as possible because even the bright ones become agitated when not writing well.

> Inevitably, I'm more lenient towards blacks. I try to avoid confrontation. I tend to ask them to do something, rather than telling them to do it.

> I recognise that West Indians have a lower flash point. Whereas I might bark at a white kid, I'm more patient with the more volatile West Indians.

Undoubtedly, there were some teachers at Hillsview School who operated with pejorative stereotypes of West Indian pupils and viewed their behaviour, academic abilities and parent culture in a negative manner. There were several occasions in interview when teachers referred to this group as 'lacking in ability', 'unable to concentrate', 'indolent', 'insolent', 'disruptive', 'aggressive' and 'disrespectful of authority'. Frequently, our respondents alluded to a cultural-deficit model when accounting for West Indian academic failure. Some alleged that 'West Indian parents do not value education as much as other groups' or said that 'West Indian parents do not support their children emotionally or educationally'. Furthermore, black resistance to schooling was often viewed by teachers as a form of deviance emanating from an authoritarian family upbringing. The following teacher's comments are typical of this genre:-

> They (West Indian pupils) are more resentful of authority because they come from a stricter background. Their parents treat them very badly. They're only supposed to speak when spoken to and if they do anything wrong they're likely to get belted ..... We're not in a position to exercise that sort of authority. They just don't see us as any sort of threat.

However, it should be stressed that there were

teachers at Hillsview - albeit a minority - who
rejected their colleagues stereotypical rationalisations of West Indian academic failure and
resistance to schooling.   Instead they offered
accounts which took cognisance of the position of
this ethnic group in a racially-structured society
and labour market.   A science teacher remarked:

> We are trying to ask West Indians and Asians
> and anyone else who's not English to adhere
> to our society, our methods of teaching, the
> way we live, the way we do everything.

Referring to the invidious position of West
Indians in the labour market, a languages teacher
recounted a conversation with some of her older
black pupils, noting:-

> There's little hope for them - In my class,
> West Indian kids say to me - 'Miss you're
> wasting your time.   School work doesn't
> matter.   I shan't get a job - I don't want
> to know'.

Whereas the teachers tended to underrate the
academic potential of black pupils, their comments
about the abilities of this group in low-status,
practical activities were often laudatory.   West
Indians were variously described as having 'a well
developed artistic ability or sense of colour' or
'greater athletic prowess then white pupils', and
as being, 'ideal for dance and drama' or 'capable
of achieving better results physically then
academically'.

Teachers' Explanations of West Indian Involvement in School Sport

During interview, teachers were shown tables
detailing the ethnic composition of school sports
teams and invited to comment upon the high level of
West Indian involvement.

Although there is a substantial body of
research suggesting that no credence can be given to
naturalistic interpretations of black sports
involvement (viz. accounts based upon speculative
assumptions about innate racial differences in
physique or motor skills), many teachers, nevertheless, explained the over-representation of West
Indians in school teams in these terms.   Often
explicit references were made to what Gallop and
Dolan characterise as 'the physiological myths

51

surrounding black athletic success' (20).   For
example, one of the science staff who also assisted
with coaching contended:

> West Indians are superior in the power that
> they can generate compared to white kids.
> They seem to possess better musculature and
> don't have the fat you often find on a
> British kid.

Similarly, a humanities teacher believes that:

> The physique of West Indian children generally,
> would appear to be in line with getting
> better results at sport.

Invariably, there were some teachers, who not
only perceived West Indians as having superior
physical endowments and skills, but who looked upon
sport as providing an appropriate channel for
compensating these supposedly 'motor minded' pupils
for their academic failure.   As one of the P.E.
staff remarked:

> West Indian pupils seem to be more muscular,
> more physically developed and have better
> physical skills than white children of the
> same age.   Only rarely does one see a weak,
> flabby or poorly co-ordinated West Indian
> child.   They have a raw talent and are
> immediately attracted to an area where they
> can excel.

Similarly, a humanities teacher claimed:

> Sport gives them (West Indian pupils) a
> chance of success.   Whereas they're not
> successful in the classroom they can show
> their abilities on the sports field.

Some teachers, often those eschewing stereotypical rationalisations of black academic failure,
offered alternative accounts of West Indian sports
involvement to those discussed above.   A few
recognised that prominent black athletes often
constitute significant others for West Indian
youth, e.g.

> There are few black heroes - especially around
> here.   West Indian pupils identify with black
> sportsmen.

> Maybe it's the influence of television.
> They have suddenly realised they're good
> at something. In school sport West Indians
> are the only ones who'll volunteer; you have
> to dragoon the others into taking part.

On the other hand, the accounts provided by
some respondents revealed an awareness of the
symbolic significance of the territory of the
school for West Indian youth (21). A drama
teacher, alluding to this, stated:

> The school provides West Indian pupils with
> something they really need... When something
> is going on after school (a dramatic production
> or sports fixture), there are far more West
> Indian kids hanging around or riding bikes.

Other teachers were more explicit than this
particular respondent. Several felt that West
Indian pupils had sought to 'colonise' the school
sports field and interpreted the growing involvement of this group in sport as an expression of
their ethnicity. According to one member of
staff:

> West Indians live in a tightly-knit
> community. It could be that one or two
> are good at sport and others practice a bit
> harder and go along to be with their friends
> ... Indigeneous children no longer want to
> participate because they feel outnumbered.
> When there were only 2 or 3 West Indians in
> each team they were accepted by other team
> members. But as the numbers became 5, 6 or 7
> this began to affect the thinking of some of
> the white pupils.

The question of 'colonisation' will be
considered later in this account when the reasons
given by pupils for taking part in (or opting out
of) extra-curricular sport are examined.

Sport as a Side-Track

There were strong indications from both pupils' and
teachers' remarks during individual interviews and
group discussions that sport provided the school
with a convenient side-track for many of its
disaffected West Indian pupils. Although the
teachers did not seek to secure a truce with
disaffected pupils by openly trading additional

<u>curricular</u> sport and a reduced academic workload
for more conformist behaviour on the part of the
pupils, it was found that sports involvement was
utilised by teachers as a control mechanism - but
in a more subtle and convert manner (22).   Whereas
one of the school rules stated quite unequivocally
that non-attenders and disruptive pupils would be
barred from taking part in school teams, it was
apparent that this rule was interpreted with a good
deal of flexibility!   For example, one teacher,
when asked 'Are badly behaved pupils or truants
allowed to play in a school team?' replied:-

> Yes - I've let such pupils off detention
> to play in a team, even though there's a
> formal school rule which says they should
> not play.

Other teachers also indicated that they felt
that the sanctions normally taken out against the
non-conformist pupil might be waived in the case
of a team member, and seemed to advocate an
'unspoken truce' with disaffected pupils, whom they
believed ought to be encouraged to play in school
teams.   Whilst some justified this practice in
the belief that success in sport would serve to
compensate low-achievers for academic failure,
others sponsored the involvement of such pupils in
school teams in the hope that it would enable them
to identify more closely with the school as an
institution, e.g.

> Lessons and playing football are part and
> parcel of the same thing.   Sport is the
> only thing that some children are good at.
> I think a case can be made for badly behaved
> pupils or truants playing in a team.   If a
> child is badly behaved in school but is good
> at football - this is a positive thing to
> build on.

> Once you reject them it's difficult to get
> them back.   Kids are kept in the mainstream
> through sport at school because, at least
> for a short period of time, they're accepting
> the rules which the school has laid down.

Many pupils appeared to be aware of this
'unspoken truce'.   As Alex, a West Indian rugby
player intimated:-

Sometimes you're stopped from playing for legging it - but if you come late or muck around in the corridors, you're still allowed to play.

Similarly, a member of the soccer team contended:-

Most of the teachers and the headteacher are not bothered about truanting - but you've got to be in school on Friday if there's a game on Saturday.

In addition to the indirect forms of sponsorship referred to above, some direct pressure was placed upon pupils to participate in school teams. This usually came from the P.E. staff themselves, or from other teachers who assisted with coaching. On most occasions, teachers appeared to rely on their powers of persuasion when recruiting players for teams. However, on others more coercive means were employed!

Female staff, cognisant of the disdain shown by many adolescent girls for team sports - though not necessarily aware of the reasons for this - said that they had made certain concessions to team members to ensure their continued support. Girls, it appeared, were no longer compelled to participate in the time-honoured ritual of communal bathing after a match!

Several pupils, mostly West Indians, reported that P.E. staff had pressurised them to take part in school teams. One West Indian girl said a games teacher 'nagged' her incessantly until she finally agreed to play hockey. Another black pupil recounted the following:-

The P.E. teachers kept on telling me how good I was at running. They worked on me (persuaded) to go along to athletics practice even though I didn't like the idea.

Sometimes consensual methods were abandoned in favour of force. As Ronald, a West Indian pupil, with commitments in several sports teams explained:

Teachers kept pushin' me around (when I was) in the first year. They threatened to lower my report if I didn't play.

Some pupils, however, told how they resisted such force. Garry, a white school rejector, recalled an incident where a teacher had 'asked' him to play in the rugby team.

> He used to threaten me by saying he'd give me a bad report and by thumping me and twisting my arms.....

but added defiantly,

> I only turned up for one game.

Let us now consider in more detail the reasons given by pupils for their involvement in (or rejection) of extra-curricular sport.

As we have already seen almost all of the female team members and about two thirds of the white male team members were drawn from the upper band in the School. In general terms, the explanations which these pupils offered for participating in sports teams reflected their more favourable position in the school hierarchy.

Both black and white female participants tended to stress the social dimension of sport and said that playing in a school team gave them an opportunity to be with their friends. A few found the competitive aspects stimulating or indicated that they 'played for fun' or 'to keep fit'. Many said that they participated because they were 'proud to represent the school' or 'wanted to do something to help the school'. The impression gained of the majority of female participants, in contrast to the findings of Fuller (23), was of conformist pupils firmly ensconsed within the consensual fold of the school.

It came as no surprise that boys (from each ethnic group) tended to look upon sport as an appropriate channel through which to express their masculinity, enhance their male identities and maintain contacts with their peers. As one boy responded when asked by he played soccer for the school: "It's a real man's game, that's all". Many boys stressed the cathartic value of sport claiming that it 'helped them to wind down', 'relax' or 'relieve tensions'. Predictably the boys gave greater emphasis than the girls to the competitive aspects of sport, saying they 'enjoyed the challenge', 'liked the spirit of competition' or found it 'fun to meet and beat other schools'. Unlike the girls, few boys expressed mainsteam –

conformist sentiments when accounting for their
involvement in sports teams. According to David,
a West Indian rugby and soccer player:-

> There's little winning for the school at
> heart. You're winning for the team - the
> school has very little part.

Disaffected white pupils at Hillsview tended to
spurn extra-curricular sport, even though many of
the boys spent much of their spare time playing
soccer or Rugby League. Their rejection of school
sport was allied to their rejection of school per se.
Thus, Paul summed up the feelings of this group,
when he said:

> I'm good enough to play in the football
> team - but I just don't bother to ...
> Sport is just another subject after school.

Unlike Paul and many of his white peers in the
lower band, a substantial caucus of disaffected
black youth played regularly in school teams, even
though their responses to other facets of school and
schooling appeared ambivalent or negative. In
contrast to their white counterparts, these pupils
appeared to regard sport as qualitatively different
from other school activities. As Roy, a West
Indian rugby player with an undistinguished academic
record, who it seemed, was at war with the school,
explained:-

> I take part because I'm not forced to do so.
> Rugby isn't like lessons. If you're sitting
> in the back of the class you're picked on ...
> but if you're playing rugby it's of your own
> free will.

How is this differential response to be interpreted? Could it be that disaffected black pupils
tended to co-operate with this form of channelling
because their rejection of school was not as
complete as that of their white working class peers?
As the authors of the report Disaffected Pupils
have observed:-

> For the white boys and girls disaffection
> meant a severing of contact with the school
> and all that it stood for, whereas for the
> black boys - even the most difficult in the
> teachers' eyes - their approach to school was

riven with contradictions. They were both
for it and against it and their hostility was
always tempered by a recognition that it was
essential in achieving the type of career to
which they aspired (24).

It would seem likely, therefore, that ethnic
specific sub-cultural factors play some part in the
high level of West Indian involvement in school
sport. Could it be, with the apparent lack of
competition from white working class pupils, West
Indians have easy access to an almost 'deserted
field'?
In addition, the apparent readiness of black
youth at Hillsview to co-operate with channelling
appeared to be related to the growth of ethnic
consciousness among this group. As I have already
suggested, there were signs that black pupils
looked upon sport as an opportunity to 'colonise'
one major area of school activity and to make it
their own. Indeed, there were indications, not
only from the school staff but from pupils (black
and white alike) that West Indians had 'colonised'
school sport and regarded the sports field as their
territory. A variety of strategies were deployed
to control this territory. According to one West
Indian team member, Joanne:-

In some teams the coloured girls are right
nasty. They shout at the white girls, who
then drop out because they're frightened that
we will make life uncomfortable for them.

Other black pupils, like Alex, informed us
that pupils often played a part in team selection
and

That white lads were frequently overlooked
unless they were friendly with coloured lads
in the team.

There could be little doubt that racial
boundaries at the school had become more sharply
delineated as a result of the sponsorship of West
Indian involvement in sport. Whilst the boycotting
of extra-curricular sport by some white pupils
could be read as a manifestation of working class
resistance to schooling, with others it was more
directly related to racial considerations. Indeed,
it could be argued that racism within this sector
of the school population played an important part in

determining the ethnic composition of the sports
teams.   As one white pupil conceded:-

> There's a lot of prejudice at this school
> .... Some kids won't play for the school
> because they just don't like West Indians.

"Sport - That's all we're good at" (or the Self-fulfilling Prophecy' at work)

The question of whether pupils at Hillsview School
shared their teachers' preconceptions of their
abilities was approached indirectly:- pupils were
asked (both individually and in groups) to account
for their school's distinguished record in sport.
From their responses, it was apparent that some
pupils - both black and white - had internalised
low expectations of their academic abilities, or
racial stereotypes of black athletic prowess and
physical superiority.   Several pupils saw athletic
success as compensating for academic failure, e.g.

> Hillsview's pupils are not very clever
> academically so they concentrate on sport
> where only physical fitness is essential
> and excel. (Andrew; white)

> Pupils don't seem to do all that well in
> academic subjects so they push all the more
> harder in sport.   (Beverley; black)

There were some who utilised racial stereotypes in their accounts, as the following extracts
indicate:-

> It's because of the coloureds.   They're
> better at sport than white people.   Most
> of them are big, fast and aggressive.
> (Michelle; white)

> In Hillsview most coloured people believe
> they're better at sport than white people.
> (Hilson; black)

> It's because of the coloured blood.   If it
> wasn't for the coloured blood our school
> wouldn't be as good as it is. (David; black)

In contrast to the above, other pupils variously explained the frequent successes of the school
teams in terms of:- the rough and tough nature of
the school catchment area; the quality of its

training and coaching facilities, or the pre-
occupation of many of the staff with sport, e.g.

> We're surrounded by a rough area.   People
> round here tend to be strong and hard.   There
> are very few middle class kids in the school.
> (David; black)

> We've got very good sports facilities;
> teachers are very involved with sport.
> (Mandy; white)

> The other teams are scared of us 'cos we're
> bigger and rougher.   Sport's the best thing
> that goes on at this school.   More goes into
> sport than other lessons. (Malcolm; white)

Aspirations : imaginary and real

Despite their heavy commitments in school teams and
although some had internalised the stereotype of
black physical superiority, none of the West Indian
pupils approached during the course of the research
seemed to endorse the chimerical notion of sport as
a viable channel for social advancement.   Whereas
a few male pupils (i.e. 7 black, 11 white), when
asked 'If you could have any job in the world what
would it be?', indicated that they held fantasies of
a career in professional sport (usually soccer),
only one (a white youth) appeared to perceive this
as a real option.   If West Indians did not hold
unrealistic aspirations of a career in sport, what
were their aspirations?   Along with Bird et al.,
Fuller and Sharpe it was found that the aspirations
of these pupils, despite their low attainment levels,
tended to be higher than those of their white
peers (25).   West Indian boys, for example, were
more likely to eschew lower status manual jobs than
white boys.   Many aspired to skilled manual work,
and indicated that they hoped a declining job market
would not prevent them from becoming engineering
apprentices, mechanics, electricians etc.
Similarly, West Indian girls gave the impression of
being more ambitious than white girls.   Unlike the
latter, they seemed to be less attracted to factory
work or routinised 'white blouse' work, and more
likely to aspire to 'careers' in such fields as
nursing, teaching or social work.   Many expressed
similar views to those of Melanie, who informed us

> I want a good education and then to get a good
> job...Perhaps a games teacher or a nurse if

I'm good enough.

Often aspirations of ambitious black pupils were tempered by a sense of realism. As Donna replied, when asked if anything worried her about finding a job:-

Employers might not like your colour even if you have the necessary qualifications.

SUMMARY AND CONCLUSIONS

In conclusion, an attempt has been made to show that the overrepresentation of West Indian pupils in school sports teams is in part the outcome of channelling by teachers who have a tendency to view this ethnic group in stereotypical terms, as having skills of the body rather than skills of the mind. By encouraging these allegedly 'motor minded' pupils to concentrate on sport in school perhaps at some expense to their academic studies and by utilising (particularly in the case of disaffected, non-academic black males) extra-curricular sports involvement as a mechanism of social control, teachers have inadvertently reinforced West Indian academic failure and, concomitantly, have thereby facilitated the reproduction of the black worker as 'wage labour at the lower end of employment production and skill'. What, if anything, can be done to interrupt this cycle?

In general terms, I accept the thesis that schooling in capitalist formations is a 'conservative force' and that the school system: (1) transmits a culture supportive of the established social order and the class interests which dominate it; (2) implicity favours those with access to power and resources; and (3) by teaching different skills, values and dispositions to different sectors of the school population, schools latently recreate the class structure with its attendant racial and sexual divisions. However, like Giddens and others who seek to distance themselves from the excessive determinism of certain Marxist and sociological accounts of cultural and social reproduction, I would stress that reproduction neither occurs automatically nor takes place 'behind the backs of social actors' (26). Schools are no more cogs in a capitalist machine, than teachers the unreflexive purveyors of the ruling ideology, or pupils, the passive recipients of know-how, values and dispositions appropriate to their future positions in the socio-technical division of labour.

The school system - along with other cultural and political institutions - is a site of struggle. The conservative face of schooling, therefore, must be regarded as contingent rather than pre-given. To accept the need for a politics of education and policy initiatives within education, whether to tackle race, class or gender based forms of educational disadvantage, is to accept the specificity of institutions such as the school and to recognise that teachers (along with other social actors), whilst not wholly free, are not 'automatoms', 'passive objects', 'cultural dupes' or 'the mere bearers of the mode of production'.

Whilst I recognise that racist attitudes, values and practices are deeply entrenched within the fabric of British society, history and culture, and acknowledge the limitations of educational reform per se, I do not accept that teachers (or other agents of cultural and social reproduction) are incapable of appraising, evaluating and - over time - changing their attitudes and practices in relation to particular social categories and groups. "Racially-explicit" policies, therefore, such as those advocated in the Rampton Report and by Kirp, Little and Willey et al. must now be pursued (27). From this and other ethnographic research, it is evident that one starting point for such a policy would be to address the issue of racism within the teaching force itself. Without such initiatives in the field of education and further interventions, for example, to curb discriminatory practices in the labour market, West Indians will continue to function as a respository of menial wage labour and as 'gladiators' for white British society.

ACKNOWLEDGEMENTS

I am grateful to John Beattie and Oliver Leaman for their helpful comments upon an earlier draft of this paper, to Tony Edwards, Haydn Davies Jones and my co-researcher Edward Wood for their advice and support and to the staff and pupils of Hillsview Comprehensive School.

NOTES AND REFERENCES

1. Edwards, H. (1973) 'The Black Athlete: Twentieth Century Cladiators for White America', Psychology Today, November edition.
2. Sargeant, A.J. (1972) 'Participation of West Indian

Boys in English School Sports Teams', Educational Research Vol. 14, pp. 225-30; Wood, E.R. (1973), An Investigation of Some Aspects of Social Class and Ethnic Group Differentiation in a School-Based Junior Activities Centre, M.Ed. thesis (unpublished), University of Newcastle upon Tyne; Beswick, W.A. (1976) 'The Relationship of the Ethnic Background of Secondary School Boys to their Participation in and Attitudes towards Physical Acitivity' Research Papers in Physical Education, Vol. 3, No. 2; Jones, P. (1977) 'An Evaluation of the effect of Sport on the integration of West Indian School Children', Ph.D. thesis (unpublished) University of Surrey.

3. For a critique of 'endowment theory' and naturalistic accounts of black sports involvement in the United States see:- Loy, J. (1969) 'The Study of Sport and Social Mobility' in Kenyon, G.S. (ed.) *Aspects of Contemporary Sports Sociology*, Chicago Athletics Institute; Edwards, H. (1973) *Sociology of Sport*, St. Louis, Mosby; Loy, J., McPherson, B.D. and Kenyon, G.S. (1978) *Sport and Social Systems*, Chicago, Addison Wesley.

4. The structural position of ethnic minorities in Britain has been analysed by several authors *including:* Sivanandan, A. (1976) 'Race, Class and the State - the Black Experience in Britain', Race and Class, Vol. 17, No. 4; Hall, S. et al. (1978) *Policing the Crisis*, London, Macmillan; Brake, M. (1980) *The Sociology of Youth Culture and Youth Sub-cultures*, London, Routledge and Kegan Paul, Chapter 4; Smith, D.J. (1977) *Racial Disadvantage in Britain*, Harmondsworth, Penguin.

5. Department of Education and Science (1981), *Interim Report of the Committee of Inquiry into the Education of Children from Ethnic Minority Groups: West Indian Children in Our Schools*, London, H.M.S.O. (i.e. 'The Rampton Report'); Coard, B. (1971) *How the West Indian Child is made Educationally Sub-normal in the British School System*, London, New Beacon Books; See Carrington, B. (1981) 'Schooling an Underclass', Durham and Newcastle Research Review, Vol. 9, No. 47 for a discussion of the central themes and issues in the race and schooling debate in Britain; and Mullard, C. (1982) 'The Racial Code: Its Features, Rules and Change', in this volume.

6. Barker, M. (1981) *The New Racism*, London, Junction Books, pp. 1-29.

7. Wellman, D. (1977) *Portraits of White Racism*, New York, Cambridge University Press, p. 39.

8. ibid., pp. 221-2.

9. Brittan, E.M. (1976) 'Multi-Racial Education', Educational Research, Vol. 18, No. 3; Giles, R. (1977) *The West Indian Experience in British Schools*, London, Heinemann; Rex, J. and Tomlinson, S. (1979) *Colonial Immigrants in a British City*, London, Routledge and Kegan Paul, Chapter 6; Rampton, op. cit., pp. 12-14; Perkins, T.E.

(1979) 'Rethinking Stereotypes'; in Barrett, M. et al. (eds.), *Ideology and Cultural Production*, London, Croom Helm.

10. Times Educational Supplement, 26th April, 1981, p.1.

11. Stone, M. (1981) *The Education of the Black Child in Britain*, London, Fontana, pp. 65-66.

12. See note (2).

13. Lawson, H. (1979) 'Physical Education and Sport in the Black Community', Journal of Negro Education, Vol. 48, No. 2.

14. Troyna, B. (1979) 'Differential Commitment to Ethnic Identity', New Community, Vol. 7, No. 30.

15. Kew, S. (1979) 'Ethnic Groups and Leisure', London, S.S.R.C./Sports Council.

16. Cashmore, E. (1981) 'The Black British Sporting Life', New Society, 6th August; Gallop, P. and Dolan, J. (1981) 'Perspectives on the Participation in Sporting Recreation amongst Minority Group Youngsters', Physical Education Review, Vol. 4, No. 1.

17. Pseudonyms have been used throughout the case study.

18. For example, Coard, B. op. cit., Black Peoples' Progressive Association (1978) 'Cause for Concern: West Indian Pupils in Redbridge', Redbridge Community Relations Council.

19. Hendry, L. and Thorpe, E. (1977) 'Pupils' Choice, Extra Curricular Activities: A Critique of Hierarchical Authority?' International Review of Sport Sociology, Vol. 4, No. 12. Corrigan, P. (1979) *Schooling the Smash Street Kids*, London, Macmillan; Hargreaves, D. (1967) *Social Relations in a Secondary School*, London, Routledge and Kegan Paul.

20. Gallop, P. and Dolan, J. op. cit.; see note (3).

21. Furlong, V.J. (forthcoming, 1982) 'Black Resistance in the Liberal Comprehensive School' in Furlong, V.J. (ed.) *Ideological and Interactional Approaches to Research*, London, Falmer.

22. Reynolds, D. (1976) 'When Pupils and Teachers Refuse a Truce' in Mungham, G. and Pearson, G. (eds.) *Working Class Youth Culture*, London, Routledge and Kegan Paul.

23. Fuller, M. (1980) 'Black Girls in a London Comprehensive School' in Deem, R. (ed.) Schooling for Women's Work, London, Routledge and Kegan Paul.

24. Bird, C. et al. (1981) *Disaffected Pupils*, Uxbridge, Brunel University.

25. Fuller, M. ibid., p. 32-39. Sharpe, S. (1976) *Just Like a Girl*, Harmondsworth, Penguin.

26. Giddens, A. (1979) *Central Problems in Social Theory*, London, Methuen, pp. 9-130.

27. For example, Kirp, D. (1979) *Doing Good by Doing Little*, Berkeley, University of California Press; Rampton

op. cit., Chapter 4;   Little, A. and Willey, R. (1981)
'Multi-ethnic Education: the Way Forward', London, Schools
Council.

BLACK WOMEN IN HIGHER EDUCATION - CASE STUDIES OF UNIVERSITY WOMEN IN BRITAIN

Sally Tomlinson

The most commonly documented characteristic of
black school students of West Indian origin in
Britain is their educational underachievement.
Pressure on the government to initiate an enquiry
into this underachievement led to the setting up of
the Rampton Committee in 1979.   The interim report
of this committee published D.E.S. statistics for
1979 which indicated that only 1% of West Indian
school-leavers, compared with 3% Asian and 3% other
leavers, went on to a full-time University degree
course.(West Indian Children in our School 1981,
p. 9.)
      Less commonly documented is that girls of West
Indian origin have tended to perform rather better
than boys in educational tests of ability, and
their school achievement does seem to be slightly
superior to that of West Indian boys.   A study by
Houghton in 1966 showed Jamaican girls scoring
higher than boys on reasoning tests (Houghton 1966).
In the Inner London Education Authority research
first published in 1968 (Little et al. 1968) girls
performed better than boys on tests of reading and
verbal ability.   Payne and Phillips, both testing
children in 1969, reported West Indian girls
performing better than boys on reading tests
(Payne 1969, Phillips 1979).   Driver,in a small
study reported in 1977, recorded greater school
persistence of West Indian girls compared to boys,
(Driver 1977) and in his more contentious research
reported in 1980, claimed that a rank overall
achievement order at five schools showed West
Indian girls coming first six times, boys only
twice (Driver 1980).   Sharpe (1976) in a study of
teenage girls in four London schools, found that
the response of black girls to schools included
placing more importance on the acquisition of

qualifications and on education itself than either
black boys or white girls. Fuller recorded that
the black teenage girls she interviewed had "an
acute awareness of their double subordination as
women and blacks, accompanied by a refusal to accept
the facts of subordination" (Fuller 1980, p. 64).
Part of the girls' refusal to accept subordination
was the acquisition of educational credentials as
a means of gaining control over their own future.
        This higher achievement of girls does seem to
extend to higher education where there is some
indication that the chance of black girls entering
higher education to pursue a degree course is
rather higher than boys, although it must be
remembered that absolute numbers of all black
students entering higher education are still
extremely small. This relative 'success' of black
girls has begun to generate some interest and
discussion. Questions have begun to be raised
as to whether black girls perceive and use the
education system differently to boys, whether
schools perceive and educate girls differently
and perhaps more favourably, and what this `"success"
means for black women in British society.
        The National Union of Students, who appear to
have been the first body to actually gather black
college and university students together to discuss
their education (1) noted that black women tended to
outnumber men in higher education, and one N.U.S.
official commented that "it seems that black women
are actually more likely to succeed academically
than men..... this seems to contradict the double
oppression faced by black women."
        The double oppression theme has assumed that
while black people and women are disadvantaged
compared to white people and men "the facts of
racial and sexual disadvantage in Britain mean
that - whatever their social class, black women and
girls are in a doubly subordinate position in the
social formation." (Fuller 1980, p. 52.)
        Theories of double oppression, and debate
about the status of educated black women have
generated quite a large literature in the U.S.A.
(Ladner 1971, Lerner 1972, Wallace 1979), particularly since the emergence of an educated black
middle class as an economically significant force
(Wilson 1979).   There is no literature in Britain
discussing black women in University education -
how they view their achievements, their problems,
position and future, and whether they feel that
their changes of combatting "double oppression" have

been improved. This paper is presented as a pilot study of a small number (8) of black women, six of them born in Britain, studying at two English Universities 1978-82, who were interviewed during 1981. The aim of the interviews was to gather information about the students' school and family background - to enquire if any specific factors had made for their 'success', and to ask how they viewed their higher education, future, and position as educated black women in British society. The only initial hypothesis made was that black university women would not be willing to accept an "oppressed condition" on either a racial or gender basis.

THE N.U.S. EVIDENCE

The only recorded discussion to date between black students in higher education appears to be the evidence (<u>Just a Segment</u>, N.U.S. 1980) presented to the Rampton Committee for the interim report - <u>West Indian Children in our Schools</u> (1981). A selected group of (17) black students also met members of the Rampton Committee to discuss the evidence. It seemed worthwhile to review the N.U.S. evidence briefly, as a point of reference for comparison with the experience of the eight students interviewed in my study.

The discussions by the college students for the N.U.S. centred round the factors which the students, - men and women, - felt had helped them to "break the cycle" of black underachievement and actually arrive at college. The students also discussed their cultural and identity problems, and the problem of being black intellectuals in a white society. They criticised aspects of the school system which they felt worked against black children - particularly the school curriculum, and made eighteen suggestions for improvement. While there was little mention of overt racial abuse, the students felt that schools and teachers lacked commitment to the welfare and aspirations of black students and that the school curriculum was geared to the "invisibility" of blacks.

I don't think they (the teachers) really cared about us.

They wouldn't really encourage you to do better.

Everybody knows all about England - all the
West Indian children are schooled on English
books, English grammer, English everything.....
I did all my education here, and I did not
study about my own country .... They've got
this mighty Empire, but they don't know anything about the people they exploit.

The students also felt that the streaming
process affected black pupils negatively:-

It was like you got thrown into the C.S.E.
stream like rubbish.

Teacher expectations about black children were
noted - one student described how he had come late
into a maths exam and was automatically given the
C.S.E., rather than the 'O' level paper.   The
women students tended to agree that at school boys
were treated less favourably than girls -

Boys seem to get the worst deal don't they ...
I don't think its because they've got no
ambition ... its the pressure they are under
... they are going to get dumped in C.S.E.'s -
go out looking for a job and get nothing.

An N.U.S. official also suggested that schools
may look more favourably on girls as being
potentially less disruptive and better behaved.

Sexist expectations of passivity among women
counteracts the racist expectations of
disruptive behaviour among blacks in general.

However, one student was of the opinion that
teachers expected as little of black girls as boys,
- she described how she had visited her old school
and told the teachers that a friend of hers with
C.S.E.'s had a job in an insurance office.

They looked at me as if to say - my God - she
should be working at Tesco's.

The students discussed the issue of dialect,
since use of dialect by West Indian children has been
put forward as a possible cause of underachievement,
both because of confusion with standard English,
and because teachers devalue dialect (Edwards, 1979).
The general opinion was that the black community
were divided as to whether dialect should be

69

encouraged in schools. Many parents felt that
while school could encourage dialect as a positive
aspect of West Indian culture, pupils may also be
disadvantaged by this. As one student put it:-
"Which employer is going to employ someone they
can't understand."

It is interesting to note that recent
research by Rosen and Burgess (1980) found that
teachers rated a higher proportion of black girls
as Standard English speakers, than black boys.

The students all felt their parents had
played an important part in helping them to "break
the cycle" of underachievement by encouraging them,
and explaining the consequences of particular
subject choices, and also in protecting the rights
of pupils against teachers.

"You have to have a parent behind you to push,
fight and spell things out clearly."

They thought that the onus was on individuals
and families to fight the schools pre-conceived
ideas of what black pupils could achieve and felt
that many black parents, who had not directly
experienced the British school system, were least
well equipped to carry the burden of helping their
children through the system. The black women
students who had been through English education
were quite clear that they would challenge stereotypes about black children and press for their
success, even at the risk of unpopularity.

> I correct my children's homework ... I ask
> them to present it to the teacher again.
> This gets the child very unpopular at school
> and so you present yourself to the school so
> the battle can be taken out on you instead
> of the child (mature student).

The N.U.S. evidence indicated that black
students do feel conflict and ambivalence about
their identity, role and status as highly educated
black people, - some students spoke of losing their
"right" to membership of the black community.

> Right now, I'm different, since I've got
> to college .... you're not one of them are
> you ... but then I have to be ... because
> there is no other way.

> The only way is to go through their system -
> because no black really feels - though some
> do ... they would like to stay here ... you

say to yourself - what am I doing here?

The black women seemed most prepared to use their advantages and success to help other black people. Several of them were preparing for B.Ed. (teaching) and social work courses.

> The reason why I decided to come on this course ... was that I was presented with so many black children wanting to come to nursing with bad qualifications. They come to take the test and they fail ... they've been born in this country and have lots of C.S.E.'s that are no use to them, ... I was sorry for my blacks, they didn't know the system and are not getting up off their back-sides to see what's happening to their children.

It may be that black intellectual women understand as well as men that "the black intellectual is one of the few in our times who does not really have the liberty to pursue his narrow and selfish academic interest ... the liberty to close his eye to the problem of his people" (Mezu, 1970, my underlinings).

CASE STUDIES OF BLACK UNIVERSITY WOMEN

Turning now to the eight students who were interviewed for this study - what was their family background, particularly in terms of occupation and education. On the basis of the occupational classification of both parents, three of the families would rate as 'white-collar' middle class and five as manual working class. Two of the families had 'middle-class' occupations in the West Indies, but six were black working-class immigrants. The 'normal' family situation was that both parents worked, although in one case the father was dead and another mother was a single parent. In one middle-class family both parents had degrees - the father having a B.A. and a law degree and having worked as a government official in the West Indies before becoming a salesman in England. The mother in this family had trained as a nurse but with her six children growing up had returned to college to take a B.Ed. degree. Five of the six children had acquired 'A' levels, three had degrees already and the respondent was in the second year of her degree. Not surprisingly, this student attributed her

arrival at University largely to her parents'
encouragement:-

> My parents had always created an atmosphere
> at home where university was considered a
> necessary part of education.

Another student who attributed her success to
parental encouragement had a father who had "worked
his way up" from London transport to owning his own
garage, - the mother having secretarial training
and working as a personal assistant. The student
felt she had been very much influenced by her
father whom she thought had very realistic
aspirations for his children.

> It was Dad's dream to go to college, he
> equated education with success. He's said
> to me ever since I was born, - you're black
> and you won't get anywhere without education.

This family had sent both its girls to private
primary schools and moved to a "white area".
Similar parental attitudes of encouragement
were evident in the working class families. In
one family where the father was a railway porter
and the mother working in an old people's home, the
respondent said "It was my father who always
encouraged us, - he had no education and had passed
no exams and he said, - you don't get nowhere
without education. My mother doesn't see
education as so important." In this family one
sister was training to be a nurse and a brother was
at technical college. The family had originally
lived in the St. Pauls area of Bristol, but had
moved out to a "white area". "My father said the
housing and schools were better away from St.
Pauls."
In the single parent family the respondent
described her mother as having an elementary
education - "then in 1957 she came from Jamaica
because she thought the streets were paved with
gold here. She worked in a business in Jamaica
and was respected - had middle-class aspirations
you might say, but here she ended up working in a
cigarette factory." Her mother had encouraged her
to work at school and was "fantastically proud
when I got to University."
It was noticeable that in all cases - whether
the parents had a higher or low level of education
themselves they had encouraged their girls to work

72

at school and had, like the students in the N.U.S. discussion reported, been willing to take action as well as provide verbal encouragement. Several parents had visited schools to "push the teachers". Only one student reported that her parents who had a 'very basic' education themselves, had not been too keen on her attending university - but this was because they regarded her chosen subject - theology - as a "waste of time".

It was interesting to note that, apart from the single parent family, all the students mentioned the encouragement from their fathers. This would seem to contradict those who are still arguing that the matrilineal focus of the West Indian household accounts for the educational success of girls (Driver, 1980). The only two students who specifically mentioned the influence of mothers on the achievement of girls were both without fathers.

One source of encouragement which does not figure in any literature, but which was spontaneously mentioned by three students, was the influence of the (pentecostal) church. One student, who had been a young preacher and had had a traumatic break with her church before coming to university, felt that during her teenage years the church had been a source of stability and encouragement. - "You hear a lot about the influence of the Rastafarians, but no one writes about the pentecostal church influence."

Another student mentioned that she had become a Christian six years previously. "The main influence on my life has been God - I believe that he has a purpose for my life." She had had to re-sit her 'A' levels, having failed the first time round, and attributed her perseverance and ultimate achievements to "God's will".

The students were asked about their school experiences, from pre-school to university and were particularly asked about teacher encouragement and expectations, and use of dialect. Three students remembered attending nursery school, - one private, two state schools. One respondent noted that: "I had a white minder who I sometimes stayed with in the week. I was the only black child in the area and when I went to the nursery it was called multi-racial!"

Three students particularly remembered being taught to read by their mothers before going to primary school.

The most striking characteristic of the primary school experience of all the students was that there were relatively small numbers of black children at

the schools they attended, sometimes literally only
one or two. They all felt they had had friendliness
and good teaching at primary school. One student,
from a middle class family, said:

> I loved my (private) primary school. We had
> a uniform, straw hats and yellow sun-dresses in
> the summer. It was tiny and prestigious -
> and there were only two black girls.

Another student reported that there were about
15% of black children in her primary school and felt
she was well-liked because she had had older
"bright" brothers and sisters at school before her.
One student felt that as the only black child at her
infant school she had been treated as a novelty.
"I got on well with the teachers - I was a pet,
- they treated me like a little black doll." Her
enthusiasm for school was rewarded by the teachers,
- "I loved reading, I thought it was a great gift
and I was praised by the teachers." However later
on in primary school she felt the teaching became
worse, there was a higher teacher turn-over and she
failed the 11+.
"I felt this was so unfair because we had no
proper teacher that year. I wrote a letter to the
education authority asking to go to the High School
and got my mother to copy it." This student felt
that her achievement in getting to university had
been a struggle from that point.
Another student, immigrant from Jamaica, said
that after the "role learning and slates in Jamaica,
English primary education had been a shock, - "it
seemed very free". From their memories of primary
school the students could not recall either overt or
subtle discrimination, and one student felt she had
been set on her university path by a primary
teacher - "a South African, who took a particular
interest in me." However, it should be recalled
that the schools were largely "all-white."
At the secondary level it was even more
striking that the respondents had attended schools
with small numbers of black children. One student
had achieved a grammar school place in an area not
yet comprehensive - "I loved it - it was like being
at a private school, - there were only three black
kids in my year." All the other students had
attended comprehensive schools with "Two blacks,
me and my sister." "Very few blacks indeed." One
respondent volunteered that: "My Mum thinks that
in a school with a lot of black children the

standard goes down. In my sheltered middle-class area my parents were actually pleased I didn't know many blacks." However, there was some ambivalence here as the student later reported that "my Dad can be conveniently West Indian when it suits him - he doesn't like me having white boy-friends."

With one exception the students all felt that they had mostly had teacher encouragement, usually from one particular teacher who had taken a particular interest in them, expected them to work and achieve, and perhaps more important, had actually explained what university was all about, and how to go about getting there.

"My sixth form tutor encouraged me and is now a family friend."

"My drama teacher encouraged me all through school and in the sixth form the religious studies teacher encouraged me and suggested I try for theology."

"By the sixth form we were all expected to go to university. The English teacher pushed me, - I was the only black girl left by then."

One girl in particular felt her own (lowered) aspirations were raised by her teachers.

"I was going to leave school after 'O' levels and train as a nurse. My form teacher told me I could get 'A' levels and helped me get a scholar-ship to stay on in the sixth form."

Another girl felt that it was the collusion of her parents and teachers who had pushed her to university.

"I would have been happy applying to Poly's but my parents talked it over with the careers teacher and they all pressured me." The student who felt she had not particularly had teacher encouragement said that she thought her teachers were "a bit afraid of me - I never really enjoyed school and never felt the teachers got to know me."

The students all said that it was following the 'normal' traditional subject-oriented curriculum, taking 'O' and "A" levels, that had brought them to university - their fellow-pupils steered into C.S.E. courses, integrated courses, or 'new' areas of study had not achieved university places. The eight students had averaged between 5-7 'O' levels each, and in two cases had actively resisted being put in for C.S.E. courses. At 'A' level they averaged C's and D's, - they had all applied for campus university except for one student whose subject took her to a prestigious London college.

Only one student felt that dialect had created problems for her at school, particularly just after her arrival from Jamaica. The other students did not find dialect an educational problem, - four used it at home but not at school. It was however, a cultural issue. One student said: "We were never allowed to use dialect - my Mum said it was common, but my brother uses it because he says it makes him feel black."

Another student said "I can use dialect for fun - to slip into the typical black stereotype for whites."

The students all expressed satisfaction with university and their courses, although they thought it required effort and hard work. One student said she had surprised herself with realising how hard she could work. They considered themselves lucky to have achieved university, both because of race and gender.

"I'm lucky to be at university, most of my school friends are doing secretarial courses, - the teachers didn't push them because they were black."

"University has helped my personal development - it's made me more aware of the pressures I'll face as a black woman."

The table below illustrates the subject the student is majoring in, and future job aspiration.

Student	Major Subject	Career Wanted
1	Politics	Youth or Community Work
2	Biology	Teacher
3	Biology	Medical Work
4	Theology	Teaching Religious Studies
5	Social Admin.	Lecturer
6	Social Admin.	Solicitor
7	Sociology	Business Studies or Journalist
8	Educational Studies	Primary Teacher

Given the amount of effort and determination these women have already put into achieving their university place, it seems realistic to assume that they will achieve their career ambitions.

In summary then, what are the factors which appear to have contributed to the 'success' of these students. Parental encouragement and support, particularly from fathers, appears to be crucial, not merely verbal encouragement but willingness to move house to 'better schools' (which in practice usually means a 'white' area), to work with or confront teachers, and generally to take action on the child's behalf. Attending schools with very few black children also seems to be an important factor. Having sympathetic teachers with high expectations of the pupils also helps, and crucially, if one or more teachers act as a 'mentor', helping the pupil in the practical business of choosing subjects and university courses, the high academic achievement is more likely. Avoiding C.S.E. streams, and speaking standard English also characterises 'successful' students.

DOUBLE OPPRESSION?

How then, do these students see themselves as black women intellectuals? How do they think other black people view them, and is there a paradox between the general doubly subordinate status of 'black women' and being academically 'successful' black women?

The experiences and views of non-white (male) intellectuals in Britain were vividly documented in a collection of articles edited by Parekh in 1974. In the introduction to this volume Parekh wrote "the editor is aware of the volume's limitations, he regrets that there are no women contributors, but that is not for want of trying." The majority of male contributors to Parekh's volume noted in some way, their feelings of alienation from black and white groups, their sense of isolation, their 'cultural schizophrenia" (Kunar in Parekh 1974). Sivanandan encapsulated their alientation and set it in its historical context.

"On the margins of European culture, alienated from his own, the 'coloured' intellectual is an artefact of colonial history - marginal man par excellence" (Sivanandan in Parekh 1974).

The women in this study mostly felt similar isolation and alienation, which was evident when asked about their problems in getting to, and being at, univeristy.

"Black women can be isolated and alienated from their black contemporaries in the process (of getting to university)."

"At college you are really isolated, if you are the only black woman, and you usually are, you either mix with whites or you mix with overseas students who are going back to Africa etc. and have their future mapped out."

"Black people easily feel isolated at University, being such a minority, it's not easy, - some

77

tutors are racist."

Two students noted that their university studies had helped them to understand and articulate the position of blacks in British society.

"I'm becoming aware of our black position in society. I was very protected and conservative. I thought we should be a bit careful in the present (race) climate, I still think blacks shouldn't parade it (their blackness) so much."

"I'm aware that there are few blacks at university, I see this as a product of the inherent inequality of the system. I don't accept it should remain this way - hopefully there will be many more but it won't be through generosity on the part of the policy-makers, but through a raised consciousness and self-help of black people."

The students' feelings of marginal status was articulated in the way they considered other black people - particularly men - regarded them.

"Some people think that having got to university we aren't black any more."

"Black boys think you are a brain box and they can't talk to you any more. I met a Rasta who told me I'd get nowhere, even if I was at university, but I think I will if I work."

"Personal experience has shown me that some black people regard you as a snob or as 'white-minded' ... but if they speak to me, they realise that I'm very aware of the problems facing blacks in Britain - particularly educational achievement - and their views change."

Several of the students felt that, despite their feelings of isolation and marginal status, they were regarded as 'role models' by black people.

"If they see some black (women) joining the professions, most black people will have the hope that their children can be successful too."

The students were asked if they could account for the tendency for black women to be rather more successful academically than men. While there was some sympathy for black men as the more obvious targets of discrimination in Britain, there was also some irritation expressed at what were regarded as black male chracteristics, which were incompatible with the effort needed to get to university.

"Men seem to be in the forefront for discrimination but the peer group also is an important influence on them - they want immediate gratification and to keep up a good front with their friends."

"Black boys stagnate - they are into having

fun, - drinking - girls, - girls aren't so rowdy, they are more settled."

"Black boys always say the system is against them, I know they have a hard time, but I worked - it can be an excuse.!"

"Possibly black women are more willing to fit into the (white) system and conform than men are, they don't cause the same amount of trouble - but boys do have more pressure from their peer group to misbehave."

Wallace (1979) reviewing the position of black women in the U.S.A. wrote dramatically of their double oppression, they were beginning to realise, she wrote, that they were "victims, not superwomen". The black women in this study did feel their sub-ordinated position, both as women and as blacks - but they did not see themselves as either victims or superwomen. They did not feel helpless or powerless to change their position, and they emerged as strong, assertive women, who had struggled against the odds in arriving at university. They were determined to continue to "succeed" occupationally and economically, while being aware of the pressures of them both as black and as women. Ironically, their careers might well be furthered by the token woman syndrome, employers might be delighted to take on a token "two in one' - black and female! They are likely to become a part of a small but growing black middle class in Britain, and since, as Wilson has pointed out (Wilson 1979) it was more highly educated blacks who led civil rights campaigns in the U.S.A. their influence may well be felt throughout the black community in Britain.

ACKNOWLEDGEMENT

I should like to acknowledge the help given by Andy Permain, N.U.S.

REFERENCES

Driver, G. (1977) "Culture, Competence, Social Power and School Achievement. West Indian Secondary School Pupils in the Midlands." *New Community*, Vol. 5, No. 4.
Driver, G. (1980) "How West Indians do better at School (especially the girls), *New Society*, 17/1/80.
Edwards, V. (1979) *The West Indian Language Issue in British Schools*, R.K.P.
Fuller, M. (1980) "Black girls in a London Comprehensive School" in (ed. R. Deen. *Schooling for Womens Work*, R.K.P.

Houghton, V.P. (1966) "A Report of the Scores of West
    Indian Children and English Children on an individually
    administrative test". *Race*, Vol. 8, No. 1.
Kuman, K. (1974) "A Child and a Stranger. On growing out of
    English Culture" in (ed.) B. Parekh. *Colour, Culture
    and Consciousness*. Allen and Unwin.
Ladner, J.A. (1971) *Tomorrow's Tomorrow - The Black Woman*.
    Doubleday, N.Y.
Lerner, G. (ed.) (1972) *Black Women in White America*.
    Pantheon, N.Y.
Little, A. et al. (1968) "The Education of Immigrant Pupils
    in Inner London Primary Schools", *Race*, Vol. 9, No. 4.
Mezu, S.O. (1970) "Towards a Progressive Pan African Studies
    and Research Programme". *Black Academy Review*. Vol. 1,
    No. 2.
National Union of Students (1980) *Just a Segment*. Evidence
    presented to the Rampton Committee Enquiry into the
    education of West Indian children.
Payne, J. (1969) "A Comparative Study of the Mental Ability
    of 7 and 8-year old British and West Indian Children in
    a West Midlands Town". British Journal of Educational
    Psychology, Vol. 39.
Parekh, B. (1974) *Colour, Culture and Consciousness*, Allen
    and Unwin.
Phillips, C. (1979) "Educational Underachievement in
    Different Ethnic Groups". *Educational Research*, Vol. 21,
    No. 2.
(Rampton Committee) (1981) *West Indian Children in our
    Schools*, Cmnd. 8273, H.M.S.O.
Rosen, H. and Burgess, T.(1980) *Languages and Dialects of
    London School Children*, Ward Lock.
Sharpe, S. (1976) *Just Like a Girl*, Penguin.
Sivanandan, A. (1974) 'Alien Gods' in (ed.) B. Parekh,
    Colour, Culture and Consciousness, Allen and Unwin.
Wallace, M. (1979) *Black Macho and the Myth of Superwomen*,
    Calder, London.
Wilson, W.J. (1979) *The Declining Significance of Race*,
    University of Chicago Press.

NOTES

1. Black students from two London Colleges were
brought together by the N.U.S. to hold discussions, prior
to submitting evidence to the Rampton Committee.

SOCIO-CULTURAL CONSIDERATIONS IN THE REFORM OF COLONIAL SCHOOLING: A CASE STUDY FROM PAPUA NEW GUINEA

Graham Vulliamy

Discussions of inequalities in education based on class, race and gender usually address themselves to the existence of such inequalities <u>within</u> a given society. In this paper, however, I am more concerned with arguments relating to the potential role which educational systems play in the maintenance of inequalities <u>between</u> nations. A central tenet of the dependency paradigm in sociological analyses of Third World countries is that their economic and social development can only be understood by reference to a global context of international capitalism. Thus racial inequalities between North and South are perpetuated by the dominance of metropolitan societies over peripheral societies via colonial and neo-colonial relationships in the cultural, economic and political spheres. A number of writers have interpreted the schooling process as an important means of helping maintain such a dependent relationship. Carnoy (1974), for example, views education as a form of cultural imperialism. He provides a largely historical analysis which 'not only relates the role of schooling to fit Africans and Asians into European colonial structures, but also how schooling was called upon to colonize people in the United States, and how these methods and experiences were and are exported back to a now 'independent' Third World' (p. 23). A similar theme characterises a more recent collection of papers on 'education and colonialism', edited by Altbach and Kelly (1978).

A general characteristic shared by many Third World countries has been the inheritance of a Western model of schooling. In practice this has meant schooling in formal institutions typified by values and practices derived from the institutional-

isation of mass schooling in the West: a hidden
curriculum reflecting hierarchy, selection on the
basis of individual competition and Western (or
rather industrial) notions of punctuality and order;
highly didactic, and often authoritarian, styles of
teaching; and an overt curriculum exemplifying what
Young (1971) has suggested are the four main
characteristics of high status knowledge - literacy,
abstractness, individualism and lack of relation to
everyday life.

The appropriateness of such a pattern of
schooling has been called into question in many
developing countries. Those committed to
socialist paths of development have recognized that
such an academically-oriented curriculum contributes
to the development of divisions between mental and
manual labour and the consequent solidification of a
class structure. On the other hand, predominantly
rural societies who are attempting to modernise
along more capitalist lines have also recognized
the sheer irrelevance of Western curricula for a
concerted economic strategy promoting rural development. Consequently, as Sinclair and Lillis' (1980)
recent book on 'School and Community in the Third
World' demonstrates, there have been numerous
attempts to introduce a more relevant, community-
oriented education in such countries. However,
such work-related educational projects have usually
failed because they have been interpreted as of
inferior status in a dual system of academic and
vocational schooling (Colclough, 1976 and Foster,
1965).

Papua New Guinea has recently embarked on a
particularly interesting attempt to reform its
colonial pattern of secondary schooling. The
Secondary Schools Community Extension Project
(SSCEP) is a five year pilot project due to end its
first phase in 1982. It is designed to test the
feasibility of providing a more relevant rural
education at the secondary level, whilst avoiding
the dangers of a dual curriculum split between
academic and vocational streams. Five secondary
schools in contrasting regions of the country were
chosen to try the project in the period 1978-82.
If the project is successful, and progress to-date
has been encouraging, the plan is to extend it to
larger and larger groups of secondary schools until
eventually they are all SSCEP oriented.

The general aims of SSCEP are very broad. They
include the production of school leavers who are
both less alienated from village life and more

capable of contributing to rural development through self-employment; the de-institutionalisation of parts of secondary schooling by both setting up out-stations, where small groups of students go for weeks at a time, and by developing community extension activities and learning programmes in local areas; the redesigning of curricula in grades 9 and 10 (approximate ages 15 and 16) so as to relate academic and practical skills in a structured way; the improvement of teaching and curriculum development skills of teachers in SSCEP schools via intensive in-service school-based training programmes; and the maintenance of academic standards in the SSCEP schools in order that the opportunities for a small number of students to proceed to higher education are not curtailed (1). SSCEP, therefore, has something in common with other attempts to integrate academic and practical work in a community related context, such as Tanzania's 'Education for Self Reliance' and the Cuban 'Schools in the Countryside' campaign.

This paper will raise some issues based upon a 7-month period of research on SSCEP in Papua New Guinea during 1979-80. The research involved participant observation in two SSCEP boarding high schools and a five week stay on a bush outstation, where groups of about forty students were taught by two teachers for periods of a month at a time. In the space available here I can do no more than use some illustrative data from my case studies, which have been fully reported elsewhere (2), to illuminate some general factors which either impede or facilitate educational change in a neo-colonial environment. In the process, however, I hope to cast a little light on what Ball (1981), in his review of sociological accounts of schooling in developing countries, has argued has been hitherto a total 'black box':

> It is both striking and disappointing to find that there are no sociological ethnographies of schooling in developing societies ... It is virtually impossible to find sociological accounts that employ the words and meanings of the 'educated' themselves as sources of data ... Sociologists need theories of schooling which articulate with the realities confronted on a day-to-day basis by teachers, pupils and administrators (p. 311).

I will begin by looking at some major

constraints on change and will then consider the
possibilities, by examining some of the more
optimistic outcomes of my research into SSCEP.
A general conclusion is that dependency theories
of education as cultural imperialism, such as those
of Carnoy (1974), suffer from deficiencies similar
to the correspondence theories of writers such as
Bowles and Gintis (1976). An emphasis on the
macro level of analysis and on over-deterministic
relationships between schooling and the economy and
wider society not only leads to over-simplified
assumptions of homogeneity at the interactional
level, but also plays down the possibilities either
of forms of resistance or of the creation of
alternatives in the pattern of schooling.

The wider social and economic context in which
any development within Papua New Guinea needs to be
viewed is one of dependency on Australia (3).   In
such circumstances educational reforms are often
sponsored by international organizations such as
the World Bank - organizations which, as Wickham
(1981) has argued, often promote reforms according
to criteria which may well not be in the best
interests of the recipients of aid.   It is important
to stress, therefore, that SSCEP is a home-grown
project funded entirely by the Papua New Guinean
Ministry of Education.   The original idea for the
scheme came from Papua New Guineans within the
Ministry of Education who were concerned to modify
the secondary school system so that it was more
supportive of the National Development Strategy of
encouraging rural development.   However, the specific details of the project, together with plans for
implementing it, have been devised by a central team
of four expatriates.   An important principle under-
lying the processes of curriculum development and
community extension in SSCEP is that such developments should as far as possible be carried out
within the schools themselves, albeit with the
guidance of the headquarters team based in the
country's capital.   There are two reasons for this.
First, the programmes in the five project schools
are necessarily different in that they are related
to very different community contexts.   Second, it
is felt that SSCEP is more likely to succeed if
large numbers of staff in the school are involved
in its planning and implementation from the outset.
In both the schools where I was conducting research,
however, such an involvement of all the staff never
materialised and one of the main reasons for this
was the potential conflict between expatriates and

Papua New Guineans in the promotion of the
innovation.   Although in each school about half
the staff were nationals, the political and administrative structure of the school tended to impede
national staff involvement in key decisions and
consequently the planning of SSCEP was no exception
to this for the national staff.   Most of the SSCEP
teachers who had been appointed specifically to
develop relevant practical projects in the schools
were expatriates.   Although the intention was to
involve all staff in the replanning of grade 9 and
10 syllabi so that skills in the core subjects of
English, Maths, Science and Social Science were
carefully integrated with skills being taught in the
practical projects, expatriates tended to dominate
the planning meetings within the school.   As one
admitted to me:

> I found the expats overpowering ... they took
> over the whole thing, because we speak quicker
> than the nationals and like eager to get the
> whole thing over and done with. We didn't
> give the national teachers enough time to
> think about it and put something into it.

For the expatriate teachers the main aim was to
produce the product, in the form of a carefully
prepared written programme for curricular integration
and practical projects, in the most efficient manner
possible.   For SSCEP Headquarters, however, the
main aim of the school-based curriculum development
programme had been to involve the national staff of
the schools especially in the process of replanning
teaching programmes.   Since the main aim of SSCEP
is to test the viability of the scheme as a model
for the future of Papua New Guinean secondary
schools, whose staff are being increasingly local-
ised, SSCEP Headquarters regard the process of
involving nationals in course development, even if
the final product is not as satisfactory, as the
more important.   But this was often not the way in
which the exercise was perceived by expatriate
teachers within the schools themselves.
The difficulty which national teachers
experienced with the curriculum development side of
SSCEP is indicative of another major constraint on
the programme.   The degree of initiative being
asked of teachers, together with an emphasis in
SSCEP on student-centred learning strategies,
conflicts with the style of teaching for which
Papua New Guineans have been tained.   SSCEP

requires that teachers operate at what Beeby (1966) has called 'the stage of meaning' and yet empirical evidence suggests that most teachers in Papua New Guinea are at what Beeby calls 'the stage of formalism' (Guthrie, 1980a, 1980b). Moreover, much of the hidden curriculum of the traditional Papua New Guinea high school works against the SSCEP aim of students taking a more active part in the learning process. This was particularly apparent at a Catholic mission school in which I was researching. The Catholic order's teaching tradition was one of exerting a tight, authoritarian control over the students and allowing them little scope to exert responsibility. There was also an air of extreme formality in most lessons and certain classroom traditions, such as students having to stand up in class when answering teachers' questions, increased students' passivity.

Another constraint which became clear as the research progressed was the various ways in which some of the aims of SSCEP were viewed as conflicting with certain aspects of traditional Papua New Guinean cultures. At one of the research schools most of the students I talked to expressed the view that, if they failed to obtain a wage job in the formal sector, then they would be happy to return home to their villages. This accords with much research in Papua New Guinea which suggests that the people are far more attached to their villages than is the case in other developing countries, a point to which I shall briefly return later in this paper. However, despite this apparent willingness to return to the village, students identified many problems about doing so, such as 'wantoks' (pidgin for 'one talk' - a reference to the members of the same language grouping who are conceived of as one large extended family), their lack of status being young, and shortages of land. Many of them feared that they would be the objects of sorcery or magic against them. This suggests that the SSCEP emphasis upon encouraging students to go back to the village and use their own initiative and skills they have learned to modernise rural life could strongly conflict with traditional culture, at least in Milne Bay Province, one of the sites of my research. Numerous students there said that they would be afraid to start a project of some kind in their villages for fear of jealousy and magic. For example, one student who had shown remarkable qualities of responsibility and leadership at the school's bush outstation told me that, if he did not obtain a job, then he would return to his village and start a tradestore. However, he went on to add that if it was successful and people became jealous of him, he would have to close it down:

> Because as far as I know native customs are different from your customs ... if a person is running a successful business somebody want to come in, you know, like make magic ... something like this to stop that successful business. So maybe if I'm running a business, somebody come and like do this to me, maybe I'll stop that business.

A few students either said magic was no longer a problem in the area from which they came or argued that, as long as one's plans were openly discussed and agreed with village bigmen beforehand, then there would not be any problem. However, for most students, magic represented a real threat to their initiative, suggesting that Fortune's assessment of the impact of magic in the 1930s on an island in Milne Bay Province still represents an accurate portrayal of villagers' beliefs:

> [Magic is used] generally "to cast down the mighty from their seat". There is great resentment of any conspicuously successful man in Dobu. There is respect for old age and for primogeniture, but nothing except anger for any differences in success due to ability. The black art is used against an over successful gardener, since he is believed to have stolen other person's yams from their gardens by magic (Fortune, 1932, 1963, p. 176).

It was clear, therefore, from my interviews that from the students' point of view, simply having the skills to promote village projects was not in itself enough.

At my second research school, a Catholic boys' school in Central Province, students did not extensively mention the problem of magic, although the latter was reportedly fairly widespread in some local villages. Nor did students often refer to problems of a shortage of land, since most of them came from areas where land was plentiful. However, there _was_ a general concern that their lack of status in the village hierarchy, together with pressure from their 'wantoks' would curtail any

economic ventures on their part. The school staff
were very aware of this problem - as one of them
told me:

> There are traditional restrictions on them.
> Until a fellow gets married, he's just a small
> boy and this is a social problem we'll just
> have to face with SSCEP. It's something I
> want the kids to face head-on and I'd like to
> see it as an important study in their social
> science syllabus. So that they know and
> understand the authority structure and they
> know and understand how to work within the
> authority structure and what their obligations
> are to the various chiefs, wantoks and so on
> ... There is virtually a group responsibility
> in the village for any action that is taken.
> Here we are trying to get kids to act on their
> own initiative, accept the responsibility for
> their own actions, which is not normal to the
> village. Our [Western] concept of blokes
> earning a living, making a living to gain some
> kind of profit as somebody individual conflicts
> with village ethics, where demands are always
> put on those who do well.

Here there was a recognition that the
individualistic orientation of Western schooling is
in conflict with a collectivist philosophy which
pervades village life. In view of this, an
encouraging feature of SSCEP at this particular
school was the way in which group initiative and
responsibility were promoted wherever possible.
Thus subsistence gardens were planned and run by
groups of students who needed to come to mutual
agreement about their course of action. The plans
for community extension work in grade 10 involved
groups of students working together on a project in
a village. For a number of years the school has
had a policy of groups of staff visiting, at least
once a year during a vacation period, nearly all the
villages which send children to the school,
including those from mountain areas many days' walk
away. Given this close contact with the local
communities, it may be that staff could encourage
groups of school leavers to work together on a
project after they had left the school. Were such
work supervised, however minimally, by staff at the
school, not only would the group of ex-students
gain a solidarity to counteract the elders in a
village if necessary but the overt support of the

school for the project might help promote widespread village support as well.

Some of these perceptions by both students and teachers of a conflict between certain aims of SSCEP and the values of local communities are highlighted by Carrier's (1980) anthropological study of the constraints on the application of new knowledge in village life on the very small island of Ponam in New Guinea.

It was found that when Ponams skilled in some technical trade returned to the island, they did not put their skills to practical use even though by doing so they could have in some sense bettered people's lives. This was because Ponam attitudes to informal exchange, together with their conceptions of equality, meant that putting special skills to use resulted in a social, and often financial, cost to the individual rather than a benefit. As Carrier puts it by way of example:

> Under the Ponam informal exchange practice, I can expect no specific repayment from you in return for my sharpening your axe. Rather, I can expect that at some time in the future you will help me. But, I could expect that future help from you anyway, because you and I are in that sort of relationship, a relationship which is independent of any specific routine gift or counter-gift (1980, p. 119).

As long as the skill in question, such as axe sharpening, is fairly widespread throughout the tribe, this poses no problem. If, however, someone acquires a skill that very few others possess, such as repairing radios, then if they make this skill known, they will be besieged by requests for help for which they are unable to claim any compensation for lost time or materials. The resulting resistance to the application of new knowledge cannot simply be put down to notions of traditionalism or 'conservative village elders' but rather to the unintended consequences of ethics and practices, which have helped maintain a society that is both caring and egalitarian.

Carrier concludes his article by looking at the implications for any educational scheme, such as SSCEP, which is designed to help rural development. He does this by considering the one exception to the lack of transfer of new knowledge to Ponam and that was the introduction of the Western skill of

baking.   There were two drum oven bakeries which
ran successfully as businesses with full community
support.   What differentiated this skill from the
others was, first, that knowledge of baking was
widespread on the island (thanks to a nearby
technical school where many Ponam girls went) and,
second, that the bakeries were licensed by the
provincial government.   Carrier concludes:

> This one example [of baking] suggests, then,
> two things.   First, the knowledge to be
> introduced should be introduced through
> several people at once, so that the demand
> on any one individual is reduced.   Second,
> it should be presented in such a way that it
> is itself seen to be set apart from the
> system of informal exchange.   Some sort of
> certificate or licensing suggests itself
> (1980, p. 124).

It would be wrong to draw too pessimistic
conclusions from Carrier's research about the
possibility of an educational policy helping support
an economic policy of rural development.   Not only
is Papua New Guinea characterised by numerous
different cultures with differing values (some of
which are positively disposed to modernisation in
the interests of raising the community's standard
of living), but also the research indicates that
even in Ponam new knowledge was introduced with
community support under certain circumstances.
However, Carrier's work does help make sense of
the kinds of reservations expressed to me by both
students and teachers in SSCEP schools.   It also
suggests that the Catholic schools' careful
selection of practical projects following advice
from local community leaders, together with their
stress on work by groups of students, was a
sensible policy to help alleviate any potential
conflict between SSCEP and local communities.
    I will now proceed to discuss some of the more
optimistic outcomes of my research, including some
findings which, I must admit, surprised me at the
time, given my prior knowledge of the fate of
similar schemes in other developing countries (4).
About 90% of the students I interviewed in the two
SSCEP schools expressed strong support for the idea
of SSCEP.   There was also widespread support
amongst the school staff, despite some reservations
such as the extra time and demands imposed on them
and the feeling that, with the extra time students

spent on practical work, teachers would have less time to cover the existing grade 9 and 10 syllabi. The finding that many students reported that their parents were happy about the idea of SSCEP, once it had been fully explained to them, was more unexpected given the documentation of parental opposition to such projects in other countries (5).

The generally very positive way in which SSCEP had been received reflects, I believe, both the careful manner in which the project has been implemented and the fact that it is argued that, despite the introduction of more practical and agricultural work, students' chances of selection for wage jobs or for higher education will not be impaired. A central aim of the project is to maintain or even raise academic standards in the SSCEP schools and thus to prevent the local community interpreting them as second best in relation to conventional secondary schools. Such an aim is hoped to be achieved by a structured integration of academic subjects with practical projects, so that skills taught in the main academic subjects of Maths, Science, English and Social Sciences are reinforced in a practical or agricultural project. This is done by careful curriculum planning within the schools, carried out by groups of teachers, and has therefore taken different forms in different contexts. For example, certain core subject skills (such as writing letters in English, areas and volumes in Maths) can be taught directly in the core projects (such as a cattle project, copra project, etc.); alternatively, some core subject skills might simply be reinforced in the core project; and core subject tachers could also change the content of their syllabi in order that the skills were taught using a similar content to that in the core project.

If the students were assessed using a conventional exam testing memorisation of the content of their core subject syllabi, then the fact that students spent less time on such academic work, coupled with the change in the content of syllabi in some cases, would undoubtedly penalise them and lead to poorer exam results.

However, the principal exams on which school leavers are assessed in grade 10 are skill-based rather than content-based, and also use multiple-choice questions to avoid strong biasses in favour of the students who, because of the areas in which they live, inevitably have a better command of English than other students. Factual information

tends to be given in the exam questions (and therefore does not need memorisation) and students' ans-
wers are dependent upon an understanding of such
information or upon skills of manipulating or
analysing it. The hope is that by reinforcing
academic skills in a practical project, students
may well do better in examinations, and the
earliest evidence from the SSCEP schools is that
their school exam results and consequent job record
for school leavers have been better since the
introduction of SSCEP than prior to it (Stanton,
1981a, 1981b). It should also be stressed here
that all the students in SSCEP schools follow the
same programme of integrated academic and practical
work with no streaming, whereas, of course, in
Britain attempts at more practical, community-related learning schemes are usually preserved only
for the less able who are not following a more conventional academic path (6).

The most common parental reaction to SSCEP
reported to me by both teachers and students who
had talked to parents was that it was a good idea
as long as their children had as good a chance as
before of getting a job. They recognised, however,
that many school leavers would not get jobs in the
formal sector, and their concern was that students
did not return to the village as 'useless bigheads'
(a common expression for young people whose heads
are full of Western ideas but who are both unmoti-
vated and incapable of contributing practically to
village life) or go to town to become unemployed
'rascals'. Although generalisations are dangerous,
given the diversity of Papua New Guinean cultures,
it does nevertheless seem to be the case that
Papua New Guineans have a far greater attachment to
village life than is found in many other Third
World countries. This is partly because traditional, and highly complex, patterns of land ownership
have remained largely unaltered and partly because
processes of modernisation, far from destroying the
traditional social structure of the village, seem
to have been incorporated within it. The legacy
of Australian, as opposed to British, colonial rule
has also perhaps contributed to this. Something
of the frontier outback mentality seems to have been
incorporated into the opening-up of Papua New Guinea,
whereas the ideal-typical British colonial in
African countries shortly before independence was
more usually viewed as an administrative pen-pusher
resident in urban areas. Thus one of the
difficulties that Tanzania has had in the implement-

ation of its education for self-reliance programme
is the inheritance of a colonial legacy, which
associates agricultural and manual work with
Africans and higher status white collar work with
Europeans. Saunders (1982) found that many
Tanzanian teachers interviewed in his research
disliked being seen 'getting their hands dirty'
with manual work, whereas in Papua New Guinea such
work is widely accepted by teachers and students
alike. For, unlike Tanzania, most conventional
Papue New Guinean high schools have a tradition of
self-reliance activities and also have agriculture
and practical skills as compulsory subjects on the
curriculum (7).
  Sociologists of education have rarely considered the literature on the implementation of curricular innovations, despite exhortations that
counter-hegemonic alternative pedagogies should be
institutionalised to help subvert the correspondence
between schooling and the wider capitalist society
(8). And yet the extent to which oppositional
practices can be maintained in schools is often
related to the particular manner in which such
innovations are managed. I will only touch upon
the question of implementation briefly here,
because the case has already been argued in detail
in a paper, co-written with Murray Saunders, which
compares the implementation of self-reliance in
Tanzania with the implementation of SSCEP in Papua
New Guinea (Saunders and Vulliamy, 1981). These
two reforms provide an interesting contrast in
modes of implementing innovations which are
essentially top-down ones (i.e. not the product of
a grass-roots reform by teachers and students
within existing schools, but rather of a government
directive). Saunders (1982) suggests that in
Tanzania there was little, if any, attempt to
specify how the policy, as delineated in Nyerere
(1967), was to be implemented at the school level.
Consequently, there was little attempt to provide
in-service teacher training on self-reliance, little
attempt to provide feedback on teachers' practices
and little extra provision in the way of resources
to schools. Little or no direction was given as
to possible ways of integrating academic and
practical work, and since the reforms were not
congruent with existing teacher practices, it is
not surprising that there remained a marked
discrepancy between theory and practice.
  The implementation strategy for SSCEP was very
different and corresponded closely to the major

approach advocated by Sinclair and Lillis (1980), following their review of 'relevant education' projects in developing countries. This involved a stepwise approach to reform using pilot schools and intensive in-service training of teachers within the schools themselves. Feedback and resources were provided for the pilot schools by SSCEP Headquarters, but the emphasis was upon the schools themselves devising their own SSCEP programmes, developing their own out-stations and so on.

While aspects of SSCEP, such as pedagogical styles, were not congruent with existing teacher practices, other aspects were, such as the previous tradition of self-reliance activities within the schools.

One of the conclusions of our analysis was that any attempts to integrate academic and practical work are filtered through the dominance of the existing assessment structure, which is based on a literary mode. Thus, whereas policy dictates require that self-reliance activities by students in Tanzanian secondary schools must be assessed, the potential of such assessment is neutralised. On the one hand, secondary schools in Tanzania are ranked nationally in every academic subject, so that teachers are therefore accountable for the academic success or failure of their students, whereas no such accountability exists for their failure to relate theory and practice. On the other hand, all students needed to pass their self-reliance assessments in order to complete their schooling successfully. Consequently, such assessments became a mere formality or, at best, a judge of general character or responsibility. By way of contrast, in Papua New Guinea the SSCEP programme, together with its attempt at structured integration of theory and practice, has been sold to teachers, students and parents as both a more relevant education and a more effective preparation for the existing grade 10 exams taken in all Papua New Guinea high schools.

It still remains an open question as to whether, through careful implementation, the literary mode of assessment itself can be at least partially eroded. One of the original aims of SSCEP was to develop some new assessment procedures which can test 'application, innovation, leadership success and a wide range of personal attributes and attitudes designed to reward those who excel in the practical implementation of the curriculum' (Stanton, 1978, p. 69). This was to be the responsibility of an assessment expert in SSCEP

Headquarters, who was to help devise these in collaboration with the schools. However, following difficulties in recruitment, an assessment adviser could only be appointed for one year of the five year pilot project. During this year (1980) he did lay the foundations in some of the SSCEP schools for an integration of the assessment of academic and practical work. In one of my research schools, for example, part of core subject assessment scores were to be derived from application of subject skills in the practical projects. But, as SSCAP Headquarters now admits, the loss of this member of the Headquarters team, together with a lack of replacement, will result in this particular aspect of the programme not being successfully implemented:

> In terms of SSCEP as a major educational project within Papua New Guinea, lack of systematic measurement of village-related skill application will leave a serious gap in the final analysis of the project as a whole (Currin, 1981, p. 6).

A lack of integration in the assessment programme proved to be an important constraint on what was otherwise one of the most interesting and successful oppositional practices generated by the SSCEP programme - the experience of schooling on a bush outstation which I was researching. Classes of around forty students spent a month at a time with two teachers at the outstation, which had been built with bush materials by contracted village labourers with the students' help. There they did a mixture of classroom work (English, Maths and Science) and practical activities such as subsistence-gardening, running a tradestore, making copra, a furniture-making project for the boys and a baking one for the girls. Attempts were made to integrate the classroom and practical work so that, for example, the maths programme was on tradestore and business maths. Students then took turns in manning the tradestore and keeping its daily accounts.

I found that, while on the one hand, students really valued their SSCEP work at the outstation and the new skills they learned, they nevertheless did not see it as 'normal' schooling. In particular, they viewed the difference between the high school and the outstation in academic-practical terms. Many of them were worried that, because they did not do much classroom work at the outstation (about three hours a day, including night study), they would have more to catch up at the high school. They also did not feel that their outstation work would help them in their exams. Similarly, teachers at the main high school complained that they had much less time to teach the official grade 9 syllabus, given the time that students spent at the outstation. To counteract these complaints, it is important that the outstation's academic programme should be clearly related to the normal high school curriculum and that there should be an assessment policy which reinforces this curricular integration. Without any guidance from SSCEP Headquarters, however, it is doubtful whether such an assessment policy will materialise.

The details of my research on the outstation have been reported elsewhere (Vulliamy, 1980, 1981c) but, in the context of this paper, it might be worth briefly mentioning those factors which con-- tributed most to the oppositional nature of school- ing there, in the sense of its providing alternat- ive practices to conventional schooling in Papua New Guinea. Students took a more active part in the learning process, both inside and outside the classroom, than they did at the main high school. They were also more prepared to use their own initiative and to work without supervision, demonstrating greater intrinsic motivation. Students also argued that the outstation was a much more suitable environment in which to integrate academic and practical activities, both because of the wider range of practical pursuits there and because practical activities at the high school were severely constrained by the rigidity of the timetable.

The outstation was characterised by an unusually egalitatian relationship between staff and students, and a general breakdown on the institutionalised hidden curriculum of the high school was facilitated by the small size of the outstation, by the delegation of much more responsibility to students in the running of the place and by its village atmosphere. The opportunities which the outstation makes available for student involvement in the local village communities is, I would argue, particularly important in terms of the attitudinal changes desired by SSCEP. One aim is to make students more positively disposed towards returning to their villages and putting their skills to good use there. To achieve this, continuous village contact is essential. Much of high school life is

oriented to town conditions: a mixture of people,
having things organized for students by staff, the
sleeping and sanitary arrangements, access to
sports, films and so on. Students spend four years
in such schools, many of them returning home only
once a year, a few never during their high school
career. Consequently, if students are not to be
totally alienated from village life, then they need
to be constantly reminded of it, or as one of the
students at the high school put it:

> We have to go out there to be used to the
> village situation and then when we leave
> school it will be a bit easier to stay in the
> village and do something for the village
> people.

The use of the local villages as an educational
resource did highlight one conflict, however, which
illustrated the limits to the flexibility with which
schooling at the outstation could be organized.
This concerned the differences between Papua New
Guinean and Western notions of time. A school
relies on punctuality, whereas to a villager time
is more inexact. An outstation can be very much
more flexible in its ordering of time than a large
school. However, it cannot be as unconcerned
about time as the village community, because
students are necessarily on the outstation for a
limited period themselves. Thus one of the
outstation teachers (an expatriate) was particularly
critical of curriculum and syllabus authors who
failed to recognize the implications of this aspect
of village culture:

> Now, for instance, the grade 9 Traditional
> Technology syllabus was written by someone
> who has never had anything to do with a
> village in Papua New Guinea ... it's obvious
> ... the guy sets out time limits for these
> village activities which is ludicrous ... he
> allows two hours to visit a village garden ...
> well it take three days ... We go the first
> day, and the village people aren't there when
> they say they are going to be there; so they
> go the second day and they get nearly there
> and then they visit someone else along the
> way. And the next day they go and they're
> gone all day long because it takes them five
> hours to walk to the gardens [which were up
> in nearby mountains], they're there for

> fifteen minutes and it takes them five hours
> to talk back ... and this is the way our
> garden survey has gone.

It therefore needs to be recognized that the kind
of community extension work which is advocated in
the SSCEP programme firstly must be able to operate
on a very flexible timetable and, secondly, will
inevitably take very much longer than conventional
school practical projects.

I have deliberately concentrated in this paper
on those socio-cultural considerations in the reform
of colonial schooling which were thrown up by ethnographic research into the perspectives of the
participants themselves. This is not, of course,
to deny that there may be influential wider structural features of which the participants are unaware.
However, I would suggest that this discussion of
the processes of schooling in a developing country
(a hitherto almost entirely neglected area - at
least from a sociological standpoint) acts as a
useful antidote to the over-determinism of much of
the dependency paradigm's analysis of schooling.
One of the contributions which sociologists can
make to the reform of schooling in any given context
is to help specify those conditions which facilitate
the adoption of oppositional practices within the
conventional school system. I have argued here
that, in this respect, there is something to be
learned from the experience of Papua New Guinea's
attempt to modify a secondary schooling system
designed by white colonisers, so that it is more
suited to the needs of its own indigenous peoples.

NOTES

1. A more extensive discussion of SSCEP, together
with some background information on both Papua New Guinea and
its educational system, is given in Vulliamy (1981a).
2. The two case studies are reported in Vulliamy
(1980) and Vulliamy (1981b), both of which contain
appendices on the methodology used, and a comparative
analysis of the two case studies, together with a
discussion of schemes similar to SSCEP in other countries,
is given in Vulliamy (1981c).
3. Amarshi et al. (1979) provide a radical analysis
of the political economy of Papua New Guinea. However, this
book has a number of deficiencies. A more balanced assessment of Papua New Guinea's development prospects can be
found in World Bank (1976).
4. Some of these findings might, of course, be put

down to the 'Hawthorne' effect, given the early stage of
SSCEP at which my research was conducted.   This is one of
the reasons why I am hoping to be able to return to Papua
New Guinea to do follow-up research in the last five months
of 1982, which coincides with the end of the pilot phase of
the five year project.

5.   The data on parental reactions are the weakest in
that they were necessarily dependent on both students' and
teachers' reports of what parents said.   Nevertheless, the
data were usually obtained from often detailed and lengthy
interviews with students and are likely to be more valid than
if such data had been obtained from students using a quest-
ionnaire.   At the first research school in Milne Bay
Province, about 90% of the students interviewed reported
parental support.   At the second school in Central Province,
only 50% of the student sample said that their parents
supported SSCEP, although teachers' reports gave a more
optimistic picture.   I argued, however, that the students'
reports were likely to be more valid (Vulliamy, 1981b, pp.
42-43).   Some tentative reasons for the differences in
levels of parental support in the two different areas are
given in Vulliamy (1981b), p. 43.

6.   In addition, unlike many other developing
countries, Papua New Guinea does not have a private schooling
system which creams off an elite of Papua New Guinea entrants.
There are, however, international schools which mainly cater
for the children of expatriate workers, following New South
Wales curricula.   They are open to anyone paying the required
fees, which are considerably higher than those for
conventional Papua New Guinea primary and secondary schools.
In 1980, about 0.37% of Papua New Guinean students were in
international primary schools and about 0.21% in international high schools.   As Weeks and Guthrie, forthcoming, note:
'these very much tend to be children of urban salary-earning
elites, and this is a sign of incipient class formation'.

7.   It is also worth adding here that, although one
of the main functions of primary schools in Papua New
Guinea is to select those students (in 1980, about 40% of
those finishing Grade 6) to proceed to secondary school, both
the philosophy and practice of primary schools stress
community-related learning, together with rural activities
in most cases.

8.   Such exhortations can be found in, for example,
Giroux (1981).

REFERENCES

Altbach, P.G. and Kelly, G.P. (eds.) (1978) *Education and
        Colonialism*, Longman.
Amarshi, A., Good, K. and Mortimer, R. (1979) ,*Development
        and Dependency: The Political Economy of Papua New*

Guinea, Oxford University Press.

Ball, S. (1981) 'The Sociology of Education in Developing Countries', *British Journal of Sociology of Education*, Vol. 2, No. 3.

Beeby, C.E. (1966) *The Quality of Education in Developing Countries*, Harvard University Press.

Bowles, S. and Gintis, H. (1976) *Schooling in Capitalist America*, Routledge and Kegan Paul.

Carnoy, M. (1974) *Education as Cultural Imperialism*, David McKay.

Carrier, J.G. (1980) 'Knowledge and its Use: Constraints upon the Application of New Knowledge in Ponam Society', *Papua New Guinea Journal of Education*, Vol. 16, No. 2.

Colclough, C. (1976) 'Basic Education: Samson or Delilah?', *Convergence*, Vol. IX, No. 2.

Currin, C. (1981) 'SSCEP: A General Curriculum Implementation Review of 1980', SSCEP Headquarters, Port Moresby.

Foster, P.J. (1965) 'The Vocational School Fallacy in Development Planning', in Anderson, C.A. and Bowman, M.J. (eds.), *Education and Economic Development*, Aldine Publishing Company.

Fortune, R.F. (1932) and (1963) *Sorcerers of Dobu*, Dutton.

Giroux, H.A. (1981) *Ideology, Culture and the Process of Schooling*, Falmer Press.

Guthrie, G. (1980a) 'Stages of Educational Development? Beeby Revisited', *International Review of Education*, Vol. 26, No. 4.

Guthrie, G. (1980b) 'Teaching Styles', Paper presented to the Extraordinary Meeting of the Faculty of Education, University of Papua New Guinea, Port Moresby, 18-19 September.

Nyerere, J.K. (1967) *Education for Self-Reliance*, Government Printer: Dar es Salaam.

Saunders, M. (1982) 'Productive Activity in the Curriculum: Changing the Literate Bias of Secondary Schools in Tanzania', *British Journal of Sociology of Education*, Vol. 3, No. 1.

Saunders, M. and Vulliamy, G. (1981) 'Practical Action in the Curriculum: A Comparative Analysis', Paper presented to the 'Sociology of Curriculum Practice' Conference, St. Hilda's College, Oxford, 21-23 September.

Sinclair, M.E. and Lillis, K. (1980) *School and Community in the Third World*, Croom Helm.

Stanton, R.J. (1978) 'The Secondary Schools Community Extension Project', *Administration for Development*, No. 11.

Stanton, R.J. (1981a) 'An Analysis of SSCEP Mid-Year Examination Results for 1981', SSCEP Headquarters, Port Moresby.

Stanton, R.J. (1981b) 'The Placement of 1980 Grade 10 Leavers from SSCEP Project Schools', SSCEP Headquarters,

Port Moresby.

Vulliamy, G. (1980) *SSCEP and High School Outstations: A Case Study*, ERU Research Report No. 33, University of Papua New Guinea, Port Moresby.

Vulliamy, G. (1981a) 'The Secondary Schools Community Extension Project in Papua New Guinea', *Journal of Curriculum Studies*, Vol. 13, No. 2.

Vulliamy, G. (1981b) *Planning for SSCEP: A Case Study*, ERU Research Report No. 38, University of Papua New Guinea, Port Moresby.

Vulliamy, G. (1981c) 'Combining a Constructive Rural Orientation with Academic Quality: High School Out-stations in Papua New Guinea', *International Journal of Educational Development*, Vol. 1, No. 2.

Weeks, S.G. and Guthrie, G., forthcoming 'Papua New Guinea' in Thomas, R.M. and Postlethwaite, T.N. (eds.), *Schooling in the Pacific Islands: Colonies in Transition*, Pergamon.

Wickham, A. (1981) 'Education Systems in an International Context', Block 2, Unit 6 of Open University course E353, Open University Press.

World Bank (1976) *Papua New Guinea: Economic Situation and Development Prospects*, Report No. 1150, 14th July.

Young, M.F.D. (ed.) (1971) *Knowledge and Control*, Collier-Macmillan.

PART TWO

RACE, RESISTANCE AND COLLECTIVE STRUGGLE

INTRODUCTION

In the first part of this book the main focus was on
the ways in which social and educational processes
condition the cultural identities of minority groups
and of groups acting in association with such
minorities.   In this section the focus shifts
towards a more sustained consideration of how
cultural groups whose members share certain
perceptions which critically challenge established
viewpoints use (or might use) such interpretations
as a basis for collective struggle.
Collective struggle is not the sole perogative
of a single oppressed group and in this second
section of this book careful attention is given in
the various papers to the ways in which we might
gain a deeper understanding of the dynamics of
collective resistance from investigations of the
contests made by different groups operating in different contexts.   Investigations of the forms of
resistance and conformity offered by working-class
boys (Willis), by groups of girls oppressively
labelled as deviants (Fuller), and by both black
and white youths faced with unemployment (Roberts
et al.), are all used in this comparative re-appraisal.
By making a re-appraisal of the nature and the
extent of collective struggle in this way, certain
key points are high-lighted relevant to a
consideration of the whole theme of this book.
Firstly, sets of cultural practice cannot be
conveniently categorised and labelled as distinctive
and unambiguous areas of specific forms of
oppression or as unique types of resistance.   The
conditions for cultural practice are more complex
than that.   Thus, the implication for both
analysts and activists is that because dominant
ideologies can be, say, both racist and sexist at
one and the same time and because these ideologies

can be selectively or generally resisted, then a collective response, in which provision is made for the accommodation of a plurality of interests, is required at both the level of description and of action.

Secondly, a great advantage of this kind of re-appraisal is that it directs a powerful spotlight on the precise nature of the established order, on what it is that is being struggled against. This might appear in the form of the strong and deeply-entrenched racist code which Mullard describes as invading the whole fabric of schools and society, or it might appear as concrete practices like repressive school regimes or distorted curriculum design, or, and this is crucial, it might appear in the form of weak codes and practices which are successfully contested and transformed by certain groups — and thus the approach helps in the identification of where the strengths and the weaknesses of the system are to be found and what forms these will take.

Thirdly, the re-appraisal has the great merit of reminding us, should we ever need such prompting, that social life is dynamic, that social order is precarious and that prevalent practices and procedures are neither inevitable nor unchangeable. But, we are also reminded that real change would only seem to be possible if it emanates from conscious, collective and concerted struggle, and we hope that the papers in this volume, in some small way, contribute to such an endeavour.

CULTURAL PRODUCTION AND THEORIES OF REPRODUCTION

Paul Willis

I'm taking the opportunity of my contribution
to this volume of the Westhill conference papers to
revisit my book Learning to Labour (1) on its fifth
anniversary. If the claustrophobia of family
reunions bores or grates, skip this chapter. If
you are reading on you'll find that I review, place
and develop some of the arguments of that book in
the light of recent developments in the literature,
and seek to rescue it from, what seems to me, a
double and contradictory fate: its inflation into
a simple 'resistance' paradigm (much in evidence at
the Westhill conference) which celebrates, roman-
tically and uncritically identifies with, an
oppositional or working class spirit; its consign-
ment to a deep pessimism (evident in much of the US
response to the book) (2) which closes off the
possibility of struggle and change. I also hope,
in mobilising for a critique of recent theory, to
place Learning and work of its kind in at least my
'brand' of the Cultural Studies tradition and to
argue for some of its continuing strengths.   It
also seems appropriate now to review and develop
some of my previous arguments concerning the
transition from school to work in the current period
of intractable economic crisis and associated and
quite unprecedented continuing educational and
institutional restructuration of the transition
into work/non-work and of 16-19 age group provision.
I deal with this in an extended conclusion to the
article.
    It may help the reader to know that I do not
come innocently to the reunion. What follows is
informed by two basic intentions. Firstly: the
admission but de-emphasis of the 'left functionalist'
side of my previous work - the over-developed
symmetry and irony of Learning, where what I called

'limitations' were draped too neatly over what I
called 'penetrations', as if accommodation could
exactly balance resistance in subordinate groups,
as if a 'spontaneous' design of capitalism 'from
below' were possible. Secondly: the re-emphasis
and promotion of a more complex, considered and
moderate version of what was always most important
and the other side of my work, what I now want to
call cultural production - the processes of meaning,
making, the alternative knowledges, the activity,
creativity and social promise of subordinated
groups, but considered now in a more internal and
dialectical relation with the structures of a
capitalist and patriarchal society. In this way I
hope to begin to work through some of the endless
antimonies between agency/structure, pessimism,
optimism, resistance/accommodation to clarify what
might be learnt from the past decade of educational
research and writing and to set a framework for
future tasks and possibilities. More of this later.
For now I turn to a brief overview of relevant
recent developments in educational theory and
research.

THEORIES OF REPRODUCTION I

Recent European and American work has powerfully
exposed the contadictions and illusions of the
social democratic 'settlement' in education
characteristic of most advanced western societies
since the war. In the UK this settlement accepted
that the post war expanding capitalist economy was
basically a benign phenomenon. It was moving most
people towards an affluent and a more middle class
life style. There were still problems: pockets
of poverty, inequality and failure. These were
left overs from the starker and more primitive pre-
keynsian capitalist system. But such anachronisms
could be removed without basically challenging the
nature of capitalism. Higher taxation and an
expanding state could be trusted to do the job.
State Education was the privileged instrument for
these reforms, and even potentially oppositional
groups, such as those in the labour movement, agreed
that no separate, non statist action was required
(3).
    Education seemed to offer the prospect of
individual human development as well as the prospect of greater social equality. Happily these
joint aims were compatible because they made the
economic system more efficient anyway: there was

a need for more skilled workers in the expanding
and high technological society. It was necessary
to 'dredge the pool of talent'. Furthermore the
over-riding aim of social integration would be
promoted because both the demands of individuals and
those of a healthy economy could be satisfied.
So great seemed to be the apparent internal
coherence of these aims that any educational
failure was repeatedly seen to be the fault of the
people at whom it was directed (4). Failure was
the fault of education's recipients, their environment, background, their early childhood experience
or their surrounding culture. Compensatory
education and the interest in 'cultural deprivation'
all aimed to top up the abilities and skills of the
poorer kids so that the 'disadvantaged' could come
up to a common starting grid in life's race. The
sociology of education, esconced at the aim of the
policy-maker, dug itself into deeper and deeper pits
by tunnelling ever further back into family, childhood, individual psychology and isolated cultural
effects to identify the source of 'failure'. Class,
and the analysis of class, really only made its
entry to designate a huge tautology - working class
people suffer educational and cultural disadvantages;
people who suffer educational and cultural disadvantage are working class. There was no
explanation of these things, nor suggestion of how
unequal class relations and capitalist production
might be centrally implicated in them.
Economic crisis, actual de-skilling in the
economy, unemployment, educational 'realism' and
the right wing backlash have severely questioned
and partially undercut the social democratic
educational settlement (3). A little critical
thought would anyway have shown that there can be
no hope of compatibility between personal development and equality when it is plain to see that
'personal development' for some leads nowhere and
for others to highly privileged positions, whilst
still others share this privileged position through
the effort only of birth. There is the world of
difference between real equality in life, of
expression and potential in all human beings, and
the mere equality of opportunity nailed to the
masthead of educational reform. This promises at
best only the fractional possibility of being in
the minority who win. What of 'equality' for the
majority who lose? Do they care where they were
on the starting grid once the race has started?
'Reproduction' theorists (outlined and

criticised in detail later) have suggested that
social democratic aims failed, not because of some
deficiency in the clients, but because working class
kids were supposed to fail.   Education was not
about equality, but inequality!   At their greater
distance from the policy makers, these theorists
suggested a systematic inversion of the social democratic objectives in education.   Education's main
purpose of the social integration of a class society
could be achieved only by preparing most kids for
an unequal future, and by ensuring their personal
undevelopment.   Far from productive roles in the
economy simply waiting to be 'fairly' filled by the
products of education, the 'Reproduction' perspective reversed this to suggest that capitalist production and its roles required certain educational
outcomes.

Learning to Labour can be generally located
within this view (at the same time, crucially, as
in a Cultural Studies perspective).   Schools may be
about many things other than 'Reproduction' and the
ethnographic project records and gives a reading to
this.   But so long as the burden of selection/sort-
ing/examination is placed on schooling in an unequal
and class society, then the 'Reproduction' perspective must be taken into account.   In fact the
book has added a qualitative dimension to the
exposure of the social democratic programme in
education.   Statistics show clearly the massively
uneven scope of provision and educational outcomes
as between the classes, but this can be explained
in a manner which leaves the logic of the original
approach still intact - it's the fault of working
class kids and their families.   Learning to Labour
added two things: firstly that it is exactly the
group of kids who most need to be recruited to the
new opportunities, who most actively reject
education.   Secondly it helps to suggest that far
from cultural responses being 'ignorant', 'anachron-
istic' and 'pathological' and in need of eradi-
cation, such cultures may in certain important
respects be in advance of the understanding of the
liberal agencies.   'The lads' culture, for
instance, is involved in making its own realistic
bets about its best chances in a class society and
about how best to approach an impoverished future
in manual work whilst their advisors are tying
themselves up in humanistic, developmental knots.

But I think the book had greater importance in
the critical qualification it made to the next
major step of the 'Reproductive' argument - how

education is <u>actually implicated</u> in producing the
opposite of 'social democratic hope', in producing
<u>inequality</u>.   There may be a justified scepticism
about social democratic aims in education, but the
'Reproduction' perspective moves too quickly to a
simple inversion, to their opposites.   Apparently
Education simply does the bidding of the capitalist
economy.   Education's main and uninterrupted purpose is the insertion of working class agents into
unequal futures.   Pupil experience and agency
become merely a reflex of structural determination.
The actually varied, complex and creative field of
human consciousness, culture and capacity is
reduced to a dry abstraction.   Capital requires it,
therefore, schools do it!   Humans become dummies,
dupes or zombies freely drawn on in their innermost
sensibilities.   The school is even the main site
for this cosmic drawing.   But for all we are told
of how this actually happens schools may as well
be 'black boxes' (5).
        To find our way through this impasse, and to
take up firmer ground for a critique of 'Reproduction theory' and for the exploration of the positive
contribution of <u>Learning</u>, it is useful to step back
from educational theory for a while and to consider
the general resources and approach of a 'cultural
studies perspective'.   This perspective also loc-
ates my book but is not bounded, of course, solely
by an educational interest.

THE CULTURAL STUDIES PERSPECTIVE

Definition is always a hazardous enterprise.   Some
of the flexibility and range of cultural studies
has actually depended on an eclecticism and
ambiguity which makes definition difficult - and
which definition would anyway limit.   Nevertheless,
as I am mobilising a sense of 'culture' to prepare
the ground for my general critique of 'reproduction
theory' some definition is due (6).
        At the broadest level I see the cultural
studies project as a particular kind of interest in
a particular 'moment' of the most general social
processes.   These are the social processes through
which people collectively produce themselves in
their production of social and material life.   This
production is always in relation to a particular
dominant, structured, Mode of Production, and is
conducted through antagonistic and structured social
relations - not least for the working class through
an antagonistic, though also reproductive, relation

to prevailing cultures and dominant ideological
practices.   Briefly, the 'cultural moment' in all
this concerns the specifically human and collective
activity of meaning making - the making sense, if
you will, of a structural location: a position in
a social relationship and Mode of Production (7).
     This is to rush the argument somewhat, and to
simplify, but it may be helpful to picture this
cultural interest as a focus upon one (for me
privileged) form amongst a variety of the ways in
which social agents are 'connected with' structure.
There are dangers in a simple 'subject/object' split
which I comment upon later, but I want to indicate
here three basic ways in which this 'connection'
can be made.   In orthodox marxist and general
structuralist thought the first and most fundamental
'connection' is the structural and historical
determination of subjectivity and culture - crudely,
to be born within a certain gender, a certain class,
a certain region, to be formed, developed and
become a social subject within a certain cultural/
ideological web and language community, to 'inherit'
a set of future possibilities.   This is more or
less fixed.   We cannot, for instance, decide to be
southern, rich, male and familied within 'cultural
capital'.
     The usual, complementary 'connection', our
second, is that such agents, formed in a certain
way, then set and behave in appropriate ways -
entering production in pre-ordained class roles,
marrying, voting and acting as responsible 'citizens'
of the bourgeois state - so as to maintain the
structures into which they were born and reproduce
them for the next generation - to repeat the cycle.
     What I want to add to these two is a crucial
'moment', so to speak, 'in between' - which
actually changes how we should anyway think of both.
This 'moment' is the specific object of an interpretative cultural studies.   It is the active,
collective use and exploration of received symbolic,
ideological and cultural resources to explore, make
sense of and positively respond to 'inherited'
structural and material conditions of existence.
Once born into and formed in a certain structural
location and symbolic community etc. (things over
which they have no choice) people also seek to
understand, 'see into' and respond to - especially
through the collectivity and part unconsciousness of
their cultural forms - these self same things.   The
first 'connection' concerns not just 'determinations'
but things also to be understood.   This is almost

112

to invert the traditional Marxist notion of base/ superstructure and of determinations running up from 'the economy' for instance. It suggests an active human capacity which runs the other way! It suggests an active and creative response, never specifiable in advance, by humans to what formed and forms them! Heresy to some ears! But for all that, perhaps because of that, a rude and vigorous indication of what I, at least, take the cultural terrain to be. Cultural studies attempts to present and analyse this meaning and sense making, this constructing as well as constructedness, this production of consciousness and feeling and of their larger, locating, cultural forms.

Of course, the granting of this 'creativity' and 'invention' cannot transcend some of the given-ness and structuring power of history, social location and inherited ideological and cultural discourses. Nor does it 'in normal times' prevent actions and behaviour which maintain and reproduce 'inherited' social structures and relationships. Indeed it may be that it is through some of these intentions, psychic and collective cultural pro-cesses, through senses of control and identity formation and their associated multitudinous, multiform, everyday decisions and compromises, that something of what we call 'structure' is produced and reproduced at all. This is why a 'cultural studies' perspective topples so easily into a 'Reproduction' perspective and can be pulled into its closure and pessimism. More of this later, and of the complexity of how we can understand the relation of cultural practice and production to social reproduction. For the moment and for our definitional purposes here, I am indicating that crucial 'moment' in larger social process which is concerned with collective meaning and meaning making, with sense and sense making and their associated cultural forms.

Within this over-arching definition it is possible to list more detailed and concrete aspects of the 'cultural level' (8). The latter includes relatively coherent systems of material practices and interlocking symbolic systems which have, according to the region, their own specificity and objectives. They constitute the ordinary milieu of everyday existence and its commonplace span of shared concerns activities and struggles through which, amongst other things, social agents come to a collective, mediated, lived awareness of their condition of existence and relationship to other

113

classes.

Characteristic features of this milieu include: 'lived collective awareness' as concrete forms of resistance; relatively rational collective responses to current dilemmas and possibilities; the immanence of unconscious and collective cultural meanings which nonetheless help to direct actions and constitute subjectivity; collective punctuations of regulating ideologies and enclosing technologies of control and domination; contradictory and complexly articulated discourses and inherited symbolic forms and practices; complex ideological effects which regulate meanings both as in-puts and out-puts of cultural forms.

However what I want to most emphasize here within the cultural studies perspective is a notion of cultural production (9). This is the active principle of the 'cultural level' and stresses a notion of social agents at their furthest from being passive bearers and transmitters of structure and ideology. They are seen, instead, as active appropriators who produce meanings and cultural forms by the transformation of materials into products with the use of tools which, at its own level, proceeds quite as material production. Cultural production is the process of the collective, creative use of discourses, meanings, materials, practices and group processes to explore, understand and creatively occupy particular positions, relations and sets of material possibilities. For oppressed groups this is likely to include oppositional forms and, what I called in Learning, cultural 'penetrations' of particular concrete sites, ideologies or regions. As an aside we may note that the uncovering of these repressed, informal forms becomes the especial province of a qualitative, ethnographic, commensurate, 'living' method - such processes do not leave their Public Records in the Bourgeois Office of Account.

The notion of cultural production, then, insists on the active, transformative natures of cultures, and on the collective ability of social agents, not only to think like theorists, but to act like activists. Life experiences; individual and group projects; secret illicit and informal knowledge; private fears and fantasies; the threatening anarchic power arising from irreverent association, and the dirty, material productions of these things; are not merely interesting additions, the open ended results of 'structural location', nor even the private recognition of structure as in

114

Wright's 'private troubles'. These things are
central; determined but also determining. They
must occupy, fully fledged in their own right, a
vital theoretical and political transformative stage
of our analysis. This is, in part, the project of
showing the capacities of the working class to
generate albeit ambiguous, complex and often ironic,
collective and cultural forms of knowledge not
reducible back to the bourgeois forms - and the
importance of this as one of the bases for political
change.

We are now in a position to return to a
consideration of the major contributions to
'Reproduction Theory'.

THEORIES OF REPRODUCTION II

It is, of course, Althusser in the celebrated ISA
essay (10) who claims for education the privileged
role in social reproduction. Education provides
the necessary skills for production, the necessary
graded ideologies for the social division of labour
and provides for the actual formation of subjectivities through the celebrated 'imaginery relationship of individuals to their real conditions of
existence'.

Now as a limited statement, at a certain level
of abstraction, this will do nicely for some
purposes and is an advance on liberal positions.
It indicates that, despite confusing ambitions to
the contrary in the Educational sphere, a social
relationship is continuously being achieved for
the purpose of the continuance of Capital formation.
But in a certain way this is tautologous - we know
from the evidence of our eyes that Capitalism
continues and that most kids go to school. Ergo-
schools are implicated in the formation of the
social relationship which is a condition for the
functioning of capitalism. For an explanatory
account which avoids this formalism and rationalism,
we need a notion of the actual formation of classes
- in relationship to each other to be sure - but
which nevertheless have their own profane material
existence and if you like, ontology. The implicit
account of what is 'doing' the relationship from
the working class 'side' for Althusser pictures the
working class as totally dominated and merely
'bearing' the structures of Capitalism. The
working class is formed by Althusser without a word
about its own cultural production.

Part of the problem here is the structuralist

conceit of the economy being comprised of pre-given 'empty' places which are then simply 'filled' by agents kitted out with the right ideologies and subjectivities. Far from structure being the result of contestation and the struggle over meanings and definition - one of whose sources, from the 'side' of the working class, is what I'm calling, cultural production - structure is an hyposthesized given in a quite unsocial world. The absolute given contours of 'places' are to be filled by agents who share no collective principles of variation or continuity of their own. With no sense of structure being a contested medium as well as an outcome of social process, 'Reproduction' becomes a mechanical inevitability. A pre-given and pre-empting structure of class relations and production is simply replaced. Agency, struggle, change - those things which at least partly, one may say, help to produce 'structure' to 'start with' - are banished in the ever pre-givenness of 'empty places'.

From a somewhat different 'structuralist' perspective Bowles and Gintis operate from within a similar paradigm of the reproduction of the social relations (as empty place filling) necessary, as a condition, for capital accumulation. Here we are faced not with the ideological operation of the ISA, but with the structural principle of the 'correspondence' (11). Even the appearance and rhetoric of autonomy in the educational realm is given-up. His majesty the Economy reigns supreme - and in his own clothes! The 'habituation' of the educational process is the same as 'habituation' to production - the one relationship directly prepares for the succeeding one. Certification adds legitimation to this socialisation for inequality. We have a prone class in its deepest ontology, cultural forms and material experiences called up and founded in the directly manipulative categories of Capital. One wonders from where the individuals, classes or groups are to come to even listen to, never mind understand, the fine call to a socialist pedagogic practice with which Bowles and Gintis conclude their book. They certainly cannot come from the world of 'correspondence'. The two halves of the analysis do not fit. Of course, the work of Bowles and Gintis is hugely important and highly impressive in its empirical scope, range and seriousness and concrete in a way which Althusser's contribution is not. Nevertheless the criticisms are now well known and also partly accepted by the authors. They constitute, again, in my terms the general charge of the lack of any notion of <u>cultural production</u> in the dominated class.

The notion of 'correspondence' omits the possibility of resistance and, through this, the constitution of working class identities at least partially separate from their ideal expression in the bourgeois imagination. 'Correspondence' omits the independent effect of the working class on its relationship with the dominant class, thus overlooking consciousness and culture as constitutive moments of social process. Human action is the consequence of quite inhuman and separate 'structures'. Thus the analysis is unable to comprehend the massive and currently evident 'misfits' between the economy and education, and finds it unnecessary to commit itself to a real analysis of what happens in schools and to the variety of the forms in which educational messages are decoded in particular student groups.

The analysis can conveniently take over much straight statistical work and bourgeois apologetics in this area, because the analysis is in a certain sense, confirming what these people believe: that it is possible to correctly identify social requirements and to effectively meet them. Against this must be placed the obvious fact that segments of the dominant group disagree anyway over industrially instrumental or humanistically developmental objectives for society, and that the 'autonomy', the 'professionalism' and university involvement in the 'educational interest', can provide alternative bases for assessment. Furthermore the 'needs of Capital' are likely to be contradictory anyway - in the current period, for some up-skilling, more de-skilling and some socialisation for unemployment even amongst the same cohorts of students.

I argue that <u>cultural production</u> amongst dominated groups of various kinds ensures that a straightforward imprint of social requirements on students - even if they were consistently defined - is impossible anyway. It also reminds us that what is often only a minimum habituation to work is actually achieved by the combination of many processes in many sites - not least gender formation in the family and the experience of production itself. It also reminds us that the school is only one in a chain of other sites implicated in many other kinds of 'Reproduction' struggles - not least gender and generation formation. We must

117

never conclude too early that the school is the pivotal site for the preparation of those warm, gendered, concrete bodies that actually enter production - still less read back this accomplished transition as a class logic of what goes on in schools.

Bourdieu's analysis marks a serious advance, in part, upon this perspective (12). We are introduced to a 'cultural level' at least for the dominating class - which really is shown to be different, and to have some autonomy, from the economic. Indeed what we can think of as finally a spurious autonomy is the central feature of education. A coherent field of rules and sets of relationships proclaiming itself as separate and objective dignifies, and makes 'official', a culture which is actually the property of the dominant classes. The higher one goes up the educational system, therefore, the most this culture is 'pre-supposed'. It is required for success. This same culture is therefore further proclaimed as the legitimate and objective one. Working class students fail not because they are working class, but because they do not have the 'objective' skills and language necessary for success. They are not 'cooled out', they are 'coded out'! Real Capital has become cultural capital; lack of capital (the possession only of labour power) becomes lack of cultural capital. Where production relations quickly show the actual social exclusion, inequality and heritability of real Capital, education guarantees the apparent equivalence, independence and free born equality of symbolic capital. Education mystifies itself, as well as others, in concealing its own basis in, and reproduction of, the power relationships in society. His majesty the Economy is willing to stand quite aside, so long as education performs this service.

We do have more satisfactory elements here towards a properly autonomous notion of how certification and legitimation might work. We are also given a detailed and plausible account of how certain crucial ideological inversions and mystifications are achieved without implicit recourse to a theory of false consciousness and the ox-like dumbness of the dominated class.

The Educational theory rests, of course, on the foundations of the larger Bourdieun system. The powerful group (apparently in any society) exerts its power to impose meanings through a 'cultural arbitrary' enforced by 'symbolic violence' in a way which hides the power relation which is its basis. This constitutes a double violence: both the imposition and the hiding. This is one of the important bases for the production of 'the habitus', 'the durably installed generative principle of regulated improvisations' (13) which provides 'dispositions' towards actions which finally 'reproduce' the original structures and power relations which are the basis for the original symbolic violence.

But it is in consideration of this general theory where we can see some of the faults which limit the value of the regional educational theory. Oddly we see a ghost of the problem behind Althusser's and Bowles and Gintis' analyses - because of the almost total separation granted to culture, and education's complicit role in its maintenance, the economy appears, though off stage, as the basic fixed universe to which culture is added. And 'the economy' makes its appearance, not as a specific Mode of Production full of contradictions, but as an abstract set of power relations, which, it appears, apply equally to <u>any</u> kind of society. That power is taken as a given, to which culture is then very persuasively added, in order to demonstrate its reproduction. But that original production of power is mythical and, finally, an assumption which allows the hall of mirrors of culture to stand and reflect at all. We have a pre-given asserted structure of power which is then reproduced culturally. What of the <u>formation</u> of that power structure, so to speak 'to start with'. What of agency in this 'Reproduction' when the question of power has been settled before we start?

It is only, I argue, in a material notion of <u>cultural production</u> working on and in the contradictions of a dominant Mode of Production that we can reach the notion of structured and durable social relations of power at all. For all the richness of the Bourdieun system, agency, struggle, variety, have again been banished from history. Capital, even for the powerful, becomes an inert possession - so much formal power, money and symbolic wealth - rather than a whole contested social relation worked through a whole Mode of Production.

The essence of the Bourdieun educational theory concerns, of course, bourgeois culture and there are, as I've said, advances here. But even here, at its strongest point, the system suffers from a lack of any notion of <u>cultural</u>

119

production in my sense. The problem of variety
and resistences amongst bourgeois children cannot be
handled under the massive weight of homogenous
symbolic violence and cultural arbitrariness. Nor
are stages of 'acculturation', their characteristic
motives, subjective and inner contradiction handled
in the general notion of 'habitus'. For all the
important advances here over a simple notion of
ideology we are left finally with a traditional
socialisation model - the Bourgeoisie transmit,
quite unproblematically, their culture to their off-
spring.
      These difficulties and inadequacies become much
clearer when we look at the Bourdieun scheme, not
for dominant transmission and reproduction, but for
subordinate reproduction and transmission. The
arguments about the cultural legitimation of dominant
culture are perhaps clear enough. But even if the
dominated accept that they have no right to cultural
privilege, this is not a full argument for their
acceptance of social underprivilege and economic
exploitation. Why should they accept the
dominance of cultural capital anymore easily than
they accept the domination of real capital? One
might as well say that they have no real capital
either, or that there is an available ideology
concerning free capacity to accumulate real capital
as well as symbolic capital, enjoyed by all. But
this does not prevent the dominated from resisting
its power. Of course there is a partial explanation perhaps in that cultural capital legitimates
itself through certification also as the right to
manage - a technocratic justification - but this
sits ill with the overwhelming literary/artistic/
humanities rather than technical definition of
culture in Bourdieu. We are still in need of
some account of why the 'powerless' apparently,
for the most part, accept their unequal fates.
Crudely, though it might be one of the conditions
for, the dominated's acceptance of their cultural
inferiority, could never be an adequate basis for
their general submission to exploitation. How do
the 'powerless' understand and accept their
position? What is their role in 'Reproduction'?
      Unfortunately Bourdieu's realm of the cultural
does not function in the same explanatory fashion
for the dominated. They become indeed the dis-
possessed. Apparently 'culture' for all that it
designates as separate and independant really does
mean Bourgeois culture. The dominated have no
culture. Their 'culture', apparently, is only the

120

medium of the transmission backwards of their
'objective' chances in life.   They disqualify
themselves because they have never had a chance.
What of autonomy here?   It was no impediment to
Bourgeois cultural production - at its own level -
that they had every chance in life!   His majesty
the Economy has entered here again with a vengeance,
and the culture of the oppressed is the same as
their structured location in society.   We do not
even have the framework of 'correspondence'.
Because neither dominant nor subordinate cultural
production and transmission had been rooted in a
Mode of Production, class struggle and contestation,
and since there are no handy common-sense items
around which proclaim themselves through aesthetics
as 'culture' for the dominated class, then the
dominated have no relatively independent culture
and consciousness.   They just recognise their
chances.   It might be theatre for the Bourgeoisie
but its betting on rigged horse racing for the
proletariat - and moreover they're the horses.
Economic life has to play all the parts in proletarian culture!   With this lack of any notion of
a specifically cultural and relatively independent
cultural production in relation to material life
and labour for the Proletariat, it comes as no
surprise that the Bourdieun system has nothing to
say about a radical politics of education.   It
presents, finally, a gloomy, enclosed, Weberian
world of no-escape.   There is no theoretical basis
for a politics of change, for the production of
alternative or radical consciousness.
      I'm suggesting generally that whilst Bourdieu
offers - though there are weaknesses - a very
important set of arguments concerning dominant
culture, its relative independence, mode of transmission and constitution of the nature of a class
and how that helps to constitute the nature of a
social relationship necessary to Capital, we are
given no real help towards understanding what may
be similar processes in the culture of the
dominated.
      For the moment, leaving aside the rest of his
oeuvre, there are some clear hints and indications
towards this in Bernstein's formulations around
educational codes and their relation to Production.
In his essay 'Aspects of the relation between
Education and Production' (14) where he deals really
only with aspects of correspondence rather than with
legitimation (to say nothing of what I'm calling
cultural production), we are presented with the

possibility for the first time of radical breaks
between the education and the production system.
The educational code with its tendency towards the
combination of weak 'classification' and 'framing',
tending, therefore, towards the 'integrated code'
feeds into an industrial system which tends towards
- especially we might say now under Thatcherism and
Reaganism - strong 'classification' and 'framing',
that is towards the 'collection code'. This
disjunction - contrary to what we might have
expected from 'correspondence theory' - is most
marked at the 'lower' educational levels (most prone
to developments towards the 'integrated code') and
at the 'lower' industrial levels (traditionally and
still marked by strong 'classification' and 'framing'): in a word for the working class and its
lower reaches - the crucial site for 'correspondence'
theories.

Now Bernstein does not develop this, but
clearly if aspects of education are disfunctional
for the Production system - do not produce in
themselves the social relation necessary to
Capitalism - but yet the 'transition from school to
work' is achieved, and by all accounts achieved most
unproblematically by this target group, then there
are other processes occuring, most likely at least
partly on the site of the school, which do achieve
such outcomes. Somewhat lopsidedly here, but
nonetheless in a very clear manner, we see the
scope for an analysis of informal forms of the
school, for the contradictory processes of cultural
production that interests me, where in our previous
theorists, there was simply no space for such
concerns. Bernstein has introduced the possibility
of the school not functioning unproblematically as
whatever variety of an ISA, but as a site of
contradictions and larger processes with cultures
and differences which are no part of its official
purposes. In fact the school may work, for some
social groups, not through its homologies with other
parts of the social system, but through its
differences, and in some ways it may function, with
respect to 'Reproduction', not through its own
categories and intentions, spinning on the axis of
its own integrity, but profanely and eccentrically
as the only partially determining site of quite
other processes of cultural production. The
school may be implicated in different ways in both
dominant and subordinate cultural production. This
suggests that some dominant interests and ideologies may not be transmitted or communicated

directly but through social and cultural dialectics, mediations and struggle. The powerful do not always impose meanings without those meanings being taken into account by the dominated - or at least an important section of them which provides opposition- al themes as a cultural resource for the rest. This dominated response takes in other meanings to those coded in the dominant transmission. Furthermore we must see that this imposition itself can, indeed must, in its turn, take into account oppositional or alternative responses.

Despite the promise of Bernstein's contribution it shows some of the same one-sidedness of other theorists considered. The economy, and its implicitly empty places, stands silently waiting for the gift of whatever educational process however understood. They - the 'empty' places developed in Bernstein's case through his own version of an abstractly multiplying formalism - are not them- selves the product of the struggle of constituted, acting classes. We are also presented with only the pristine simplicity of one form of domination, class, with no mention of Patriarchal and race domination and how, at least aspects of their ideological forms may intersect with class.

All the theories also deal most basically with power, rather than with a Mode of Production in relation to material interests, experiences and culture. Power is somehow idealistically seen as, in itself, _bad_, as synonymous with domination. Without a fully inward notion of struggles through power, and without notions of countervailing power and of working class resources constituting 'their side' of the class struggle, as intrinsic features of the theoretical position, we are left only with untheorised or asserted notions of mechanical ideologies simply imposing themselves to stand in the place of what I have called for - more dynamic notions of cultural production. Pessimism, in different forms, reigns supreme.

THE DIFFERENCES BETWEEN CULTURAL PRODUCTION AND 'REPRODUCTION'

It is precisely this pessimism from which I want to free my previous work - or one side of it. Although Learning to Labour is, in part, associated with the 'Reproductive' perspective and is fully addressed to the importance of real educational outcomes, it is actually more centrally addressed to questions of cultural production. The 'Reproductive' effects

which I notice only arise partly through the self
activity of 'the lads' in their own culture.   The
book deals with a major transitional point, the entry
to work, as one of the classic 'choice points' where
'structure' and 'agency' most crucially meet - not
where 'structure' overpowers 'agency'.   The aim of
the ethnographic chapters is not just to dryly
prepare readers for a magical 'Re-production', but
to demonstrate and recreate something of the close
grain and creativity of a culture as it is
thoroughly enmeshed in, though far from directly
determined by, its structural location.   The
chapters also aim to show something of the specificity by which some general themes and discourses are
worked up into the particular shape of a 'cultural
form' in the detail and materiality of its locating
institution.   It is the material arrangements,
social organisation and educational paradigm of the
school which help to form the specific dynamics and
structure of the counter-school culture - just as
we might say that very important aspects of the
school organisation are influenced not by some
abstract needs of Capital but by the very real
problems of containing, controlling and regulating
this culture.
        The essential point is that Learning to Labour
starts not with 'Reproduction' but with cultural
production, 'Reproduction' proceeds through
cultural production in its analysis (15).   The
problem with the 'Reproduction' theories of
various sorts we have looked at is that by
articulating the analysis on general 'Reproduction'
from the beginning they have collapsed notions,
or implied highly mechanistic notions, of cultural
production.   In my view we must, so to speak,
logically conclude with socially contested reproduction of the conditions for Capital accumulation - not begin with this point and therefore
write out the space for a dynamic analysis.
        The distinctiveness of Learning to Labour, then,
is not in its provision of another version of how
general processes continually refill emptying but
fixed places.   It is in its emphasis on the
moment of cultural production in a specific example
even if it becomes implicated in 'Reproduction'.
Cultural production's contribution to 'Reproduction'
is an ever repeated creative process which each time
carries no more guarantee than the last, and which,
in different material or political circumstances,
can produce different outcomes.
        My suggestion is, therefore, that for a

properly dialectical notion of 'Reproduction' one
starting point should be in the cultural mileau,
in the everyday span of the material practices,
productions and practical consciousness of lives in
their historical context. We should investigate
the form of living collective cultural productions
that occur on the determinate and contradictory
grounds of what is inherited, and what is currently
suffered through imposition, but which are nevertheless creatively and actively experienced as new
by each generation group and person - believed and
occupied, 'marked', precisely because of such
things. 'Reproduction' directs us only towards
general features of a relationship and not to the
internal features of a class, or a tight specificity
of the 'conditions' required by Capital. A range
of possibilities within cultural production, with
quite different specifications of social groups,
their qualities and nature, could satisfy this
general abstract social relation - though some,
clearly would not.
     It is absurd in my view to think that something
called Capital could coherently think out its list
of tight social conditions - these and no other -
still less imprint them on a malleable class. It
is not to say that the Capitalist Mode of Production
does not set certain limits on cultural production,
or that its historic forms of settlement with real
cultural processes do not supply powerfully
formative inferences. Furthermore, ideological
processes are undoubtedly involved in cultural
production and certain elemental features of the
logic of the capitalist labour process do materially
imprint themselves on living experiences and
meanings. On the other hand, it is to say that all
of this is not of the order of a specification, or
direct determination. Capital cannot really 'know'
what are the fundamental social and cultural
conditions of its dominance - partly because these
are anyway always changing with the help of
categories, meanings and substances supplied, often
through struggle, actually from below. Capital
will accept ever new arrangements that allow it to
work and we may say, that now, for instance,
schools with other sites are 'blindly' and
'profanely' forging new arrangements that another
generation of 'Reproduction' theorists in the
future will take as the rigid conditions for the
functioning of the then capitalist labour process.
In an awesome reverse of the Medusan myth,
'Re-production' theorists look back to cultural

production and turn it, not themselves, to stone.
'Reproduction' should direct us to the limited, bare,
truly open, 'teeth gritting', elements of the
conjunction between cultural production and the
minimal maintenance of the Capitalist social
relation - not to a wholesale theory of social
generation which is always much, much more than
this.   And if cultural production, in the school
for instance, directs us towards some of the ways
in which 'Reproduction' is achieved we must also
include under 'Reproduction' several other processes and other sites: the condition of wage
labour itself; the labour process; the state and
its organs; the police; the media; leisure
institutions.
     The militant distinction I am making between
cultural production and 'Reproduction' also guards
against a creeping functionalism.   In the first
case, of course, one of my basic arguments, the
motives and intentions of cultural production concern the specifics of its own level, opposition
and what I called in the book 'penetrations' for
instance, amongst the oppressed, rather than
functional harmony.   More formally, however, in
the case of male counter-school culture, subordinate cultural production does help to provide
some of the social conditions towards the overall
Capital relation.   But it is, actually a highly
inefficient and hardly intended method of
'achieving' these aims - even when considered at
its abstract 'pure' best - quite apart from the
obvious social dislocation and unease it produces.
The space, the school, in which it occurs is paid
for by taxes, some of which are from the proletarian wage.   This payment is supposed to be for
something to happen - yet manifestly often nothing
happens.   This can lead, as we tragically see
currently, to the danger of all classes being
suspicious and resentful of state education, what
is being returned, in the public apology of these
things, for all that money?   More technically we
can say that the massive amount of 'extra' schooling supplied mainly so that a good proportion of
the class can do nothing (i.e. beyond the point
usually where very basic numerical and literacy
skills are acquired) is in fact a 'gift' (insofar
as the taxes are not from the wage) to the working
class.   Of course the technical argument runs
that such 'extra' schooling contributes to an
increased value of labour power.   But since the
content of this 'value' is ambiguous (from the

126

point of view of valorisation) to say the least,
and since by the latest MSC figures in the UK for
instance, Capital is unlikely to be able to realise
this value (never mind expect a contribution to
surplus value) for well over 50% of school leaving
students, this extra value given to labour power
has been poured down the drain.   Individual
capitals may have historically trusted the State
to do what competition prevented them from doing
for themselves - cf. the length of the working day,
training for skills etc. - but they still expected
to be able, eventually, to realise charges made on
them through exploitation of higher value labour
power.   The costly forms of 'Reproduction' I'm
indicating here are undoubtedly partly responsible
for the crises in accumulation, the fiscal crisis
of the state, and the current strategy to shift many
state expenses back on to the family, on to
domestic production of the value of labour power
there, and to move the exploitation of workers in
employment up a whole gear in intensity.   This
form of contested 'Reproduction', therefore, far
from being functional for the State and Capital
Accumulation is, actually, currently one of its
problems.   If Capital would 'warehouse' or 'freeze'
young people between 13-20 it would undoubtedly
attempt to do so, rather than allow the continuance
of cultural and social processes it anyway barely
understands.

THE CONNECTIONS BETWEEN CULTURAL PRODUCTION AND 'REPRODUCTION'

The previous arguments deal basically with the
separation and distinction between cultural
production and 'Reproduction'.   Things are more
complex when we try to detail the nature of their
connection.   Clearly - my whole point - this is
not through the 'needs' and determinations of
'Reproduction' simply shaping the form and content
of cultural production.   In the case of the school,
for instance, the resistance of 'the lads'
sufficiently makes the point that domination and
mental inculcation are certainly not automatic and
direct.   'The Lads' caried and developed, sometimes anti-social, culture is hardly straight from
the Capitalist Design Office.
    But the 'penetration' and 'limitation'
formulation by which Learning tries to make the
link, besides being sexist, is also misleading.
It is misleading both in its mechanistic separation

of what is all of a piece in cultural production
and in its tendency to suggest closure.   Over-
ridingly, there is a danger of the simple inflation
of 'penetrations' into a libertarianism or
'triumphalism', or of the reduction of 'limitations'
into an automatic self regulating pessimism.
     I now argue that we need a more unified view of
cultural production as both challenging and confirming.   In a way it is irrelevant to insist that it
should be either pessimistic or optimistic, either
accommodational or oppositional, either revolutionary
or reactionary.   We should have had enough of
'either-or-isms'.   Nor can we say that some things
simply reproduce a given society and that others
challenge it.   That society is always moving,
always self transforming, always giving of the
appearance of public stability only through a
thousand uncertainties.
     We need some patience in trying to understand
cultural production.   Before pronouncing on its
political or reproductive potential, it should be
no intractable contradiction, no silliness, to say
that two or more contradictory things may be true
of it.   Once we have grasped something of the
contradictory flow of social process, then we may
realistically proceed to place 'cultural forms',
forsee the possibilities;   judge the grounds that
could be won;   the grounds that cannot be lost.
     I am proposing that we must seek within a more
unified notion of cultural production a more
intrinsic connection between what I called before
'penetration' and 'limitation', and of how it
becomes implicated in 'Reproduction'.   One
important possibility here is that the very
strength of cultural struggle, the very success of
subordinate cultural production, is related to
processes which help to reproduce some of the
essential ideological frameworks and categories of
society.   Cultural production indicates a degree
of agency.   It frames experiences, and life trans-
itions as in some way broadening and liberating -
a practicised field of 'choice'.   The very
experience of resistance and collective strength
may mark and stamp identities with a confidence and
distinctness.   But the 'fixing' of symbolic
materials, activities, and attitudes in confidence
and struggle may also produce orientations and dispositions which help to produce entrapping decisions
in a sufficient number to grittingly meet the
requirements of 'structure' and so help to
reproduce it - though be it noted in a minimum,

128

largely unillusioned manner which is far short of the 'ideal' abstract requirements of Capital.

If we take the example of the male counter school culture, some of the activity and strength (non-speciability from the point of view of the dominant) of its cultural production can be seen in a number of ways analysed by Learning to Labour. There is a clear resistance to the school and to its attempted control through what I termed the 'educational paradigm' (the exchange of obedience for knowledge and hoped for qualifications). Their challenge questions whether the 'knowledge' on offer is any kind of real equivalent to what is to be rendered in the exchange - the loss of vital capacities skills and freedoms: what obedience actually amounts to. Certainly for most working class kids such knowledge will not be in the form of certificates which offer real mobility - only a fraction of the working class 'succeed' through educational means. A scepticism about qualifications amongst 'the lads' constitutes a kind of awareness that no amount of certification amongst the working class will produce more jobs or more mob mobility, but that it might produce social legitimation for those who seem to have succeeded through them - and preparation for job discipline for those who have not.

Also the attitude to work amongst 'the lads' - indifference to particular forms of labour; lack of interest in its intrinsic quality or variety; a rough and ready masculine confrontation with the task; scorn of 'cissy' work - can be seen as a creative and productive response, to the nature of modern work for the majority: its standardisation, de-skilling, and steady disappearance. In these and other fields the cultural productivity of 'the lads' works at a natural level of collectivity. It responds to their position and social location within a collective working class logic, rather than within the individualism of practical consciousness and of rational calculation of market chances. Individual working class kids may succeed in education - never the whole class. Individual jobs might be interesting, better paid, worth competing for - never the condition of wage labour itself. For the class as a whole, for its collective experience, it is the general labouring condition which has salience and relevance. Their culture tells them this is no-one else.

But the very strength and success of this cultural production brings some profoundly

129

reproductive consequences. The vigour of the struggle against the school equates mentalism in general with something to be resisted. This acts as a kind of innoculation against the mental competences and aspirations required for 'middle class' jobs - 'cissy' anyway - and produces a real orientation towards manual work. This is a cultural, not officially directed, production of the mental/manual division of labour - indeed a corner stone of the class society but not produced simply by oppression or participation in the labour process. Furthermore the vibrancy of the counter school culture manages to associate academic 'underachievement' with worldly precocity. This 'worldliness' induces and attracts 'the lads' forwards - but into adult relations of exploitation too. They want adult consumption and behaviour, they get jobs. They want, so to speak, 'the world' - despite that its cost is its loss.

Learning to Labour also charts how, in the counter-school culture, some unremarked but profound themes of masculinity are taken up into a sense of self and into the experiental forms of labour power and its manual expression. It is masculinity which gives an edge to resistance in school and rounds and fills an identity located in a social position often emptied of all other worth and value. But it is also masculinity which helps to discredit mental life and which, by giving it some displaced meaning and dignity, leads to an acceptance of heavy work. It can also oppress women and lead to the reproduction of conventional gender roles in the family. Creative cultures are where styles of accommodation are learned, where they hold and form. The future can be where they tie and bind.

From the 'cultural studies perspective' what is to be noted here is the internality of the ways in which some of the structures and essential ideological architecture of a patriarchal capitalism are experienced and reproduced. 'Reproduction' and contradiction are not abstract entities or forces. They are embedded dynamically within the real lives of people in a way which is not simple 'correspond-ence' or 'reflection' of unchanged, somehow deeper structures. The lived internality of structured forms, and of this psychic mechanisms of recognition and control, is evident in the way that 'the mental/manual split is produced for 'the lads'' vigorous response to school. It is evident in the way that their sometimes virulent masculinism, and its intertwinings with a manualist sense of

their labour power, is appropriated as a personal
and collective accomplishment. It is evident
finally in that an acceptance of a future in manual
wage labour is taken as no defeat.

Incidentally, we may also note that for all
their 'oppositional' or 'reproductive' consequences
much of this is also experienced as 'fun' and
'excitement'. Short of being able to provide the
outlines of a 'socialist' lived culture which is
vibrant, fun, and amusing, we should take care in
our assessments. We should not force upon this
cultural production an undialectical rationality
which becomes a socialist tombstone to 'fun'. We
should not make of our encounter with cultural
production the rainy funeral afternoon for its
participants of coping with distant relatives on the
make - for the 'class' inheritance.

SOME NEW TERMS

Though this is only preliminary and runs all the
dangers of violence in 'new' thinking, it may be
worthwhile to try to systemmatise some of these
connections between cultural production and
'Reproduction' in the hope that their generalisation
might aid application to other areas. It can be
suggested that these processes fall into four kinds
of basically related and mutually reinforcing
categories: locking, destressing, transformation
and isomorphism.

Locking might be used to indicate the surprising processes whereby the 'fixing' of one set
of meanings, attitudes, symbols and associated
behaviours in relation to surrounding systemmatic
practices, or to a locating institution, have
consequences for other, perhaps future, regions and
processes. A cultured 'configuration', worked up
in relation and logic to one site, 'reads over' in
its 'locked' form to other sites where a different
configuration may actually have been more relevant.
The locked culture nevertheless organises similar
behaviour in the new site as if its nature were the
same as the original - producing the possibility of
all kinds of 'Reproductive' effects. I am
thinking in our concrete example, for instance, of
the ways in which anti-mentalism and masculinity
in the school, and the furnacing of a sense of self
and culture there through a particular combination
of the mental/manual split and of gender, help to
produce orientations to manual work and to the
family which are no direct part of their original

131

'logic'.

By destressing I mean the associated effect whereby the more or less self conscious struggle against a particular kind of regime or institution - in our concrete case the school - and the particular nature of cultural forms produced in such a context, lead to a kind of identification of and guard against certain oppressions, but also potentially to a simultaneous relative demotion - a destressing - of other possible oppressions and associated fates which might finally be more serious and fundamentally trapping. Crudely, to oppose and successfully resist some things may be to accept equally oppressive other things. For instance the successful cultural production of 'the lads' identifies the tensions and problems of the school, but not the oppressions of the social and sexual division of labour. It may well be that a pre-occupation with a cultural response to the pressure of the state school leads many kids to de-stress what should perhaps occupy them more - their whole future in a class society!

What I call transformation is directly connected. It is the rendering of certain specific kinds of, perhaps future, oppression and exploitations into the different terms of an immediate, local and sensuous culture. It is a consequence of locking, if you like, for the perception and understanding of destressed social issues. For instance a future of class oppression amongst 'the lads' is partly treated and understood by them through the structures of gender, informality and anti-mentalism. These are some of the terms of dignity, some of the building bricks of a viable project in life, which are of the least importance to Capital, welcomed by it or inflicting least damage upon it. Its basic and fundamental conditions are met no matter what the terms in which people understand this 'necessary' behaviour. It may also be, for instance, that it is through the terms of 'romance' that many girls see and interpret, partly no doubt finally live through, their future of domestic oppression (16). It may be in the hope of 'nice secretarial work' or a 'good marriage' that an essentially class future is accepted and mediated through gender and sexuality.

The connection of presents and futures in this way, and the continuities which connect them (so aiding basic requirements of 'Reproduction') can be seen as a kind of cultural isomorphism. By this I mean the experiental and real connection between cultural forms that aids the human passage between

the locating sites.   Some fundamental 'decisions' amongst subordinate groups, which seem to be self limiting, to be without 'aspiration', are not votes for the social order.   They are votes to be with the same kind of people, votes for a certain kind of cultural solidarity.   They are votes, in part, for a _familiar_ future - which 'happens' to be oppressive. Working class kids, for instance, do not want working class jobs, so much as they want to be with the people who are in them, to be with the working class.
This detailing and specification of the complexities of cultural production should not push it again wholly into a 'Reproduction' perspective and into a consequent replay of the split between pessimism and optimism, determinism or voluntarism. To be clear my argument here is _not_ that _locking_, _destressing_, _transformation_ or _isomorphism_ cancel out, negate or render purely ironic any sense of _struggle_, and therefore of potential change and development.   Quite to the contrary.   Rather it is to suggest no struggle can take place except within and among the profane and complex material of history and of pre-existing social relationships and dis- courses.   It is to suggest that no social category or discourse lives and continues except through struggle, except through the social relations within, through and by which it _is_.   The 'worst' of my case is perhaps a necessary and trenchant implication that there is no _pure_ struggle of the oppressed, no pure resistance, no utopianism, which does not work through the contradictions and contrary effects of its own production.

CONCLUSION

The qualifications and elaborations I am making around the notion of struggle and cultural product- ion can be seen finally as an aspect of a broader view of the most basic struggle in society, class struggle, and of how this is related to some of the basic social categories and ideological 'archi- tecture' of a capitalist society.
For me now this is essentially that some essential structures of capitalism are not _given_, or simply _externally_ imposed, with perhaps some marginal resistance.   They are produced _through_ struggle, and in the collective self formation of subjects and the working class.   This is to say that the structure of Capital is not external and separate from the everyday life of society.   Struggle does not go on 'somewhere else' from structure.   By

133

the same token, the working class is not something
separate and apart from the capitalist system.   It
is not on holy ground, subject for the moment to
the 'oppression' and 'exploitation' of the capitalist system, waiting to be released and set free -
unchanged - upon its destruction.   The working
class is formed in and through, and through its
struggles importantly helps to produce, the
structures and characteristic forms of a capitalist
society.   Perhaps contentiously, this is to say
that the working class necessarily partly has a
stake in the system - it knows no other - and must
work through the contradictions of the system and
its own self transformation, to come to a future
minutely born out of the capitalist experience.
'The lads' culture, for instance, is a form of the
class struggle mediated by balances within the
school and by its 'educational paradigm', and yet
it helps to produce the division between mental and
manual labour through its anti-mentalism.   'The
lads' subjective insulation from the world of work;
their cynical manipulation of it to yield the
maximum cash;   their devotion to consumption and
pleasure, and later to ease in the 'sanctuary' of
the proletarian home, through the wage but at the
furthest reach from where it is earned;   are all in
their way vigorous and assertive struggles for the
rights of the 'free labourer' to be as independent
as possible from Capital.   But at the same time
they make a future in wage labour subjectively
possible, as well as directly contributing to the
profound divisions between work and leisure, between
work and the home, which are so distinctive of
capitalism and through which Patriarchy takes its
material forms.
     Part of what I'm saying is that our general
theoretical view should not be to pose authentic
'class subjects' against hostile, surrounding but
separate symbolic and material structures - 'subjects' who can be inflated into working class heroes,
or deflated into working class dummies, depending on
whether they are seen as squashed by or as squashing
'structure'.   In fact neither structure nor agency
is understandable alone - they need each other in
order to be comprehensible at all.   In my view
there has to be some kind of dialectical relation -
not between free subjects (knowing and centred) and
determining structure (external and objective) -
but between subjects formed in struggle and
resistance to structures in domination, and
structures formed in and reproduced by struggle, and

134

<u>resistance against domination</u>. The key link and
common ground between the two terms, 'subjects' and
'structure', is struggle. Just because some of the
subjective and cultural moments seem 'invisible',
especially to a dominant view, and can lead to
reproductive 'effects' should be no reason to
collapse the distinctive field of human struggle
into the abstract operation of structures somehow
'thinking' themselves, absorbing all varieties of
resistance into functional 'positions' within them.
     Just because structural causation and formation
seem abstract and distant, and their analysis sometimes yielding 'subjects' as puppets on the theoretical stage, should not lead to a collapse of
human struggle and the social relations, material
and history through which it is lived, to self
inventing, humanist individuals.
     And although the main axis of analysis here is
around class, the notion of <u>cultural production</u>
indicates the complexity of how many structures of
oppression combine in experiental and cultural ways.
<u>Cultural production</u> signifies not the contours of
formal categories outlined by the theorists, 'sex,
race, class' and their dry, one might say vegatative
propagations, but the profane, living, properly
fertile, often uncontrollable combination of these
elements in real cultures, actual collective life
projects, decisions and changes. A characteristic
of this may be that 'submission' to one domination
may reveal or resist another, or that dominant
placement in one kind of 'discourse' may reveal
other kinds of submission as well as to reproduce
the original or yet others. This is the actual
stuff of the creation and recreation of material
and social life which can only then be re-classified
out by the theorists 'sex, race and class'. It is
only in understanding these tense cultural combinations in different groups that we can properly
analyse what (and how) different sections and
interests have in common and how they might be
generally mobilised on common fronts and alliances.
     We should be concerned with specific oppress-
ions, of course, and with their particular forms of
struggle and solidarity. But we should also be
concerned with the <u>variety</u> of <u>relations</u> of
oppression, not just as categories of domination,
but, taken together, as categories out of which
oppression is fought. Their combinations help to
form concrete subjects and cultural forms, and to
give the scope for action, change and the
exploration of contradictions and tensions between

oppressions.   In a way this is the other side of locking and transformation.   It is the use of the combination of quite unlikely items to give expressive power, to use any of those discourses and materials which are at hand to struggle, act and make meanings of some kind.   There can be a solidarity in part arising from cultural isomorphism which can turn some social power, expression and illumination - configured in whatever surprising ways - on previously de-stressed items.   For instance, it may be through structures of masculinity that class oppressions of both the school and the factory are fought.   Women at work may draw on their femininity to make qualitative demands of work, for better conditions, safety in products and childcare.   Race, for instance, a category of oppression in its own right, can also be a prism through which class is experienced and 'new' aspects of the structure of Capital exposed - its attempt to produce an international division of labour, its tendency to separate and stratify the metropolitan workforces to produce almost a 'caste' at its lower reaches.   Blacks are living a class experience which is partly organised by race, but this can expose that class structure - and also provide a pool of images, meanings, resources, cultures to resist it.   Currently we see in massive youth unemployment a particular organisation of age to the structures of capitalism but so do we see something of it exposed;its tendency to over-production and to the production of a 'reserve army of labour'.   And these things are likely to be further explored, exposed and resisted through the resources of youth, of youth cultural forms.

    This becomes rather abstract and hectic. Certainly the argument is not rigorously and 'scientifically' presented.   That would anyway require whole volumes and is beyond me.   But my purpose is not to lay out a consistent theory. It is to suggest a particular view of subordinate cultural production.   It is a way of asking for the recognition and development of working class and oppositional knowledges and struggles which avoids collapsing them into opposites - simple reproduction or simple opposition.

    Struggle and contestation is a whole mode of the existence of 'democratic' capitalism. Certainly many 'resistances' fall far short of challenging basic social structures - but to ask for their success is to ask for an epochal shift every Sunday afternoon!   We've been exploring the possibility of a middle course which avoids saying that just because resistances do not overthrow a dominant system, then they are related only to its support. Resistance may be deeply implicated in accommodation, but <u>not</u> in a way which is inevitable, planned and wholly programmed as a pre-existing function of dominant institutions and ideology. Resistance is part of the wide field of a general human praxis, where human beings are created as they create collectively their conditions of life, showing <u>always</u> the 'mismatch', 'ragged edge' and unpredictability of the relation between what is 'reproductive' and 'confirming' in their actions, and what is dissatisfied resistant and challenging. Here is scope for change, for politics, for <u>becoming</u> - not for utopianism or despair.

NOTES

1. Published now by Gower Press. I try to deal more specifically with criticisms of the book in some other recent publications. See the Introduction to the American edition of the book, published by Columbia University Press: and my article in the recent edition of *Interchange*, I:4, Toronto, (1981).

2. See for instance the recent edition of *Interchange*, *op.cit.*

3. For a full and detailed account of this see, CCCS Education Group, *Unpopular Education: Schooling and Social Democracy in England since 1944*, Hutchinson (1981).

4. See the string of official reports on education in the UK from the *Early Leaving* report in 1954 to the Plowden Report in 1967.

5. A point well made in a lucid review of *Learning to Labour* by Michael Apple. 'What Correspondence Theories of the Hidden Curriculum Miss'. The Review of Education, Vol. 5, No. 2, Spring (1979), USA.

6. For a similar, though extended, definition on which I have drawn, see R. Johnson, 'Cultural Studies' and Educational Studies: Contributions and Critique', CCCS Stencilled Paper (1982).

7. I do not wish to imply that such meaning is cognitive, rational or located in individuals. It can be located in structures, in the implicit and lived meanings of 'cultural forms'. See the conclusion of *Profane Culture*, RKP (1978).

8. I take the general term 'cultural level' to include specific <u>cultural forms</u> as well as language, practical consciousness and more individual ways of making meaning. 'Cultural forms' designate either texts of some kind, or a relatively tight set of symbols, discourses and texts in

relation to the routine activities and practice of a specific set of agents in a specific site - counter-school culture, shop floor culture.

9.   See also Raymond Williams' comments on the materialism of culture in *Marxism and Literature*. The general terms here can apply equally to middle class as well as to working class culture. Working class <u>cultural production</u>, however, is likely to be qualitatively different, and produce different kinds of forms and knowledge, from middle class production. For a discussion of this see, 'Orders of Experience: the differences of Working Class Cultural Forms, *Social Text*, 4 (1982).

10.   L. Althusser, 'Ideology and Ideological State Apparatuses', in, ed. B. Cosin, *Education: Structure and Society*, Penguin (1972).

11.   S. Bowles and H. Gintis, *Schooling in Capitalist America*, Basic Books (1976). I do not deal here with Bowles and Gintis' recent statement and apparent partial qualification of 'correspondence'. Their more recent arguments do not anyway really bear upon the internal operation of educational practice. See S. Bowles and H. Gintis, 'Education as a Site of Contradictions in the Reproduction of the Capital-Labor Relationship: Second Thoughts on the 'Correspondence Principle', in, *Economic and Industrial Democracy*, Vol. 2, No. 2, (May 1981).

12.   See P. Bourdieu and J. Passeron, *Reproduction*, Sage (1977).

13.   P. Bourdieu, *Outline of a Theory of Practice*, Cambridge University Press, (1977), p. 78.

14.   In *Class, Codes and Control*, Vol. 3, 2nd Edition, RKP (1975).

15.   The general emphasis on <u>cultural production</u> as the starting point in *Learning to Labour* is also making a theoretical point in general. Although the book did not focus on the conformists, ethnic groups or girls, the case for the distinctions I've outlined applies in different ways to <u>all</u> groups and their cultures and, through an example, points to a general feature of the <u>contested</u> nature of cultural and social Reproduction across the board. Though I didn't supply the data the <u>approach</u> I've outlined does not block but <u>enable</u> such study.

16.   See, for instance, 'Working Class Girls and the Culture of Feminity', in Women's Studies Group, *Women Take Issue*, Hutchinson (1978).

THE RACIAL CODE: ITS FEATURES, RULES AND CHANGE

Chris Mullard

Perhaps above all else, the recent street experiences
and actions of blacks last summer in Brixton, Mosside
Southall, Toxteth and in at least thirty other inner-
city areas in Britain clearly demonstrated the
existence of two important social realities (1).
Beyond the doubt of certainly those young blacks at
the centre of the so-called 1981 'riots' and in
spite of Scarman's conclusion to the contrary, they
showed, firstly, that Britain is not only a racist
society but also that institutionalised racism is
in fact a relatively permanent feature of British
society (2).   Secondly, and in many ways more
significantly, they projected a commitment on the
part of the racially oppressed and exploited to
intensify resistance against all aspects and
agencies of racist authority;   a form of resistance
that, according to Sivanandan and others, rapidly
escalated into a state of rebellion (3).
    Whether or not this was so is only of
importance to those commentators, academics and
researchers who wish to spend their time and energy
sorting out, formulating and reformulating an often
contradictory assortment of conceptual quibbles.
For what matters in the final instance for social
scientists interested in race relations and
especially for those of us who are concerned with
the issue of racism in education is that these two
social realities can no longer be ignored or foot-
noted as examples of aggressive hyperbole;   accounts
of black definitions of reality and reaction that
somehow only possess symbolic as opposed to analytic
import (4).   If a political or even educational
sociology of racism is to be at all relevant and
meaningful, these two realities have to be built
into the very texture and conceptual structure of
all formulations, models, and accounts of racism in

society.

Given this, it is clear that the scope of this paper will have to reach beyond the task of attempting to establish the general nature of what might be termed a racial code, or a set of racially construed features, relationships, principles, and rules that appear to regulate the production and reproduction of, and reactions to racism.   Inevitably, it will have to context politically the debate on racism in education within a framework of socio-political reaction to racism.   It will have to move critically away from any over-simplistic or determinate model that either suggests an exceptionally high degree of correspondence between the production and reproduction of racism in capitalist societies or, over-romanticises the cultural existence, nature and consequences of reaction.   Thus, in almost total opposition to the cruder forms of Bowles and Gintis's otherwise perceptive thesis, it will be suggested here, firstly, that the two principal forms of reaction are themselves an integral part or feature of the racial code and, secondly, that these two forms of reaction, protest and resistance, in organised and structured relations of power in fact shape over time the actual nature of the code itself (5).   That is to say, as structurally located and expressed reactions, they, unlike Willis's notion of cultural 'productions' or by any other name, resistances, are more than theoretical descriptions of the behaviour of social actors (6). Instead they are interactionally grounded descriptions and articulations of the motor of both social control and change.

OVERVIEW

In order to provide an indication of the significance of these reactions and hence the kind of relationships that exist between the processes of production, reproduction and reaction, it might be useful at this stage to present an overview of the discussion that follows.   Rather formally this can be set out in terms of what I call here the composite and component forms of the racial code (7).

The first of these two forms can be diagramatically portrayed as follows:

$$\text{cr} \begin{bmatrix} P \longrightarrow RP \\ \hline R \end{bmatrix}$$
$$\text{rc}$$

The second or component form, which represents an
attempt to separate out the two principal modes of
reaction and to show how these two codified modes
are related to each other, can be presented in the
following way:

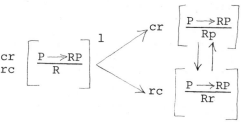

(Key: P = production;   RP = reproduction;
R = reaction;   cr = class-race;   rc = race-class;
Rp = reactions of protest;   and Rr = reactions of
resistance.   Continuous arrowed lines reflect both
the existence and dominant direction of the
relationships between processes whereas the brackets
indicate that all that is contained within them is
structured and qualified by an underpinning set of
class-race (cr) and race-class (rc) relations.)
  Although the above formulations raise many
questions that range from the very usefulness or
otherwise of diagrammatic presentations of what
appear to be extremely complex phenomena, processes
and relationships to critiques that in one way or
another all return to the charge of reductionism,
they do, however, possess the value of presenting
quite unequivocally the three main questions that
have to be resolved in order to establish both the
existence and possible sociological value of a
racial code.   Employing these questions as concerns
around which to unfold the central argument of this
paper, namely that the principles of the management
and demanagement of racism are located in the
operation of the racial code, they can be summarised
in the following order:
  (i)   What are the features of the racial
code and how are these features, as distinctive
social and racial processes, related to each other?
  (ii)   How are they regulated: or, more
precisely, what are the various rules that appear
to regulate the operation of these features or
processes?
  (iii)   What constitutes the motor force
within the code or how are changes in the management and demanagement of racism achieved?
  But before we can even begin to embark upon

answering these three questions, we need now to
establish more clearly just how we propose to
define and use the concept of code.

The important thing that needs to be said about
this is that throughout this paper the concept of
code is employed in two inter-related ways.
Following Bernstein's creative conceptualisation of
the conditional basis of social change and control,
firstly, it is used here as a regulative principle
(8).   Deeply analytical as a concept which contains
within itself the power to express and reflect a
dialectical depiction and explanation of social
control and change, a code in this sense is more
than a tacitly acquired regulative principle which
selects and integrates meanings, realisations, and
contexts.   It is in itself 'a regulator of the
relationships <u>between</u> contexts and through that
relationship a regulator of the relationships within
contexts' (9).   Given that is is essentially a
dialectical construction rather than social description of the processes of social control, change
and the specific role of the process of cultural
reproduction, it follows from this that all codes,
whether class, race or gender specific, presuppose
a concept of irrelevant or illegitimate meanings,
forms of realisation and contexts.   Thus, according to Berstein, 'the concept of code is inseparable
from concepts of legitimate and illegitimate
communications' (10).

The second way in which the concept of code is
used here reveals that, as a powerful metaphor, it
possesses a set of meanings and, in turn, evokes a
set of socio-political prescriptions for action.
In other words, a code, especially in its racial form,
is no more or less than a set of representations or
system of signals, messages and relations combined
together in a social form to camouflage broader
social or narrower racial realities.   Thus rather
crudely the 'cracking' of any code is a necessary
precondition for, firstly, the establishing of the
principles that support and guide radical and hence
possible structural changes, and, secondly, for the
launching of strategies of socio-political action
designed to bring about required changes.   Just
how effective these strategies will be in either
the short or long term will depend of course upon
a number of complex factors, including the relative
and absolute power of those groups ideologically
locked in a relationship of struggle (11).   But
that the 'cracking' of the code enables the
discovery of the principles of challenge is in

142

itself something that decisively helps to recast
the analytical dimensions of code identification,
construction, and relationships, a la Bernstein,
into fairly discrete dimensions of prescriptive
and consequently political action.

By bringing together these analytical and
metaphorical qua political dimensions, it is
possible to postulate that both general and
specific codes are operative as well as positioning
devices. A code in the combined senses employed
here is therefore not by definition a static conceptualisation of the principles, relationships,
contexts and conditions of control and change.
Instead, it is itself in perpetual change, giving
rise over time and in structures of power to a
plurality of code forms or variants which in turn
and under specific conditions generate the
principles for the reformulations if not the actual
transformation of the general or specific code.

But before any serious attempt is made to
address what at this stage seems to amount to a
cyclical process, it is necessary to introduce the
main features of the racial code.

CODE FEATURES

In essence, the three major features of the racial
code refer to the three interconnected social processes of production, reproduction and reaction.
What distinguishes them as racial as opposed to
class or gender processes is that all three are
concerned with the superimposition of racial
categorisation and criteria on, over and above any
other form of categorisation or set of criteria.
Further, as I shall show in a moment, each process
represents and seeks to produce (production),
perpetuate (reproduction) and change (reaction) a
racial construction of social reality, a racial
division of the general social division of labour,
and a racial structure of power based upon racially
construed relations of production, reproduction and
reaction. To put this in a slightly different way,
the racial character of the processes and hence the
code is largely governed by the relative political,
social and economic importance attached to racial
forms of differentiation by powerful groups in any
social structure, irrespective of whether it is
characterised by capitalist or socialist modes of
economic production and political organisation.

i) Production

In the case of the production process which provides,
conditions and evokes the explicit economic or
material context of racism, the racial forms of
differentiation are immediately observable.   For
instance, black workers are not only to be found
over-represented in unskilled, menial, poorly paid
jobs, at the bottom of the occupational structure,
in times of relatively high employment or on the
dole and in a state of what Howe terms 'wageless-
ness' during periods of relatively high unemployment (12).   But of far more sociological interest
than this, they are in relative degrees of
permanence positioned in these locations, not as a
sub-class, sub-proletariat, or, in Rex and
Tomlinson's use of the term, 'underclass', but as I
shall describe later, they are positioned as racial
groups within overall class categories (13).
Although this positioning is in part a product of
the demand or non-demand for labour within economies
based upon a high degree of occupational special-
isation and division of labour, its relative
permanence results however from the way in which
beliefs, values and attitudes on race are formed,
used and built into the structural fabric of
economic, political and social life.   Embracing
biologically and culturally determined notions of
white superiority, black, inferiority, they are
produced and employed as an ideology of racism
within the relationships that give rise to and
implicitly govern the dominant mode and relations
of economic production.
     From its historical emergence in pre-capitalist
societies, its massive mobilisation and institution-
alisation during the development of western capitalism, to its structural role in advanced or late-
capitalist societies, racism, as an ideology, has
been consistently used to position, control,
exploit and, furthermore, justify the exploitation
of black groups (14).   Historically, it arose out
of the quest to maximise profits and hence the need
to regulate the social relations of production.
For the same basic reasons, its continual production
within mainly the wider economic and political
processes of capital accumulation can be readily
observed today in not only descriptions of the
racial structure of a society's labour force but
also in the way in which this structure has been
maintained despite or, perhaps, in spite of
increased race relations legislation and policy (15).

ii)   Reproduction

Given that in all societies there exists historical and political forces to reproduce the essential conditions, structures and social principles for long term survival, the actual identification of a reproduction process is neither revelationary nor something that is in itself problematic.   Simply, because it happens to be concerned with the cultural transmission of the conditions, structures and principles of capitalist or socialist formations, it is not by this fact automatically a problem. This is to be expected, and constitutes a legitimate function of the state's various agencies of reproduction.   What however is problematic and of immediate concern to us is a group of issues that relate to the degree of correspondence that appears to obtain between the production and reproduction of racism.

Despite the many recent attempts on both sides of the Atlantic to portray the existence of a close or high degree of correspondence between the production and reproduction processes, in relation to particularly the socialisation of a class to labour in capitalist societies, it would appear that what is often lacking in these analyses is any suggestion that the reproduction process is also a productive one (16).   For it would appear logical to assume that in the very act of reproducing there results a secondary production which, certainly in the case of the reproduction of racism, is qualitatively different from the primary production. Made different, as I shall show below, by the intensity and types of reaction found inside and outside the relationships that form the reproductive system, these new though secondary productions symbolised in, for instance, the development and meaning of ethnicism and multicultural education, alter over time both the nature of original or primary productions and the general character of the racial code (17).

Even though this contingency is theoretically allowed for within the so-called relative autonomy debate in education, the part of the debate that sees educational institutions as being only loosely related to other institutions in society, the problem with this debate is that it rarely attempts to show just how loosely or partly related institutions are to each other.   The emphasis always appears to rest on the autonomous rather than the relative aspects of the relationships between institutions.   Again, in the case of the

reproduction of racism, it is more often than not
assumed by theorists and practitioners alike that,
within the school setting, programmes of racial
harmony, however designed and pedagogically executed,
can be promoted untouched by the wider structural
context in which they are unquestionably conceived
and in which schools evolve, operate and survive (18).
Indeed, it is as much like assumption as it is that
which underpins the view of a direct transmission of
racist beliefs, values and attitudes that rests at
the centre of the reproductive processes of racism.
      To expand this point a little further, it is
this very tension between the two opposing positions
within the debate that enables racism to survive
intact, to be reproduced by and within educational
institutions.   For, simply, those who see a close
correspondence between the production and reproduction of the conditions, relations and processes
or racism are already theoretically committed to
demonstrate in practice that this is in fact so.
Whereas those who start from the opposite position
are already theoretically committed to proving that
changes arising from within educational institutions,
as responses to racism, can in practice effect and
ultimately lead to other institutional changes.
In other words this latter position needs to evoke
the existence of the former in order to establish
its claim of autonomy.   As an outcome of this and
admittedly in often the somewhat disguised form of
ethnicism, racism is invariably reproduced in the
actions, policies and practices associated with
this position in the context of the school (19).

iii) Reaction
Clearly what is at issue here is that both the
processes of production and reproduction of racism
cannot be solely identified as distinctive or even
wholly separate code features.   They are more
complex than some authors would have us believe.
They are not only almost inextricably related to
each other, acting upon each other in relation to
wider international contexts and shifts of power
and purpose in the ongoing evolution, decline and
struggles within and between capitalist and
socialist formations: but they are also in turn
severely qualified if not completely changed in
social character by organised reactions to racism.
      As a process in their own right and as the
third main feature of the racial code, these
reactions are observable on two fundamentally
different levels.   Firstly, there are those which

emanate from mainly <u>white</u> educational administrators,
policy makers, teachers and pupils and, secondly,
there are those which derive mainly from <u>black</u>
parental, pupil and political or community group
responses to racism.   Although these levels can be
broken up even further into, for instance, sub-
groups of teachers, administrators, parents, pupils,
community-based political groups and so on, it is
their racial specificity and consciously chosen
forms of reaction that remain crucial for an understanding of the overall process of reaction.

As I suggested earlier, the two principal forms
of reaction tend to manifest themselves as reactions
of <u>protest</u> and reactions of <u>resistance</u>.   In the
case of the former which embrace the majority of
white responses to racism it is possible to discern
several features which in effect define protest as
a mode of <u>legitimate</u> reaction.   Firstly, all
protest reactions appear to assume two things: they
assume that there is essentially nothing wrong with
the system as a whole and that the system, usually
interpreted as the main institutions and agencies of
the state, possesses the ability if not always the
will to modify its practices and policies and
through this process of modification to effect
piecemeal changes.   Secondly, all protest reactions
seem to reflect not only a belief in the fundamental
values and institutional structures of society but
they also exhibit positive support for the normal
way as laid down by traditions, laws, or con-
stitutional directives, of achieving limited
objectives and changes.   All in all reactions of
protest are in the last analysis both actions of
support for the continuation of the system in all
its basic forms and reflections of the perceived
acceptance of protesting groups as legitimate and
therefore relatively authoritative parts of the
system itself (20).

Reactions of resistance, on the other hand,
express quite a different set of assumptions and
aims.   Firstly, they assume that the system as a
whole is structurally at fault and, because it
relies on racism to maintain a mirage of structural
stability, it neither possesses the ability nor the
will to bring about the kind of changes demanded by
resisting groups.   Secondly, all reactions of
resistance reflect an opposition to the dominant
beliefs, values and institutional structures that
characterise the social, economic and political
being of a society.   Consequently, instead of
supporting they deny the basic validity of the

147

accepted, normal and constitutionally legitimate
ways of accomplishing small or large-scale changes.
Reactions of resistance are then both actions
against the continuation of the system in its present
form and reflections of the illegitimate or, when
protest becomes resistance, delegitimate status of
resisting groups in society (21).

Apart and in a relationship of struggle, these
two racially prescriptive forms of reaction organised
around competing definitions of what actually constitutes the problem of black pupils in white schools,
black disadvantage or white racism, appear at all
times to mould and qualify the relationship between
the production and reproduction of racism (22). How
they precisely do this I shall come to later, but at
this stage in the discussion it is possible to state
that as well as shaping the social personality of the
racial code they exist as an integral feature of the
code as opposed to merely acting as symbolic
expressions of powerlessness and/or opposition.

The analytical distinction already drawn between
the two types of reaction is of vital importance for
the understanding of how changes occur within the
racial code and, further, how changes in the
character of the code come about over time and within
a racial structure of power based upon relations of
class and race.   As it is virtually impossible to
understand the social location of the code outside
of its structural context, a closer examination of
these class-race, race-class relations is therefore
needed.   This is also required because the three
processes themselves cannot in any social sense
exist without reference to their interest-bounded
and governed derivations.   The code in its nuclear
form is only meaningful when it is viewed in
relation to these derivations which are organised
and expressed in terms of patterned class-race,
race-class relations (23).

The problem of just how they are organised,
expressed and patterned is one that inevitably
leads us back to an earlier point made in
connection with the relevance or otherwise of
describing the position of racial groups in
capitalist societies as that of being an 'underclass', in the sense employed by Rex and Tomlinson
(24).   Here it is necessary not only to expose the
essentially Weberian roots of such a formulation,
as Gilroy in particular and Bourne and Sivanandan
in general rightly do, but it is also necessary to
ask whether or not it is even historically possible
to talk about 'underclasses' or 'sub-proletariats'

in the history of western capitalist formations (25).
For to do so is, in my view, either to subsume racial
groups under Marx's somewhat questionable notion of
the lumpen-proletariat or, more seriously, to deny
the class validity of the contribution blacks have
made historically, as slave, indentured, and wage
workers, to the development of the capitalist
formation.

Although the precise designation of black
workers can in part be resolved in respect to their
actual relations to the ownership of the means of
production which, if followed through, would cast
them as a class group along with all other wage
workers, this does not, however, firmly locate them
within a specific class or say anything about their
special relationship to established white classes.
It only defines them as a class group. What,
however, appears to do both things is a definition
of their position in terms of the international
division of labour, organisation and development of
western capitalist formations. Once such a world
perspective is adopted, one taken by Frank in
respect to the development of western capitalism
and by Fannon in respect to the liberation of
colonised Africa, then one thing at least becomes
much clearer (26). Not only do black groups form
an integral part of the world's working classes,
neither <u>under</u> (under-class) nor <u>removed from</u>
(lumpen or sub-proletariat) the established and
recognised class structure of capitalism, but also
that from <u>within</u> this class structure they form a
special group in which a combination of conscious-
nesses, class and race, race and class, act upon
each other to determine the precise position of
black groups and their relationship to other groups
in the class structure. Extracting and emphasising
the economic and structural aspects of positioning
from the implicitly culturalist perspective offered
by Hall and others, it is, I suggest, this combination of consciousness which in effect patterns
class-race, race-class relations in ordered
structures of power and dominance (27). In
addition to this and at any given point of time, it
also anchors, governs and modulates all expressions
or forms of the racial code.

Just how this is accomplished and just how,
once accomplished, the position of black groups in
the class structure is maintained and justified is
a matter that I am able now to address more
directly in a discussion of the three sets of rules
that regulate the production, reproduction and

reactions to racism.

RULES OF REGULATION

Arranged relationally into the composite form of
the racial code, as set out at the beginning of
this paper, the three processes of production,
reproduction and reaction are regulated by a set
of rules that position (value rules), maintain
(appropriation rules), and justify (identity rules)
the positioning of black subjects or groups in a
predominantly white and racist society.

i)   Value Rules
In respect to the production of racism, value rules
are chiefly concerned with the principles of the
placement or the positioning of black subjects or
groups in the social structure. They incorporate
racially construed assessments and costings of the
precise economic value of a unit of labour. When
broken down into specific social items, these
assessments and costings include such items as
disruption costs (e.g. trade union membership,
political activity, etc.), ameniability costs
(migration, dispossession, etc.), non-expectation
costs (minimal training, non-promotion, etc.) as
well as what might be termed the market value of
the racial unit of labour. Whereas these rules
tend to possess an objective dimension, those that
appear to underpin the reproduction of racism and
thus regulate the expected positioning of black
pupils in the economy tend to reflect a far more
subjective dimension. For instance, they
incorporate racially construed assessments of the
intellectual or academic value of black subjects or
groups, a mode of regulation and often subjective
assessment of their potential value and ultimate
place as units of labour in society. The specific
racial criteria evoked in these assessments include
amongst other things racially conditioned and/or
biased knowledge on intelligence, educational
achievement or underachievement, literacy, numeracy
and, to translate Coard's original insights into
concrete criteria, the expected educational
behaviours of subjects or groups (28).
      Somewhat more difficult to isolate precisely
because of the rhetoric associated with reactions
of protest and resistance, the value rules that
regulate the hoped-for, even ideal positioning of
black groups in the social structure, relfect in
a sense the structural base of the two organised

political expressions found in the process of
reaction.   Whilst both expressions incorporate
positive assessments of the intellectual, academic
and socio-economic value of black subjects or
groups, reactions of protest seem to reflect
class-race (white) and reactions of resistance
race-class (black) considerations.

For instance, reactions of protest appear to
evoke explicitly class and so-called ethnic criteria
on which assessments are made;   criteria which
emphasise the worth of subjects or groups in respect
to the contributions blacks made to the social,
political, cultural and economic life of the society
in which they are permanently settled.   Further,
they appear to discount all negative valuations of
the intellectual potential of black subjects by
separating out actual value, calculated as a result
and within the framework of the structural conditions
of racism, from the potential value that would be
released and actualised once racism in its present
form has been exchanged for an ideology of ethnic
pluralism - an ideal situation in which class would
take precedence over race and in which black subjects
would be placed into their class positions determined
by criteria other than race (29).

In contrast, reactions of resistance are
informed and regulated by value rules that evoke
positive as opposed to negative racial criteria in
which the real class position of blacks in racist
societies is arrived at through and understanding
of racial oppression and the role of racism in
advanced industrial societies.

ii) Appropriation Rules

If value rules refer to the positioning or placing
of black subjects in the social structure, then the
way in which these positions are maintained is
dependent upon just how subjects are socially
appropriated.

Within the production process these appropriation rules refer specifically to the ways in
which units of black labour are disconnected on the
basis of racial criteria from white units of labour
and to ways in which black workers are connected
racially to prescribed conditions of employment or
unemployment.   In the case of the disconnection
principle they include rules that relate to the
perceived marginality, insecurity, and, in the wake
of new nationality laws and increased calls for
repatriation, settlement uncertainties of black
workers.   The connection principle, on the other

hand, is subsumed in rules that reflect the patronage, favours, altruism and types of economic philanthropy that are exhibited in the phrase, 'you are lucky to have a job at all' or, if unemployed, 'at least you can remain in this country'.

Similarly, within the reproduction process, these rules refer to the ways in which black pupils are disconnected from white pupils on the basis of racial criteria.   But like their counterparts within the production process, they also refer to the ways in which black pupils are maintained in or connected to prescribed conditions of 'passing time' or, in Corrigan's phrase, 'doing nothing' in schools (30).   In respect to the disconnection principle, these rules include the ways in which the academic marginality of black pupils in a white educational system is continually stressed in the school curriculum, types of school organisation and banding or streaming decisions.   More often than not they seem to reflect a racially exclusive conception of the kind of pupils of which state and non-state schools were set up to benefit, place and maintain future workers, managers and professionals in a racially differentiated power and economic structure.   Inversely, the connection principle is grounded in rules that regulate the conditions of and what is acceptable for blacks to do in schools. They include racially deduced but socially recon-structed aspects of the assumed physical and other prowesses of black pupils.   The playing field, gymnasium, theatre, photography club or black studies corner rather than the academic classroom become the only legitimate sites for the survival and conditional acceptance of black pupils in schools.   As Carrington shows in the case of sport, these rules connect and maintain black pupils in racially perceived, defined and structured positions (31).

Whilst performing the same overall function, the appropriation rules located in the reaction process differ in one important aspect from those that regulate the other two processes.   Rather than being based on overt racial criteria, they refer to the ways in which black subjects are connected on the basis of non-racial criteria to white groups and to the ways in which they are disconnected from racially defined situations and conditions. Within reactions of protest, the connection principle is enhanced through rules that seek to deracialise the sportsfield and the academic classroom.   This is achieved through rule-governed practices that emphasise the similarities rather than the differences that exist in the biographies, interests and educational objectives of all pupils. The disconnection principle, on the other hand, is transmitted through the operation of rules that attempt to dismantle or prevent the emergence of racial conditions, situations and structures from arising in the first place. In brief they are designed to maintain black subjects within an integrated, culturally diverse, or racially non-conditioned class structure.

Where these rules in reactions of protest reinforce existing class relations of power, in reactions of resistance they in fact undermine them. That is to say the connection and disconnection principles are inverted. Positive rather than negative attempts are made to racialise the sports-field and the academic classroom; if need be in the shape of Saturday Schools, as described by Stone, or all-black schools, but always on the terms of black pupils and parents themselves (32). Positive rather than negative attempts are also made to struggle for an environment and set of race-class relations that disconnect from dominant patterns in order to discover new patterns based upon principles, practices and relations of social equality.

iii) Identity Rules

In contrast to the other two sets of rules, identity rules are largely predicative in as much that they predicate the racial settings and processes in which value and appropriation rules are constructed. They refer to the beliefs held on what constitutes the essential racial, religious, linguistic or, more generally, cultural characteristics of any society. More ideological in form and effect than either the value or appropriation rules, their chief purpose is to provide justifications for the social positions occupied and the way in which black groups are placed and maintained in these positions in society.

Whilst these rules in the three processes of production, reproduction and reaction perform much the same task of generating and regulating the racist justifications advanced for the situations and conditions of racial inequality that persist, it is only necessary here to discuss them in terms of the latter two processes. This is so because in the case of the production process they are more or less self evident in that they refer to all that is often taken for granted as constituting racist

beliefs, values and attitudes (33).   Whereas in
the other two processes, this is not always the case.
     For instance, within the reproduction process
and particularly within the school setting, these
rules not only define what distinguishes black from
white pupils, what characterises his or her identity
as a black pupil, and the degree of acceptance or
rejection black pupils experience, but they also
define the actual racial identity of the school.
Irrespective of its racial composition, its identity
is conveyed through the operation of rules that
equate or bring into a closer relationship the
internal and external racial context of the school.
In schools which are predominantly white there
resides little if any conflict at all between these
two contexts.   Whereas in schools which are mainly
black or in those which view themselves as being
'multiracial', the situation is quite different:
always convert and often overt conflict pattern so-
called multiracial conceptions of identity.   In
these schools the conflict between the two contexts
tends to be managed, even contained, as I have
suggested elsewhere, through the medium of multi-
cultural education (34).   Or to reformulate this
observation in terms of pedagogic and curriculum
practices: there appears to be only a change in
the content of what is taught and not in the context
in which it is taught.   Thus the identity rules
which regulate the justifications for the continuation of the contexts differ only in focus and not
in purpose from those that justify the positioning
of blacks in the system of economic production.
     Again taking quite a different focus the
identity rules that regulate the justifications
socially hatched in the reaction process appear at
all times to reflect an ideal conception of a 'to be
worked for' set of social relations.   In respect to
reactions of protest they project an identity based
upon a number of realities that are seen to
endorse the apparent multiracial and multicultural
nature of society at large.   In other words and
encompassing an ideology of cultural or ethnic
pluralism, they consist of rules that regulate and
project images of a future society in which racial
considerations will always remain subordinate to
culture factors, which in turn will dominate and
minimise the impact of class considerations.   More
specifically, these rules include justifications
that draw upon factors such as the permanence of
black settlement, the cultural and linguistic
richness and diversity of black groups, historical

associations, membership of an internationalised community, and, possibly most crucial of all, the inalienable right of black groups settled here to full citizenships, equal treatment and educational opportunities (35).   Whilst these rules appear to emphasise the need to adjust behaviours to apparently objective conditions as projected in the view that Britain is a multiracial, culticultural and multilingual society, those which justify reactions of resistance tend to emanate from quite a different structural and experimental base (36).

In the first place they appear to relocate the experience of blacks in white societies outside these societies and within a broader historical context of racial oppression.   Thus the experience of blacks throughout the world, from Anzania to the Americas, has become an integral part of black conceptions of self and hence of the web of justifications for resistance.   From such a position, the identity rules then, secondly, seem to project an image of not an ideal society somehow grafted on to its present structural base but rather an ideal society that in its making seeks consciously either to destroy or radically reshape the old.   Therefore, they are rules which tend to project and justify a vision of a new social order based upon egalitarian principles of production and distribution;   principles hewn from black history, from the racial consciousness of and participation in race-class, class-race struggles (37).

Obviously, these three interdependent sets of rules which appear to regulate the processes of production, reproduction and reaction need to be discussed in greater depth than is possible to do here.   In fact all I have been able to do is to identify them in relation to the processes they regulate and suggest their general character and purpose (38).   In the doing of this, I have tried to keep afloat a notion of the non-static nature of the racial code.   This has been necessary to do because, whatever else might be said about the code's features or rules of regulation, it is patently clear that over time the racial code itself appears to undergo certain changes, and it is therefore to a consideration of these changes or the code's internal dynamic structure that I shall now finally turn.

CHANGE AND CONTROL: THE CODE CYCLE

The racial code's dynamic quality does not arise, as

might be immediately expected, from either broadly
based changes in class-race, race-class relations or
from reactions to racism per se.   Although theoretically the code operates within the boundaries of
structurally established relations at any given
time, it does seem to change rather than to be
changed by these relations.   Similarly, reactions
themselves formed into a specific code feature and
process do not appear to effect the code's social
profile: they only suggest rather than account for
the dynamic quality inherent in the code.   As an
essential part of the structure of the code, the
dynamic aspect is instead embedded within the code's
component forms.   To be seen in the daigram of the
code cycle below, these forms are distinctively
shaped by two types of reaction and by a hierarch-
ically structured relationship that bonds these
reactions of protest and resistance into an overall
feature and process of reaction.   In other words
the dynamic quality of the racial code results from
and is a feature of the relationship between socially
organised and <u>dominant</u> reactions of protest and
socially organised and <u>dominated</u> reactions of
resistance.

THE CODE CYCLE

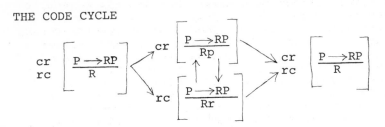

To expand upon this a little further, the socio-
political significance of the distinction I have
already drawn between reactions of protest and
resistance is evidenced in the type of relations of
dominance and struggle.   Articulated in the
struggle for supremacy over modes of thought and
views on racism or what in fact constitutes the
real problem, these relations are in a constant
state of flux, tension and conflict, and consequently
provide the code's social motor.   They reflect the
social basis and structural context of the
organisation, expression and promotion of the two
types of reaction.   In the case of the dominant
type, reactions of protest, they are formed and
maintained out of and are responses to a social

engagement, overtly or covertly entered into, with
the various black groups, bodies or agencies involved in resisting racist authority and liberating
themselves from racial oppression. Effective in
the reactions of state sponsored or officially
sanctioned bodies, agencies, or groups, they are
essentially relations of control; orchestrated and
managed to control and dominate the discourse and
space that is generated, as largely a result of
resistive struggle, within and between the overall
relationship that brings together the two types of
reaction into a general process of reaction (39).
In the case of the dominated type, reactions of
resistance, they are formed as a result of the
social engagement just described. As relations of
change they are then orchestrated and managed by
black groups in struggle to change the dominant
discourse and, if at all possible, to restructure,
occupy and control the space or social territory
that either results from resistive struggle itself
or, as phoney or colonial space, that results as an
officially sponsored or approved product of the
reactions of protest (40).

Historically organised in structured relations
of power, effective protest then depends heavily
upon the support of the institutional and state
controlled agencies of production and reproduction.
Reactions of this kind are thus not only located
within the acceptable boundaries of the state's
concern and protection but, informed by and
dependent upon the role of liberalism within the
institutional structures of the state, they also
become translators and conveyors of revised
interpretations of dominance. That is to say, as
reactions that draw upon the mould two oppositional
sources of interests into legitimate protest, the
dominant class socio-economic interests of the state
and those of the racially oppressed, they appear at
all times to be engaged in the work of redefining
racial oppression, racism, the racial discourse, in
terms of dominant class interests and, conversely,
these interests in terms of the socio-political
aspirations of the racially oppressed (41).

While the effect of this role and kind of
engagement can be readily seen in the recent
interventions of the state and hence the sudden
conversion of the state to multiculturalism, the
Rampton Committee's Report, the Home Affairs
Committee's recent deliberations on 'racial
disadvantage' and even in the Queen's 1981 Christmas
address, it would be misleading to assume that this

effect arises entirely from a rediscovered liberal
awareness, one alledgedly based upon humanitarian
values and a sense of justice and decency in human
relations (42).   Quite the reverse: it has arisen
as a direct result of a long history of black
resistance that reached just one of its climatic
points on the streets of Brixton and Toxteth in 1981.
It arose as a result of a struggle between competing
conceptions of racial reality reactively organised
in actions of protest and resistance.

Reflected in demands for non-racist education,
black pupil and parental resistance has therefore
always existed in contrast and opposition to
official policies and practices in the field (43).
It has set not only the social tenor of the
relationship in as much that black resistance
against racist authority within and outside
education has had to be taken into account in all
protest reactions.   But, just as crucially, it has
shaped the relationship between protest and
resistance reactions in two further ways.   Firstly,
it has established and to some extent controlled the
social dimension and objectives of protest reactions,
something that has been achieved through its own
consciously determined fluctuations of intensity,
strategies and demands.   The equation has been
simply that as resistance has intensified then
protest too has developed.   Or to put this in
another way: as the reactions of resistance have
demanded x the reactions of protest have interpreted
x as y to the relevant agencies and institutions of
the state which, in turn, have reacted with policies
and practices x.   Although the precise terms of y
and z cannot be calculated beforehand, at the time
when demands x are made, the likely range of y and z
responses is in the majority of cases known.   It is
the realisation and understanding of this as a
mechanism internal to the relationship that makes
the relationship in the first place meaningful and
necessary for both the relative control and change
of conditions and, even possibly, situations.

It is this feature, the most visible, that
constitutes the post facto expression of the second.
For as resistive demands are stated and interpretations and adjustments are made by individuals
or groups engaged in protest reactions then the
whole relationship experiences a shift.

Stimulated more by reactions of resistance
than those of protest, these shifts, which are
sequentially related and experienced by
individuals, groups or agencies involved in the

production and reproduction processes, ultimately result in a change in the overall racial code itself. Thus, for instance, over the last two decades which have witnessed major changes in educational ideologies and responses to racism, there have been at least three changes in the expressive or variant if not fundamental structural form of the code; a social career which can be diagrammatically represented by merely extending the code's trajectory as shown in the figure above until it is possible to write out:

$$\begin{array}{c} cr \\ rc \end{array} \left[\frac{P \longrightarrow RP}{R} \right]^3$$

CONCLUSION

Although it is possible to go on writing out variations of the racial code in this way, it is not necessary to do so in order to arrive at a point where I can draw together some of the issues and themes raised in this paper (44). In the first place and despite the reservations and qualifications already alluded to, I have tried to show that not only does such a thing as a racial code exist, but that, through the operation of value, appropriation and identity rules, it also effectively regulates the production, reproduction and reactions to racism. Moreover, I have also attempted to show that the code itself is a dynamic entity and structure of relations, one that contains within itself and between its variant forms the preconditional and conditional basis for the control and change of class-race and race-class relations. But of more immediate political and, against the backcloth of Summer 1981, policy value, I think I have arrived at a conclusion and beginning that, if heeded, should alter the course of future 'race relations' policy and practice in and outside of education.

As the main political implication and message of this paper, this conclusion can be summarised in the following way:

Reactions of protest = the management of racism.

Reactions of resistance = the demanagement of racism.

NOTES AND REFERENCES

1.   This paper represents an initial attempt to discuss some of the specific issues raised in a research project funded by the Social Science Research Council on 'The Social Management of Racial Policy and Practice'.   It should therefore be viewed as a modest theoretical contribution to and integral though small part of this broader project. For a chronological account of the 'major incidents, marches, confrontations, demonstrations, disturbances and gatherings (some peaceful, most involving violence)' that made the headlines in the seven months from March, 1981, see Mary Venner (1981), 'From Deptford to Notting Hill: Summer 1981', *New Community*, Vol. IX, No. 2, pp. 203-207.

2.   Lord Scarman (1981) *The Brixton Disorders 10-12 April 1981: Report of an Inquiry by Rt. Hon. The Lord Scarman, OBE*, HMSO, London, especially p. 11, para 2.22.

3.   A. Sivanandan (1981) 'From Resistance to Rebellion: Asian and Afro-Caribbean Struggles in Britain', *Race and Class*, Vol. XXIII, No. 2/3, pp. 111-152.   In this special double issue of *Race and Class*, entitled Britain 81: *Rebellion and Repression* see also the papers by Louis Kushnick, Paul Gilroy and, for a broader historical treatment of 'revolt and repression', Frances Webber.

4.   For an account of the kind of 'dismissal' I have in mind, which tend to pepper white accommodations to black definitions, see Peter Ratcliffe (1981) *Racism and Reaction: A Profile of Handsworth*, Routledge and Kegan Paul, London, p. 284-286.

5.   Samuel Bowles and Herbert Gintis (1976) *Schooling in Capitalist America: Educational Reform and the Con-tradictions of Economic Life*, Routledge and Kegan Paul, London.   For a more complex and subtle account of their current position, see the paper by Herbert Gintis given at this conference.

6.   See Paul Willis's paper in this volume.

7.   Both these forms stem from what I term the <u>nuclear</u> form of the racial code which can be written out as:

$\frac{P \longrightarrow RP}{R}$ Rather simply this form merely represents the relationship of the production of racism to the reproduction of and reaction to racism.   The significance of R in the code or 'under' P and RP is that it is opposition-ally related to and consequently effects both the production and reproduction processes.

8.   Basin Bernstein (1971) *Class, Codes and Control: Volume 1, Theoretical Studies towards a Sociology of Language;* and (1977) *Class, Codes and Control: Volume 3, Towards a Theory of Educational Transmissions*, Routledge and Kegan Paul, London.

9.   Basil Bernstein (1981) *Codes, Modalities and the*

Process of Cultural Reproduction: A Model, Department of Education, University of Lund, Sweden, p. 3.

10. *Ibid*, p. 4.

11. It should be noted that this paper is not directly concerned with the effectiveness of strategies that might appear to follow from the analysis offered here: it is only concerned with the arriving at a point where it is possible to conceive of such strategies.

12. D. Howe (1973) 'Fighting Back: West Indian Youth and the Police in Notting Hill' *Race Today*, Vol. 5, No. 11; and for a broader theoretical discussion on the nature and role of black labour in capitalist society, see Stuart Hall, *et al.* (1978) *Policing the Crisis: Mugging, the State and Law and Order*, The Macmillan Press, London, pp. 348-396.

13. John Rex and Sally Tomlinson (1979). *Colonial Immigrants in a British City: A Class Analysis*. Routledge and Kegan Paul, London.

14. For a longer exposition of this argument which provides a definition of racism and draws an analytical distinction between the ideological and structural aspects of racism see Chris Mullard (1980) *Racism in Society and Schools: History, Policy and Practice*, Centre for Multicultural Education, University of London Institute of Education, London.

15. Theoretical and empirical elaborations of this point can be found in the following 'reader' which includes a 'diverse' range of papers, documents, and other materials on the subject: Peter Braham, Michael Pearn and Ed Rhodes (eds.) (1982) *Discrimination and Disadvantage in Employment: The Experience of Black Workers*, Harper and Row, London.

16. Symptomatic of this tendency in the United States is the initial position of Samuel Bowles and Herbert Gintis (1976) *op cit* and in the United Kingdom, Paul Willis (1977) *Learning to Labour* Saxon House, Farnborough. Although these authors have since heavily revised their early positions, (see their papers in this volume), their work nevertheless has given rise to on both sides of the Atlantic a sprouting tradition of ill-organised and poorly conceptualised research which eulogises rather than explains the conditions of and reactions to class, race and gender oppression.

17. See Chris Mullard (1981) 'The Social Context and Meaning of Multicultural Education', *Educational Analysis*, Vol. 3, No. 1. In this paper I tried to show that multi-culturalist theory and education, 'as a socially recon-structed set of theoretical constructions, seeks to resolve and describe if not explain the capital/class-race contra-diction in terms of the cultural representation of the ideological form of racism - ethnicism' (p. 133). I went on to explain that in essence ethnicism (represents the exchange of a largely racially-determined set of ideas and beliefs (cultural determinism) to justify specific practices and

protect specific interests. As the cultural representation of the ideological form of racism, ethnicism then constitutes a set of representations of _ethnic_ differences, peculiarities, cultural biographies, histories and practices which are used to justify specific courses of action that possess the effect of institutionalising ethnic/cultural differences. In doing this, ethnicist policies and practices also tend to obfuscate the common experiences, histories and socio-political conditions of black groups and hence the degree of commonality of experience that might exist between black and certain white class and gender groups in society' (_Ibid_).

18.   Although this assumption informs much of the research, educational policies and teachers' practices in the field, it is most recently and perhaps best exemplified in an Open University book of readings that will unfortunately have more than a small impact on how, at least, O.U. students will be introduced to the area of study: Alan James and Robert Jeffcoate (eds.) (1982) _The School in the Multi-cultural Society_, Harper and Row, London.

19.   See note 17 above.

20.   A fuller account of the way in which I describe the concept and meaning of _protest_ can be found in Chris Mullard (1975) _Aboriginal Resistance: A Study of its Social Roots and Organisation_, Unpublished M.A. Dissertation, University of Durham, Durham.

21.   For further elaboration of the meaning and the understanding of _Resistance_ see Chris Mullard (1980) _Race, Power and Resistance: A Study of the Institute of Race Relations 1952-1972_, Ph.D. Thesis, University of Durham, Durham. A revised and shortened version of this research will be published as Chris Mullard (1982/3) _Race, Power and Resistance_, Routledge and Kegan Paul, London.

22.   It should be noted that _all_ recent official accounts and reports view the problem as one of 'racial disadvantage' and not one of 'racism'. This is to suggest that the so-called problem arises from the fact of being black (a social pathology model) rather than that of historically and institutionally structured white responses to the fact of being black. For instance, see Interim Report of the Committee of Inquiry into the Education of Children from Ethnic University Groups (1981) _West Indian Children in our Schools_, Cmnd 8273, HMSO, London; Home Affairs Committee (1981) _Racial Disadvantage_, HC-4247, HMSO, London; and Report of an Inquiry by the Rt. Hon. The Lord Scarman (1981) _The Brixton Disorders 10-12th April, 1981_, Cmnd 8247, HMSO, London.

23.   The nuclear form of the racial code is set out in note 7 above.

24.   See John Rex and Sally Tomlinson (1979) _op cit_, especially Chapter 1 and Note 9 to that chapter in which they extend within a Weberian frame of reference both Myrdal and

Baran and Sweezy's conception of the term.   For an account
of these two derivative conceptions see: Gunnar Myrdal (1964)
Challenge to Affluence, Gollanz, London and Paul Baran and
Paul Sweezy (1966) *Monopoly Capital.   An Essay on the
American Economic and Social Order*, Monthly Review Press,
New York.

   25.   Paul Gilroy (1980) 'Managing the Underclass':
Race and Class, Vol. XXII, No. 1, and Jenny Bourne and
A. Sivanandan (1980) 'Cheerleaders and Ombudsmen: The
Sociology of Race Relations in Britain', *Race and Class*,
Vol. XXI, No. 4.

   26.   Fanon, Frank (1970) 'The Wretched of the Earth'.
Penguin, Hammonsworth; Arghiri, Emmanual (1972) 'Unequal
Exchange: A Study of Imperialism of Trade'. New Left Book;
Frank, André (1980) 'Crisis: In the World Economy'.
Heinemann Education; Frank, André (1981) 'Crisis: In the
Third World'. Heinemann Educational.

   27.   Stuart Hall *et al.* (1979) *op. cit.*

   28.   Bernard Coard (1971) *How the West Indian Child is
Made Educationally Sub-Normal in the British School System:
The Scandal of the Black Child in Schools in Britain*, New
Beacon Books, London.

   29.   For a critical discussion of the ideology of
ethnic pluralism see Brian Bullvant (1981) *The Pluralist
Dilemma in Education: Six Case Studies*, George Allen and
Unwin, Sydney.

   30.   Paul Corrigan (1980) *Schooling the Smash Street
Kids*, The Macmillan Press, London.

   31.   See Bruce Carrington's contribution to this
volume.

   32.   Maureen Stone (1981) *The Education of the Black
Child in Britain: The Myth of Multiracial Education*, Fontana
Paperbacks, London.

   33.   For further exposition see Chris Mullard (1980)
op cit.

   34.   Chris Mullard (1981) (a) *op cit.* (1981) (b) 'Black
Kids in White Schools: Multiracial Education in Britain'
Plural Societies, Vol. 12, No. 1/2 and (1982) 'Multi-racial
Education in Britain: From Assimilation to Cultural Pluralism',
in John Tierney (ed.), *Race, Migration and Schooling*, Holt
Saunders, London.

   35.   The social and ideological drive behind much of
the work and research in the area of multi-ethnic or multi-
cultural education reflects the operation of these rules and
is consequently based upon these justifications.   For an
extremely sophisticated example of what I mean in the
sub-field of 'linguistic and dialectic diversity' see in
particular H. Rosen and T. Burgess (1980) *Languages and
Dialects of London School Children: An Investigation*, Ward
Lock Educational, London.

36.   This viewpoint informs the whole work of the
£350,OOO Linguistic Minorities Project based at the
University of London Institute of Education under the
direction of Verity Saifullah Khan.   As the largest single
grant made by the DES or for that matter any other body,
including the SSRC, for work in this field, perhaps,
rhetorically, the question needs to be asked - Why?
37.   This constitutes the ideological terrain of the
post-1972 Institute of Race Relations *(Race and Class)*, the
Race Today Collective, and a number of other black community
and political groups.
38.   Other theoretical research tasks necessary to
complete before it is possible to be more conclusive would
inevitably include the whole question of the relationship
that might exist between the three sets of rules, their
precise location and basis within the processes they regulate,
and their actual specificities vis-a-vis the change or control
of race relations.
39.   For an elaboration of this point and particularly
for a definition and discussion of the concept of space see
Chris Mullard (1980) (1982/3) *op cit.*
40.   Examples of phoney or colonial space can be seen
in the establishment of local community relations councils
during the 1960's and 1970's;   the setting up of units and
centres for multi-ethnic or multicultural education in the
DES, LEAs and institutions of higher education;   and, last
but not least, the provision of slots or space in the school
curriculum to teach and discuss multicultural issues.   What
all these developments or, more accurately, 'products' share
in common is that they have been provided by powerful white
groups as a response to essentially white perceptions and
definitions of what constitutes the problem in schools and
society - hence my designation of this kind of space as being
colonial.   Some further thoughts on this are to be found in
an, as yet, unpublished paper called 'The Colony of Space'.
41.   For further proof of this it is necessary to
consult the documents and policy statements produced by
state controlled or sponsored agencies.   An interesting
starting point in this kind of critical research work would be
an examination of the publications of the Commission for
Racial Equality, the Select/Home Affairs Committee on race
relations and immigration, and, in education, the various
statements produced by ILEA since the 1979 publication of
ILEA 269.
42.   Interim Report of the Committee of Inquiry into the
Education of Children from Ethnic Minority Groups (1981), *op cit,*
Home Affairs Committee (1981), *op cit*;   and Her Majesty Queen
Elizabeth II (1981), an address to the nation broadcasted by
the British Broadcasting Corporation on 25th December.   In
this Christmas address the Queen emphasised the harsh treatment and disadvantage that commonwealth (black) groups were

164

experiencing in the United Kingdom and called for some effort, action and change in attitude on the part of the majority of her subjects.

43. See Fairukh Dhondy (1978) 'Teaching Young Blacks', *Race Today*, May/June, pp. 80-85; the Institute of Race Relations Submission to the Rampton Committee (1979), IRR, London; and the various statements produced for instance by the Black Parents Movement and the Black Students Movement.

44. It should be noted again and finally that in this paper I have only been able to outline in general terms the nature of the racial code but this, I believe, is enough to sustain the conclusion(s) I offer.

QUALIFIED CRITICISM, CRITICAL QUALIFICATIONS

Mary Fuller

> Deviant pupils will always merit the attention
> of the sociologist of education since, on the
> basis of a relativistic conception of deviance,
> they can be interpreted as 'cultural critics'
> or 'political dissenters'.

> ... it is held that deviant pupils'
> opposition is a rational response grounded in
> their partial demystification of the social
> systems of which they are members.
> (Hargreaves 1979)

I want in this paper to examine young people's
criticisms of and dissent from the social systems in
which they operate.   Specifically I shall be
looking at fifth year pupils' dissent using some
research carried out a few years ago in a comprehensive school.   Since the young people were
attending school I shall start by looking at their
standing as pupils, but will, in order to make
sense particularly of the young women's viewpoints,
need to encompass aspects of their lives outside
school.   I shall examine the definition of deviance
as currently employed in the sociological literature
concerning adolescents and particularly young people
at school.
     I shall look at the linkages between young
people's criticisms of 'society' and their stance
as pupils within school, focusing especially on the
extent to which a pupil's dissident position in
relation to school is associated with a critical
view of the other social systems of which s/he is a
member.   I do this because there is a strong sense
in the literature that deviant pupils are cultural
critics not only of education/schooling but also
that this criticism extends to some if not all other

aspects of their lives. The obverse of this, though not usually explicitly stated, is that those pupils who are not deviant are conformers in school and, by extension, within the other social systems of which they are members.

Throughout the paper I shall be drawing on the fact that my research involved males and females and included pupils of white British, Afro-Caribbean and Indo-Pakistani parentage, which enables me to discuss acquiescence and opposition as these are manifested by pupils who are differentially located in the same social systems. By coming at this discussion from two different angles I hope to show that a more complex analysis is required of the relationship between in-school behaviour and pupils' critical attitudes to their lives outside school. I shall look first at the incidence of deviant and other pupils at the school which I call Torville, trying to relate their dissidence concerning school to their attitudes of life outside school, taking their critical awareness of two forms of domination (sexism and racism) as the focus for establishing their degree of acquiescence or opposition to the social system generally. Then, taking those people who are resisting sexual and racial domination, I shall look at the extent to which they demonstrate the kinds of behavioural and attitudinal orientation which is recognised as criticism of school culture.

I shall be re-examining some research which I completed in 1978 which came up with some information about whose interpretations I have remained un-satisfied. The problem was how to reconcile others' writing about girls' conformity and acquiescence (actually in most cases an impression left by their failure to be mentioned in the literature concerning school deviants rather than an established fact) with my own observations of young women at Torville school being actively critical and contemptuous of much that was going on around them in and outside school. Indeed, in regard to many aspects of their current and likely future lives some of the fifth year girls were markedly <u>more</u> critical and politically soph-isticated than most of the boys. Yet in terms of overt 'sympto ns' within the school the girls' opposition to what was actually and what in the future they thought was likely to be happening to them, did not come across as obviously oppositional or troublesome in the terms that others describe 'troublesome' male pupils.

The school was a large, mixed multi-racial comprehensive in the London borough of Brent. For

the Autumn and Spring terms in 1975/76 I observed
the school lives of a group of fifth year pupils.
Wherever possible I also participated in that life.
My role was as a non-teaching adult, a kind of
'honorary pupil' who attended lessons, socialised
with pupils outside the classroom (within school
hours) and who in the second term more obviously
engaged in research in that I administered questionnaires and more formally and systematically interviewed pupils using a tape recorder.   (Full details
of the project can be found in Fuller 1978, and
information about specific aspects in Fuller 1980
and 1982.)
    During the two terms in which I was daily
observing and participating in their school lives.
I kept a running record of information about pupils
which I used to build up a reputational profile of
each pupil.   There was a fair degree of overlap
concerning any particular pupil's reputation among
the teachers who taught him/her and a more than
expected consensus between pupils and teachers
concerning the reputation of each particular pupil.
Most pupils also, when asked in interview how they
were seen by staff, had a pretty accurate understanding of their status in teachers' minds.
Although I made attempts to obtain systematic
information about each pupil and was able to generate
a primitive typology of pupils on the basis of this
material I also recorded teachers' comments about
every pupil from the pupils' most recent school
report, a source of information which was relatively
free from biases introduced by my own skills and
weaknesses as an observer, and also, since it was
not written with my research interests in mind,
relatively free of systematic distortion in the
direction of what teachers knew my research
interests to be.   Using only the reports I was able
to devise an independent typology of pupils,
according to the total number of positive and
negative comments each received on their report.
(Full details of this in Fuller 1978.)   In a sense
this provided independent confirmation of the
typology based on hearsay and pupils' observed
behaviour in the classroom.   Pupils could be
described as one of the following: good, bad,
conspicuous and unobtrusive.   In some measure all
except the first category were troublesome to
teachers, though not (even among the 'bad') exclusively or mainly troublesome in terms of being con-
frontationally antagonistic to schooling and/or
teachers.

Bad pupils included all those who were overtly antagonistic but this category was not made up exclusively of such pupils. A pupil could be seen as bad in terms of having undesirable 'personality' characteristics and not solely on the basis of simple behavioural resistance. Good pupils were those who worked hard and effectively, who 'contributed to the school' but who did not draw their positive attitude to school to the teacher's attention. Unobtrusive pupils included the few recent arrivals, but also some whose lack of connection with teachers and school routines meant that they were hardly known to the teachers. They were a puzzle to the teachers but not a 'problem' in the sense of being troublesome enough to greatly exercise teachers' attention. The conspicuous were, in terms of effort and achievement, similar to the good pupils but in addition, unlike the good, they came in for a disproportionately large number of negative comments as well. Well-known to the teachers, they were also a puzzle, being a mixture of 'bad' and teacher-approved behaviour and attitudes. What lay behind this mixture was the view 'I can get something (vocationally worthwhile) from school even though school work is itself boring.'

Table 1 distinguishes male and female pupils in each of the categories.

Table 1: Teacher-generated Categorisation of Pupils

	Good	Bad	Unobtrusive	Conspicuous
Girls	19	13	7	5
Boys	26	31	15	6

Rather more boys than girls are defined as bad pupils, a finding which in itself is unsurprising given what others have written about pupil resistance. Of considerably more interest is the relatively high proportion of girls as bad pupils by the teachers at Torville, and the fact that the difference between the sexes is not statistically significant. This categorisation of pupils does not isolate the overtly antagonistic but includes them with other pupils who are defined by teachers as educationally problematic because of certain disapproved of characteristics. Nevertheless all 'bad' pupils deviate from Torville teachers' concept of acceptable attitudes and behaviour, a concept which, as already mentioned, was shared by many of the pupils (including the 'bad' ones).

At Torville school there seems to be no support for the view that girls are massively more approved by teachers, nor that being troublesome in educationally relevant ways is the perogative of boys. It is also important to note that there were no significant differences between the female and male pupils in terms of why they were viewed as bad - the types of attitudinal and behavioural characteristics of which teachers disapproved were more or less equally evident in their reports about both girls and boys. At least at Torville there did not seem to be any evidence that teachers were working with dual notions of the good male as distinct from the good female pupil nor that certain types of behaviour would only be seen as bad in one particular sex.

I feel fairly confident that the typology bears a close relation to that of other researchers in the sense that it is associated with certain other pupil characteristics in ways that are consistent with others' research about different types of pupil. For example, a much higher proportion of good pupils aspired to taking a large number of public exams ('O' level and/or 'CSE') and a much larger proportion of bad pupils had low aspirations in this respect. Others have noted a close association between teachers' perceptions of a pupil and that pupil's attainment at school. Although a relationship of this kind could be established in the Torville study, it broke down when specific groups of pupils were analysed. Of relevance to the present paper is the fact that Afro-Caribbean girls' high levels of attainment bore no relationship to the way teachers saw them. It was when I started to try to make sense of these findings that I became aware of some of the limitations and conceptual confusions surrounding conformity and deviance in school settings.

Wilkinson (1975) has suggested that black youth in America 'must still contend with social issues that never confront white youth'. Black youth in Britain - female and male - experience relations of racial domination and exclusion, a 'social issue' never far from the surface of their discussions with me when I was carrying out the research already mentioned. Women, whether black or white, experience relations of sexual domination and exclusion and this, too, was central to their thinking about their lives inside and outside school.

One of the major themes emerging from inter-

views with fifth form girls at Torville school was
that of control.   For girls of all ethnic groups
there were three inter-related aspects of their
discussions.   Firstly, their being controlled by
others in and out of school;   secondly, their wish
for control for themselves at some time in the
future;   and lastly, (and perhaps paradoxically)
their need to exercise forms of self-control and
suppression of resentment now in order to achieve
self-determination later.   In all these respects
girls, whether white, Afro-Caribbean or South Asian,
consciously compared themselves with boys of their
own age and ethnic group as a means of examining
their experiences and reflecting on their schooling.
Most of them had brothers, all had friends with
brothers, some had boyfriends and all were attending
a co-educational school.   In short, they were all
speaking from direct experience of sexual differences
in social relations.
     The girls almost without exception described
their lives as 'restricted' and lacking in 'freedom',
a state of affairs for which parents were held
mainly responsible.   For some there was the knowledge or hope that as they grew older their parents
would reduce the areas of control, though none felt
that the simple passing of time would bring them the
degree of freedom their brothers or male peers could
expect.   Thus they saw young women older than themselves enjoying more freedom of movement than they
themselves had, but even so being still subject to
more parental attempts at control than male peers.
For many more, and this applied especially to ethnic
minority girls, even small gains would have to be
struggled for.   This is not to suggest that black
parents are more repressive than white parents, but
to recognise that they saw that as women of colour
their prospects of obtaining some degree of
independence through work outside the home as being
considerably restricted.
     To wrest small gains meant adopting various
strategies - some self-denying - such as 'biting
back' their criticisms and resentments or acquiring
characteristics of, for example, deceit or 'tough-
ness' about which they were somewhat ambivalent.
Interestingly, when completing the Bem Sex Role
Inventory (Bem 1974) both Indo-Pakistani and Afro-
Caribbean girls endorsed the following characteristics as applying to them: self-reliant, defends
own beliefs, independent, athletic, has a strong
personality, analytical, self-sufficient and
ambitious.   These are all, according to Bem's

trials, supposedly masculine traits and were certainly less frequently endorsed by white girls at Torville.

Schooling and education provided an alternative and less undermining possibility in their search for greater freedom and control. Concentration on education as a way out was something which all the black girls whom I interviewed stressed, though as will be seen and as they pointed out this strategy had its drawbacks. In particular the vocational aspects of schooling and further education were attractive in their achievements in these areas were thought to lead to better prospects of a 'good' job. Being aware of both sexual and racial discrimination the girls did not assume that good educational performance was the sufficient requirement for obtaining such jobs, but they did believe it was a necessary one.

It is for these reasons that I describe qualifications as 'critical' for these girls. And it is partly because of the critical importance of qualifications in their current thinking about the future that the girls themselves qualify and temper their criticisms of both their school experience and their treatment by parents. This much the girls had in common, but I want now to look in greater detail at each group in turn. The following accounts depend on the girls' own words and on their ways of representing the dilemmas they face and of thinking their way through them. It is not possible to say whether these girls are representative of the young, female black population in Britain, because there are so few accounts of young women's lives in school and among those that exist there is hardly a mention of young black women.

AFRO-CARIBBEAN GIRLS

Parents were judged more or less 'strict' or 'old-fashioned' according to whether they placed numerous or relatively few restrictions on their daughter's life out of school. By this yardstick the parents of all but one girl were described as strict. This showed itself particularly in a double standard in which boys were positively encouraged to be out of the house and were allowed considerable freedom of movement, while girls were given little option but to remain within the home. According to Michelle, West Indian parents are:

More protective over girls, they reckon that

the boys from the time they hit 13, they should be out, mucking around playing football. If they do anything 'boys will be boys', but girls (are) supposed to stay at home and sit there. They do anything wrong, you're behaving badly, you're not behaving like you should. 'Boys will be boys', but the girls it's different. ... My mum keeps going on at my brother, when he was younger she kept going on at him, wondering what he was doing in the house. She expects him to be out, but if I ask to go out, good grief, hits the roof. She wants to know where I want to go, why, and I must be back at a certain time, who am I going with, and I must leave a phone number, all that sort of stuff.

Within the home girls are kept busy: as one girl succinctly put it, the choice is 'housework or homework'. Christa says of one of her friends:

... her mum told us that Marcia likes work, she's always got a maths book, always got some reading, some book with her. ... She does that excuse to get away from the house-work.

Considerable arguments take place between girls and their mothers and brothers at the differential expectations concerning domestic tasks. Boys are apparently expected to help very little around the house:

The work that my brother does, that mum sets him in the house, it's just the bins. (Christa)

I have to tidy up behind him (brother), so I suppose he thinks I'm like a maid or a slave. (Joan)

They are resentful, vociferous in their dislike of such 'favouritism', but also take pride in their domestic skills; especially as they believe it indicates greater competence than their brothers have and as they appreciate the degree of overwork to which their mothers are subject.

Despite having considerable criticisms of the sexual division of labour within their own families all the girls expressed great fondness for their mothers. Mothers were the ones who talked to and encouraged them, to whom they could talk and who, much more than fathers, interpreted the world outside the family. Talking about friends who have both parents living with them Christa observes:

> ... their mother is always first, their mother is more like their .... It's like they haven't got a father at all, their mother is just there.

In similar vein Janice declared 'It always comes back to my mum!'
Several other girls talked about their fathers as not so much uninterested in them as being the parent who basically laid down the rules, but was not around to ensure that they were complied with. That task was left to mothers. Once some of the girls had realised this they had decided to stop rebelling directly, bide their time and then enlist their mother's support in sidestepping their father's attempts at controlling them. In this they had sometimes been successful, but the resulting better relationship with their mothers was accompanied by ambivalence at their deceit and an increased sense that it was not possible to achieve what they wanted by rational argument with their fathers.

> ...I've settled down, because you see before, my friends have a lot more freedom, they can go out and all that kind of thing, whereas I wasn't allowed to at that time, and I used to moan about it and kick up a big fuss. But then I went quiet and just left it and I think well maybe they feel she's grown up a bit now ... (Beverley)

> ... somehow women seem nicer than men! ... I would say that women are more understanding, they can reason out things with you. There's only a few men that can do that. Men, they lose their temper ... Men are more stronger than women ... Women are more advanced, but men are more physical. ... she's better at talking and explaining than my dad. He stutters - well he doesn't explain himself properly. ... I mainly just talk to my mum. (Monica)

The inability of males to engage in rational arguments and their resort to physical forms of

control was an important part of the girls'
discussions about relationships with boys of their
own generation.   Although none of them looked to
marriage as bringing greater autonomy (as many white
girls did), and indeed only two looked forward to
marrying, most supposed they would marry in the
distant future.   When that time came they would want
their husbands to be black.   Janice speaks for a
number of others in describing marriage as follows:

> Well you're tied to one person, that can be
> boring, you can get tired of it.   You're
> restricted in what you can do, what you can't
> do, then the kids come in.   ... That's what
> you get married for, really, just that it will
> be legal for the kids.

Even where they were not allowed or did not themselves yet want boyfriends the girls nevertheless
considered black boys an important source of
friendship.   Boys were claimed to resort frequently
to 'beating' girls in order to establish their
dominance over them and to retain their reputation
with male peers.

> ... he might feel a bit embarrassed because I
> think boys feel more like that than girls. If
> they're with a group of boys and a girl calls
> him and they go over to her, they say things
> like 'She's calling you, she should be coming
> to you' because they reckon they're boys and
> the girl should come to them.   If he was on
> his own he would go over, but seeing as his
> friends are there and they start .... going
> on about her calling him, he'll start going
> on about 'You should come to me' ... When
> their friends are with them they mostly feel
> that's what they should mostly do - if they go
> after the girl it's a bit of a let-down.
> (Michelle)

> You know most coloured boys tend to knock
> their girls about.   ... They've got this
> vicious streak in them, so I warn them 'If
> you think you can knock me about, you've got
> another thought coming, because I'll knock
> you back then I'll walk off'. (Janice)

> ... well most West Indian boys ... definitely
> aren't going to let a woman dominate them or
> tell them what to do.   They firmly believe

> that they're the boss and she has to do
> everything they tell them. I think West
> Indian women are more aggressive because
> there's this thing that as soon as a women
> gets out of place they hit her for it....
> (Beverley)

Consequently the girls felt they needed to acquire
some skills to back up a reputation for not being a
'softy'and to become at least partly inured to
boys' violence - actual or threatened. In so
doing a number were described by the black boys at
Torville as girls who 'like to try to bully about'.
In addition girls were often divided from each
other by competition for boys, sometimes engaging
in physical but more often in verbal attacks on each
other. As Marcia, in her own words 'a well-known
softy', explains:

> If someone did come up against me I'd try my
> very best to beat them and show them that I
> can actually fight. Because that would be
> a real achievement for me because I try to be
> tough because people really trample on you if
> you're not. I'm soft in nature.

Looking to boys for friendship had other hazards -
many of the girls felt they had to keep their school
and job ambitions to themselves for fear that if
they were discovered they would be subject to
undermining ridicule from their male peers.

> I find that most boys do have ambitions but
> they're influenced by their friends so they
> never get put into practice anyway ... I think
> the girls are more ambitious but if they want
> to do something they don't feel embarrassed
> about it except when boys, when they hear
> you're doing 'O' levels, they won't come out
> with it and say you're a snob but they treat
> you a bit differently and you can feel it ...
> (Joan)

Marcia describes the pressures from boys in the
following way:

> I've always got my head in a book. I don't
> think they like it because they are always
> commenting on it and they say 'You won't get
> anywhere', and sometimes I think that they
> don't want me to learn or something like that,

> you know, but I spoke to my mum about it,
> and she said I shouldn't listen and I should
> keep working hard.

The experience or expectation of ridicule from boys
is not confined to Afro-Caribbean girls. Shaw
(1980) argues that it is a fact of life for girls to
be the butt of boys' abuse and scorn in school,
especially the nearer they come to challenging male
dominance. Shaw and Coleman (1961) point out that
the result of this is that girls either withdraw
from the competition or adopt various dissembling
strategies. These black girls most certainly did
not withdraw and it is to their attitudes and
behaviour in school that I now turn.

Having described these in greater detail
elsewhere (Fuller 1980, 1982) I shall give only a
broad outline of their attitudes and behaviour.
They had an instrumental orientation to education,
believing that it could offer them something useful
(paper qualifications) in their longer terms
efforts to obtain a measure of control over their
lives. So long as it was providing those
opportunities they were prepared to conform
minimally within the classroom and maximally in
terms of doing the work that was set. But beyond
a certain point they felt constrained by boys'
disapproval for showing enthusiasm for school.
School itself was 'trivial', 'boring', a place in
which it was vital to introduce an element of
'liveliness', partly for its own sake, partly to
mask their ambitions.

> ... I talk to me friends in the corridor and
> if they talk about something interesting I'm
> not going to rush off to my lesson, am I?
> I want to hear what they say first before I
> go, so that makes me late sometimes ... Miss
> G., well sometimes I go late to her lessons,
> but when I go to the classroom if she's not
> there so I go out again. I try to get back
> in again before she comes ... Just go and
> talk to your friends - if their teacher hasn't
> come in as well, you do in and talk to them
> and then you keep an eye on the door to see if
> your teacher's coming and when you see her
> coming down the corridor you just rush in
> quick. You know that she sees you but you
> still rush in. (Michelle)

They were frequently in conflict with teachers as a

result of this 'bad' behaviour and because they
would insist on teachers 'doing their job properly'
even though they might subsequently appear to ignore
the teaching. The girls hoped to obtain 'good'
jobs (within the restrictions of traditional women's
work) and talked of the need to be ambitious if they
were to avoid unemployment or dead-end jobs. Janice
was aiming to become a Personal Secretary because it
paid well and because it is the kind of job where
'most of the work depends on you, you know you're
relied on to use your initiative'. The value they
placed on educational qualifications as a necessary
preparation for work was clearly related to their
knowledge of high unemployment levels nationally
and locally and to their certainty that they would
face discrimination in the job market. As part of
their attempts to sidestep discrimination all the
girls remained in full-time education for at least
one year beyond the statutory school leaving age.
Those who, at about age seventeen, had taken up work
all mentioned that they were continuing their
studies on a part-time basis. By the time I had
completed the study the girls had obtained a mean
of 7.6 passes at 'O' level or CSE and generally with
creditable grades.

Their commitment to achievement through the
job market can be seen in the following extracts:

> I want a proper job first and some kind of
> skill so that if I do get married and have
> children I can go back to it: don't want just
> relying on him for money, cause I've got to
> look after myself, there must be something
> I can do.   (Michelle)

> I should go out to work because, really, if
> I don't start learning to get on with it, I
> maybe will just have to leave home, get
> married and depend on the husband and I don't
> want that at all ... Maybe I'll be a house-
> wife or something like that, but I always
> picture myself working.   (Monica)

I would suggest that the girls' cherished hopes of
greater control over their future lives and their
consequent emphasis on acquiring qualifications
and a 'good' job are not some form of individualistic self-improvement. Rather, they are necessary
strategies for survival where the poor employment
prospects and low wages which black males can
command make it essential even in intact families

for women to contribute financially to the family
income.   Whether to seek employment is not a real
issue for most black women, but how to maximise
their wage is.   The young women at Torville are
aiming to have some choice about the type of work
they obtain and the conditions in which they carry
out such work.   Unless their efforts to circumvent.
racial and sexual exclusion in employment are
successful they are likely to find themselves in
unskilled and semi-skilled jobs and being paid at
even lower rates of pay than their male counterparts.
    Some already have experience of attempts to
exclude them from the job market:

> When I first went for the job I was very
> crafty when I wrote the letter I put that I
> was a student and they thought I was coming
> from university and I did it in perfectly
> good English so they wouldn't think it was
> a foreign person.   And then when I went and
> they actually saw I was coloured I think they
> were a bit shocked, so they kept stalling and
> said 'Come back tomorrow'.   They said 'The
> person isn't in, can you come back next week'
> and I wouldn't give in.   Every time they
> said come back I'd go back and I'd go back.
> My dad was backing me all the way and in the
> end I got through.   (Christa)

It is perhaps not surprising that, taken up with
their resistance to sexual and racial exclusion,
the girls much admire perseverance, stamina,
resourcefulness and a thick skin.   In the
circumstances it should not be too surprising that
few of them have a clear idea what specifically
they will make of their 'freedom'.

> My grandmother .. she's another one who had
> things tough so she's always going on at me
> to succeed ... I know what I want out of
> life, I know where I'm heading.   I think
> all I really want to do is just succeed.
> I don't know what I'll do when I do succeed
> though!   (Beverley)

ASIAN GIRLS

I shall use the term Asian in referring to these
girls who were of Indo-Pakistani parentage.   One
girl was British born, three had been born in the
Indian subcontinent, and seven had been born in

East Africa and so were, at the time of the study, relatively recent arrivals in Britain.

Their reflections on their current and future lives were framed much more in terms of sexual than racial politics. This is not to suggest that they were unaware of social relations of racial domin- ation - indeed some had been subject to racial attacks on their way to and from school. But as far as they were concerned these would (and did) impinge on them less than relations of sexual dominance and political forces within their own group. So, for example when talking about employ- ment they were exercised about whether they would be allowed or discouraged from working by their future husband or mother-in-law: racial exclusion in the job market was, at that stage in their lives, a concern of secondary importance.

Marriage would be a fact of life, as Nirmala among several others stressed: 'In our culture, we have to get married, we can't stay at home'. As young women of fifteen or sixteen they were approaching (if they had not already passed) the age when their own mothers had married. From my interviews marriage emerged as the central fact which organised their thinking about their present lives at home and their opportunities at school. Their present strategies at home and in terms of education could be best understood as attempts to manoeuvre for themselves some choice within some definite and basically accepted constraints. Girls might be critical of the most traditional aspects of arranged marriages, and sometimes discussed a particular marriage which did not seem to be working well:

> I saw some marriages that were arranged and they were disasters, for the girls especially, she had to suffer. ...On the surface many marriages look nice and they try to look happy. (Sadhana)

Whether to marry was not at issue - the girls knew that they would and that their husband would be chosen for them by parents. As a principle, and despite some worries about it in practice, the arranged marriage system was something they supported:

> If I like a boy I wouldn't want to get serious with him, but if it can't be helped ... but even in the end I would marry the

> person my father said.   I wouldn't want to
> hurt my parents.   (Ila)

Uppermost in their minds was how to obtain a measure
of control about when and whom they would marry.
They wanted to marry at a later age than their
mothers (the early twenties was the commonest preference) and hoped for a boy who was not 'traditional', by which was meant a boy from the subcontinent.
These could be matters for negotiation depending on
whether the girls perceive their parent as 'modern'
or 'advanced' (that is, willing to consult and take
into account the girl's opinions about particular
prospective husbands) and partly on their ability
to persuade parents to 'trust' them.   Beyond this
their futures were much more uncertain - a future
husband and/or mother-in-law, both of whom would
have considerable say in what she could do, might
turn out to be sufficiently 'old-fashioned' as to
want to prevent her working outside the home.

> ... honestly, if you ask any Indian girl at
> the present 'If you get married what would
> worry you the first thing?', the husband
> would be modern type but the mother-in-law
> they are sort of old fashioned, they prefer
> it happens as in old fashioned times, you
> see .... I wouldn't like to get married yet,
> especially in our Indian marriages.   If you
> get mother-in-law, all they want from us is
> to cook food and not to go to work ... (Amita)

Being a 'traditional' wife was not a cherished
dream and to avoid the situation outlined by Amita
they believed having a 'decent' job would help in
negotiating a less traditional role.   Consequently
they were aiming for jobs which could not be
dismissed as unrespectable (as nursing or any work
involving night shifts) but which might be seen in
a positive light.
     Girls could strengthen their bargaining
position with parents now and in the near future
and, they hoped, with in-laws in the more distant
future by successfully pursuing certain aspects of
education which will be discussed later.   'Trust'
was a more complex issue.   It was certainly one of
the main areas for complaint about parents'
differential treatment of girls and boys in the
family.   Girls talked as though they were assumed
to be inherently untrustworthy or at the very least
so weak-willed as to be readily led astray.

> My mum treats my younger brother really well
> than she treats me.   It's not really fair,
> so I have to argue.   I say 'It's just because
> he's a son and we're daughters that you don't
> let us go out' and all that.   So they say
> 'If you were a boy we would let you go out,
> but you're a girl and boys do sorts of things
> to you these days'.   She says 'I know it
> wouldn't be your fault if you went out with a
> boy ... but boys give you such a lot of energy,
> and they heat you up in such a way that you're
> bound to get up to something with them and
> things are bound to go wrong'.   ... boys have
> more freedom, they have more respect than
> girls do.   (Meena)

Since their parents' belief in them as untrustworthy did not appear to be based on specific
incidents of bad behaviour the girls found it
puzzling to know how this reputation could be
refuted, other than by the most stern self-control.
The girls complained bitterly of a double standard
which granted boys some latitude, but blamed girls
for bringing dishonour on the family when they
attempted to behave in similar ways.   According
to the girls family honour rested more heavily on
their shoulders, but boys could afford some lapses.
Everything a girl did, especially in public, had
direct bearing on her future marriageability, and
within her own family on her bargaining position
about marriage.

> ... if I were to run away with a boy, and the
> time comes up for my little sister to get
> married people would say her sister was one
> of those flirts so she might be one .. they
> say it runs in the family, so my sister
> wouldn't find a nice bloke to get married ...
> So that's how the family reputation gets
> ruined - they think bad of my parents for not
> bringing me up the way they should have.   ...
> boys get girls to marry easily, but girls have
> to suffer because it's girls that can get
> pregnant when they go round with boys ...
> (Meena)

There was much criticism of the unfair sexual
division of labour within the family and of the
greater freedom of movement which brothers enjoyed.
However the girls tempered their criticisms at home
because they believed such sentiments might be

interpreted as a wish on their part to be more 'westernized' and so bring down further restrictions on them.

But their criticisms are not only qualified by these considerations. The girls believed that their parents were sometimes prevented from being as 'modern' as they would choose: firstly, by the fear of gossip with its potential for ruining a family's reputation; and secondly, because England is less 'decent' than the subcontinent and East Africa and so their children must be protected more here.

While some girls described their parents as 'modern' in the sense already described, they took it for granted that parents and children had some-what distant relationships with each other. So none looked to parents as people in whom they confided or with whom they would consider discussing 'personal' matters. Support of this kind was sought from sisters, cousins and friends of about their own age and was offered to those younger than themselves.

> ... I've got a little sister, so I would have to look after her ... and explain to her and generally look after when she gets into trouble. Things she can't tell my parents she will have to tell me, won't she, because there are certain things you can't tell your parents. (Ila)

With homework and housework commitments and with some restrictions on visiting friends, opportunities for conversations about the matters they could not raise with parents tended to be limited. This was one of the values of school - parents could not disapprove of them attending, so special pleas to meet friends were unnecessary, and it was a place which afforded frequent opportunities for discussions in mixed or girls-only groups. It is perhaps not surprising that in these circumstances the girls were less critical of school than Afro-Caribbean girls nor that they engaged in fewer openly con-frontational incidents with teachers or other pupils. The majority were seen as 'good' pupils, but they were by no means docile conformists. For example they could be highly critical of teachers who, as they saw it, failed to keep classes in order, did not explain work adequately, or who expected too little of pupils.

> ... sometimes I have a tiff with Mr. Jameson

> ... we had an argument and he thinks I'm an
> outspoken girl just trying to be big-headed
> or something.   I'm just hot-headed and I
> think he's not very confident about his
> teaching methods.   I've seen him in class and
> when he has failures he doesn't know how to
> react, he gets embarrassed quite often.   And
> sometimes I'm horrible and say things like
> 'I'm a failure again, how did you become a
> teacher?' and thinks like that.   It hurts him
> sometimes.   (Sadhana)

> ... they are quite good teachers really, but
> some they can't control the class and some are
> really nasty ...   Mr. Grieves, for instance,
> I can't stand him, he doesn't encourage you.
> If you make a mistake he won't say 'You've made
> a mistake here, I will tell you how to correct
> it and you must concentrate on that now',
> he'll take your paper, rub it all out, do it
> for you and then start hollering at you.   I
> don't like that, but some teachers are weak in
> controlling the class ..... (Zargoona)

Both Zargoona and Sadhana were seen as good pupils.
    The girls also placed high value on what the
school could offer in other ways.   They had an
instrumental orientation to education for reasons
which were somewhat different from the Afro-
Caribbean girls'.   While they were certainly hoping
to obtain academic qualifications and consciously
doing so as a means to finding 'respectable' work,
they had other reasons for putting so much effort
into their school work.   They believed that parents
would want to arrange their marriage soon after the
girl had completed her formal education.   All the
while she was being reasonably successful she could
hope to persuade her parents to let her stay into
the sixth form and maybe beyond, thereby buying
herself some time and putting off the time of a
marriage till nearer the age she would prefer.   It
was not just a question of being successful, but
also of pursuing prestigious courses of work at
school.   Eight of the eleven girls were taking
science courses (i.e. physics and chemistry) and
intended to continue these studies beyond the fifth
year.   This was a much higher proportion than
other girls and was similar to the proportion of
Asian boys taking science courses.   Knowledgeable
about science-based careers, the girls believed such
careers enjoyed high prestige among parents here and

in the sub-continent.

> I'm not very much particular about what kind
> of job I want, what kind of career, but I
> want something interesting that has promotion
> aspects as well. ... I haven't got much choice
> because in the medicine world there are about
> three or four degrees which are counted as very
> high. Medicine is out because I'm not capable
> of that. Dentistry perhaps I could if I work
> really hard, but pharmacy is in between very
> good and a bit lower than average, degree-wise.
> There's biochemistry, and I'm not really
> interested in that. I've got quite an interest
> in optics ... (Sadhana)

By pursuing prestigious subjects the girls thought
their parents might be disinclined to interrupt
academic careers with premature pressures to take
up a domestic one.

By the time I had completed my study the girls
had achieved a mean of 6 passes at 'O' level/CSE -
a rather low number for the fifth year as a whole,
but with average grades higher than any other group
at the school. All those about whom I have
information remained at school beyond the statutory
school-leaving age and were as committed to some
form of higher or further education.

****

Those who have researched the school lives of
young people have been mainly working in the
interpretive tradition in which the researcher is
aiming to 'make problems' rather than 'take problems'.
That is, the task is to make the everyday exotic and
to take nothing for granted in the ordinary worlds
being studied.

There is now quite a history among British
researchers of work of this type in schools and
among those studying deviant youth cultures.
Although this has produced some interesting
achievements those achievements have their limitations. The limitations are of two kinds - technical and conceptual - and both have implications
for what we know about the experiences of girls and
young women inside and outside educational
institutions. The first concerns a failure to
rigorously suspend common-sense understandings
throughout the research process. Previous
researchers' emphasis on the male is my starting
point, because it indicates some important ways in

which they have failed to make the taken-for-granted problematic and have instead taken the everyday world for granted.   Most of those researchers have been male.   They have not made sexism problematic - their own or that within the institutions or cultures they write about.   And many continue not to do so. Documenting the existence and effects of sexual divisions has in the main been left to those who are most sensitised to it through their own experience - the women who are beginning to research and write in this field and the women whom they study.   Another way in which this research can be seen to be based on taking rather than making problems is that its focus is interestingly consistent with teachers' perspectives, though that has not been what researchers have set out to do, nor the way in which their research is written up. In defining the male experience as most interesting, important and worthy of explanation and description researchers (maybe unwittingly) are working within teachers' definitions.   That is, they take as their problem that which is 'a problem' for teachers - boys' behaviour.   Drawing on Douglas' work Blackstone (1976) summarises teachers' views as follows:

> Teachers find boys difficult and unresponsive, and are much more likely to categorize them as lazy or poor workers, lacking in concentration or both.   By contrast teachers expect girls to be more docile, attentive, diligent and less adventurous.   (Blackstone 1976, pp. 210-11)

Reviewing the extensive literature on teachers' behaviour and attitudes towards male and female pupils I have concluded (Fuller 1978) that more boys than girls are referred to outside agencies (e.g. child guidance clinics) by their teachers because of unacceptable behaviour within school; boys demand and receive greater attention from their teachers;   teachers nevertheless show marked preferences for their male pupils in the secondary years;   and teachers seem to value their male pupils more highly than the girls, considering the teaching of boys both more important and more interesting.   Researchers have shown a marked preference for studying secondary rather than infant or primary schools and have given the lion's share of their attention to one specific group - the visible, troublesome male pupil.

   This brings me to the second (conceptual)

limitation of such studies, which has important
sociological consequences and has been usefully
summarised by Hargreaves (1979). Hargreaves
discerns three emphases in the study of deviance
in educational (mainly school) settings: a focus
on deviance as an expression of values and behaviour
originating outside school; an emphasis on the
process by which deviant labels are produced in
educational institutions; and thirdly, deviance
as 'cultural criticism' in which there is a concern
with the rationality of pupil deviance and on the
experience of school deviants. He argues that
researchers need to be more sophisticated in their
conceptualisation of deviance and conformity. This
would entail recognising that the deviant pupils on
whom researchers have so far spent so much time are
considerably less sociologically interesting than
other pupils. The overtly antagonistic, resisting
pupil ('the opposition' he calls them) are the
normal deviants - 'those who mark the boundaries of
our moral rules' (p. 22) and whose activities serve
to both underline and underpin the status quo.
(Willis' (1977) 'lads' being a case in point.)
   Researchers have been slow to see the sociological significance of other kinds of pupil, who in
not being defined as deviant are relegated to the
realms of the sociologically uninteresting and
unremarkable. To use Hargreaves' terms, the
'committed' raise important issues about how and
why people come to wholeheartedly accept the prevailing and dominant norms, values, and forms of
conduct; they deserve more than to be dismissed
as conformist (a categorisation which is not, in
any case, explanatory). Those who are 'indifferent' or 'instrumental' are more deviant, more
threatening to social order and consequently of
greater interest for the researcher than the
oppositional pupil whose existence and stance is
thoroughly predictable. Instrumentalists are not
committed to school norms but 'know' (I would say
'believe') that school can offer them a great deal;
the indifferent are also uncommitted, being bored,
but offering no active resistance to schooling.
Although they may be numerically more typical than
the oppositional pupils, they are (sociologically)
abnormal because they exhibit egoism and anomie
which is inimical to social solidarity. Their
deviance is therefore more undermining than that of
the overtly antagonistic.
   It is not part of Hargreaves' project to look
at the implications of his argument for the study

of girls and young women - his major concern seems to be to encourage researchers to take more seriously their debt to Durkheim and the study of deviance in the context of social solidarity - but for those who feel justification is required for researching women, it may be useful to remember that Durkheim suggested that the social/sexual division of labour has something to do with solidarity in organic societies; and there are those who believe that schools may have a hand in the reproduction of the division of labour.   Hargreaves, then, is concerned with the sociological sterility of concentrating on oppositional pupils.   Others (see Acker (1981) for example) have drawn more political conclusions from research in this tradition, pointing out that the effect of concentrating on 'deviance' as popularly understood, is that we have numerous accounts of boys in educational settings but know virtually nothing about girls.   Another way of putting this is to say that until very recently research in this tradition reflects the kind of marginalising or ignoring of women which is common for many women (teachers as well as pupils) in educational institutions.

   I am not suggesting that researchers should be trying to set the record straight by looking for girls who are deviant in the sense of being overtly antagonistic and challenging of school - though clearly some such could certainly be found and doubtless it would make for interesting reading. Nor am I suggesting that there is no interest in further studies of such boys defined in this way as deviant.   Where studies of this kind are still undertaken it behoves the writers to be more explicit about the limitations of such an enterprise - firstly to disclose that their definition of deviance is a commonsense one and secondly that studies based on one gendered group cannot be passed off as studies of 'pupils', 'kids' etc.   In practice this means that writers should stop writing in such a way that assumes boys are in some way above gender and that only girls are gendered.   Researchers concentrating on female pupils do not appear to fall so frequently into this trap.

   Another thing which seems important to me is that current definitions of deviance have the effect of presenting girls as uncritical.   It may well be true that girls make up an insignificant proportion of those pupils who are overtly antagonistic - a fact (if it is one) which is in itself interesting and worthy of some analysis.   Ignoring girls in discussions of deviance at a school leaves an impression that their acquiescence (supposed or actual) is unproblematic - a sign of their non-criticism of schooling.

Anyone who bothers to listen knows that this is not the case and knows equally that the girls' criticism cannot be readily accommodated into a definition of deviance or resistance that relies on the flashy, visible and physically confrontational. It should be possible to start from a position of understanding sexism and knowing that it is unlikely to be absent either from one's own thinking or in the educational settings to be studied. We can be confident that there are few if any manifestations of human behaviour which are restricted to one or other sex, only manifestations which show themselves differently because females and males are encourages to differentiate their behaviour in certain systematic ways. Put another way, it seems likely that both female and male pupils are deviant, both in the popular sense and in terms of Hargreaves' 'instrumental' and 'indifferent' typology, but that there will be systematic differences in the proportion of girls and boys who are oppositional, in the proportion who are 'instrumental' and so on. Just because girls do not, typically, confront, does not mean they do not have their criticisms of schooling. What it suggests to me is that the form their criticism takes (and their resistance) is integrally related to and shaped by their having been successfully engendered as feminine. Their forms of critical/resisting behaviour will be more feminine than masculine. In other words there is such a thing as passive resistance, a form of behaviour which reflects both criticism and the gender constraints within which most young women work. Similarly, because boys (most of them) will also have been successfully engendered, being masculine, their typical form of resisting behaviour will reflect this. Their resistance will show itself in more visible ways and in forms more consistent with traditional definitions of masculinity.

So, in concentrating on other pupils as well as the oppositional I would suggest it becomes less defensible to exclude girls/women from analysis since it seems likely more girls will fall into forms of behaviour typified by Hargreaves as 'truly deviant' even though it may be the case that the great majority of oppositional pupils are male. I would suggest that in concentrating on pupils other than the opposition we can get away from seeing pupils' cultural criticism as residing solely or even mainly in overt resistance to schooling. It may be that girls are too busy resisting other aspects of their life that resistance to schooling has a lower priority for them.

ACKNOWLEDGEMENTS

I should like to record my thanks to the teachers and pupils at 'Torville' school. My especial thanks to the young women whose accounts appear in this chapter, and to Ann Caro, Frances Hudson and Myna Trustam.

REFERENCES

Acker, S. (1981) No-Woman's Land: British Sociology of Education, 1960 to 1979. *Sociological Review*, 29, 77-104.

Bem, S. (1974) The Measurement of Psychological Androgyny. *Journal of Consulting and Clinical Psychology*, 42, 155-162.

Blackstone, T. (1976) The Education of Girls Today. In J. Mitchell and A. Oakley (eds.) *The Rights and Wrongs of Women*, Penguin, Harmondsworth.

Coleman, J. (1961) *The Adolescent Society*, Free Press, New York.

Fuller, M. (1978) Dimensions of Gender in a School, unpublished Ph.D. thesis, University of Bristol.

Fuller, M. (1980) Black Girls in a London Comprehensive. In R. Deem (ed.) *Schooling for Women's Work*, Routledge and Kegan Paul, London.

Fuller, M. (1982) Young, Female and Black: The World of Difference. In B. Troyna and E. Cashmore (eds.) *Black Kids*, Allen and Unwin, London.

Hargreaves, D. (1979) Durkheim, Deviance and Education. In L. Barton and R. Meighan (eds.) *Schools, Pupils and Deviance*, Nafferton, Driffiels.

Shaw, J. (1980) Education and the Individual: Schooling for Girls, or Mixed Schooling - a Mixed Blessing? In R. Deem (ed.) *Schooling for Women's Work*, Routledge and Kegan Paul, London.

Wilkinson, D. (1975) Black Youth. In R. Havighurst and P. Dreyer (eds.) *Youth*, University of Chicago Press, Chicago.

Willis, P. (1977) *Learning to Labour*, Saxon House, Farnborough.

RACIAL DISADVANTAGE IN YOUTH LABOUR MARKETS

Ken Roberts, Jill Duggan and Maria Noble

THE REPRODUCTION OF DISADVANTAGE

Britain's ethnic minorities are over-represented in
unskilled occupations and among the unemployed.
This has been 'discovered' in so many enquiries that,
in some quarters, the costs of recession falling
most heavily on such already disadvantaged groups
has become a problem to live with rather than solve.
However, evidence of racial disadvantage being
reproduced among generations born and educated in
Britain (1) can still be relied upon to stir self-
interested if not principled concern. Even in
the long-term, time alone appears unlikely to
deliver racial equality and harmony. Earlier
analyses that attributed ethnic minorities' disadvantages to their positions as immigrants, lacking
relevant qualifications and skills, and envisaged
their gradual assimilation, are being confounded.
In 1981 some young people in Brixton, Toxteth, Moss
Side and other multi-racial inner-cities began to
share their discontents, and the costs of their
expression, with the wider society. Who believes
that Britain's minorities will accept their subordination as an inevitable fact of life, even for
another 'short-term'?
    The following passages unravel some of the
processes, operating among entrants into the workforce, that reproduce and sometimes accentuate
racial disadvantage. The evidence is from 551
interviews, conducted during 1979-80, with 16-20
year olds who had completed full-time education,
and who were contacted by exhaustive household
canvasses in six multi-racial neighbourhoods - in
Brixton, Harlesden, Shepherds Bush, Liverpool's
Toxteth, Manchester's Moss Side, and Wolverhampton
(2). The subjects are far from representative of

all young people in the United Kingdom.   The
survey neighbourhoods were all inner-urban, and were
selected for their multi-racial characters, with
West Indians the main minority, and their reputations
as unemployment blackspots.   White respondents are
highly untypical of their age group.   Britain's
ethnic minorities, in contrast, tend to be concentrated in 'deprived' inner-city areas, and,
while not a random sample, our black informants will
be more representative of their ethnic group than
the whites;   a point to be emphasised later in the
analysis.
      Educational attainments in all the survey
neighbourhoods were modest.   Most of the young
people had left school at 16.   'Qualifications'
usually meant CSEs, sometimes strengthened with one
or two 'O' levels.   The overwhelming majority,
blacks and whites, had entered the workforce at the
first opportunity, with modest or zero qualifications.
Their early jobs were mostly unskilled or special
measures, and even these 'opportunities' were in
short supply.   Unemployment rates, measured as
proportions of respondents' total time in the workforce, ranged from 17 to 45 percent in the different
localities, and even in the districts with
relatively 'full' employment, at least two-thirds
of the young people were gaining some experience of
joblessness during their early working lives.
Transitory spells out-of-work following school-
leaving, then between subsequent jobs were 'normal',
not exceptional, in every neighbourhood.
      The young people in all these areas were dis-
advantaged by their social origins - working class
on any definition, by attending low-achieving
schools, and by entering local labour markets
offering mostly unskilled jobs, insufficient in
quantity to maintain full employment.   But even
'the disadvantaged' become internally stratified
during the transition into the workforce.   Risks
of joblessness varied by gender, educational
attainment and race (see Table I), which interacted
to produce a very unequal distribution of
unemployment.   Unqualified black females had been
unemployed for 61 percent of their 'working' lives,
whereas white males who left school with (usually
modest) qualifications had an unemployment rate of
'only' 11 percent.
      This analysis focuses upon the causes and some
consequences of racial disadvantage, rather than
how and why being female and/or unqualified is
related to unemployment, but in the labour market,

RACIAL DISADVANTAGE IN YOUTH LABOUR MARKETS

Table I   Unemployment Rates

	WMQ*	BMQ	WMU	BMU	WFQ	BFQ	WFU	BFU
Percentages of time in the labour market spent unemployed	11	19	22	41	19	22	34	61
n(of respondents)	54	84	83	46	65	113	69	37

*W: White; M: Male; Q: Qualified; B: Black;
F: Female; U: Unqualified.

as opposed to statistical analyses, none of these
statuses affect job-chances in isolation.   'Race
effects' vary by gender and educational status.
Among males with and without qualifications, and
unqualified females, blacks' unemployment rates ran
at approximately double the whites' levels, whereas
black females with qualifications entered labour
markets where they were no less successful than
white girls from the same neighbourhoods and with
identical educational attainments in avoiding
unemployment.   The 'solutions' available to young
people with employment problems vary by race, gender
and educational attainment, once again operating in
combination.   Among white females, a still popular
solution is withdrawal from the work-force
following parenthood.   Black women are given less
encouragement to seek economic security via menfolk,
and, according to our findings, are more likely to
remain in the labour force (though often out-of-work)
when they become mothers.   If these differences
receive scant attention in the following pages (3),
this is not to deny their importance, but in order
to concentrate upon how racial disadvantages are
not only reproduced, but often widened during the
entry into employment, and to consider some
implications for Britain's race relations.
     Britain's young blacks are disadvantaged by
their concentration in areas where all young people
enter labour markets offering limited opportunities.
Then within thse local labour markets, overall,
black school-leavers fare less favourably than their
white neighbours, themselves disadvantaged members
of their ethnic group.   Our evidence makes it
possible to specify the processes, that are responsible for young blacks' spectacularly high levels of
unemployment, then explain why disadvantaged blacks
and whites are not being united by common 'class'

193

interests, but are being provoked towards different 'solutions', even when their predicaments appear objectively similar.   Part of the explanation has already been disclosed: the blacks are by far the more heavily disadvantaged, but as we shall see, this is less than the whole story.

UNEMPLOYMENT AND RACE

The strength of the race-unemployment relationship among our subjects invites allegations of instit- utionalised racism and all-pervasive discrimination, but these blanket indictments will not stick.   The odds are not stacked against Britain's ethnic minorities during every stage in the attainment process, and our evidence can distinguish phases, as young people move from their homes, through education and into the labour market, where racial disadvant- ages mount, from 'havens' where these handicaps are contained and sometimes (marginally) reduced.
    Firstly, black respondents' relatively high rates of unemployment were not due to their lack of educational success and credentials reducing their competitiveness, vis-a-vis local whites, on entering the labour market.   Throughout Britain as a whole, there is no doubt that blacks under-achieve in school (4), but according to our evidence, this could be attributable entirely to residing in districts and attending schools where the attain- ments of all pupils are below-average.   Within our areas, black youth (especially the girls) were leaving local schools better-qualified than whites (see Table II) (5).   The schools in our survey

Table II (in percentages)
School-leaving Qualifications

	WM	BM	WF	BF
At least one O-level or CSE equivalent	19	20	24	37
CSE(s)	20	45	25	38
None	61	35	51	25
n (of respondents)	137	130	134	150

areas were not failing their black pupils;   at least, not to any greater extent than whites were failing. Blacks were not being 'held down' while their white peers acquired credentials to improve their job prospects.

Secondly, black informants were not being channelled away from higher status, skilled, pro- gressive and relatively secure levels of employment, and forced down the labour market into unskilled, insecure jobs, where rates of job-changing, and therefore exposure to the risk of unemployment are more frequent. The jobs entered by black res- pondents were just as likely to be non-manual, or involve training leading to skilled status, as the whites' occupations (see Table III). We will explain below that black informants took longer, on average, to obtain work of any type. We are not disputing the prevalence of racial discrimination in the labour market. But according to our evidence, any discrimination operates with similar results throughout all the occupational levels to which our subjects were seeking access. Discrimin- ation did not operate selectively, filtering blacks away from the more attractive opportunities, into 'secondary' labour markets.

Table III (in percentages)   Occupations

	WMQ	BMQ	WMU	BMU	WFQ	BFQ	WFU	BFU
Non-manual	8	7	3	–	37	43	8	10
Apprenticeships	39	32	13	18	9	4	1	3
Other	45	46	73	66	43	44	77	66
Special measures	8	15	11	16	11	9	14	20
n (of jobs) =	85	117	160	79	95	167	111	59

As with educational attainments, there is no doubt that, across the country, young blacks' levels of occupational attainment lag behind the norm. But once again following the education picture, the downwardly skewed distribution of young blacks' prospects could be entirely due to their concent- ration in local labour markets where most jobs available for all young people are unskilled. According to our evidence, whites who live in multi-racial, inner-city neighbourhoods are no more likely to obtain apprenticeships and non-manual jobs. Previous studies have consistently suggested that black school-leavers are disadvantaged in the competition for such types of employment, but these enquiries have covered young people from wider ranges of neighbourhoods than our respondents (6).

Some factors identified as indirectly discriminating against black shool-leavers, such as not having fathers in skilled occupations who can 'pull strings', and living in areas from which employers prefer not to recruit, operated to most of our white informants' disadvantage.

Thirdly, black respondents had found the statutory employment services as accessible and useful as whites. The services may sometimes be implicated in the transmission of discrimination, without their staffs necessarily becoming aware of this role, but there is no evidence, from our own or previous research, of the services actually aggravating young blacks' disadvantages. Black respondents had visited the services as frequently when unemployed, expressed similar opinions about their treatment, and had obtained a greater proportion of their jobs through these agencies than whites (7).

When levels of unemployment vary between two or more groups, whatever their composition, there can be any combination of three contributors. First, the mean duration of unemployed episodes might differ, with some groups taking longer than others to obtain work. Second, the risks of individuals becoming unemployed upon school-leaving, and following any subsequent job departures, may vary. Third, rates of exposure to any 'risks' can differ. All young people run some risk of unemployment when stepping from full-time education into the labour market. Thereafter their rate of exposure depends on the frequency with which they change jobs, whatever the reasons for their departures.

Table IV examines the roles played by these contributors to levels of unemployment among our black and white respondents, while controlling gender and qualifications. The figures show that the duration of episodes was related to race. Except among qualified males, blacks took longer, on average, to find work whenever they became jobless. All groups of blacks ran the higher risk of unemployment upon school-leaving, but not when subsequently changing jobs, except unqualified males. Finally, every group of black respondents had been exposed to the risk of unemployment more often than its white equivalent, because the blacks changed their jobs the more frequently. This was not due to the blacks' occupations being less 'worth keeping'. We have seen that informants' levels of employment did not vary by race. Nor was it due to the blacks experiencing the higher

Table IV   Contributors to Unemployment

	WMQ	BMQ	WMU	BMU	WFQ	BFQ	WFU	BFU
1. Duration Average length of unemployment (in months)	3.8	3.7	4.7	5.4	3.5	4.3	6.4	8.8
2. Risk a. Percentages unemployed on school-leaving	38	62	43	59	53	58	50	68
b. Percentages of job departures followed by unemployment	51	44	57	73	54	40	68	71
3. Exposure Average length of jobs (in months)	12.6	10.2	9.4	6.5	9.6	8.4	8.1	5.1

rate of involuntary dismissals.   The proportion of all job departures that were voluntary, approximately two-thirds, did not vary by race.

Secondly, according to our evidence, young blacks in inner-urban areas are more ambitious than local whites.   The former's higher levels of aspiration are partly 'justified' by their superior educational attainments, but not entirely.   With gender and school-leaving qualifications controlled, blacks remain the more ambitious, especially unqualified males (see Table V).   We are not accusing black school-leavers of nurturing 'unrealistic' aspirations.   We have no reason to believe that our subjects' ambitions were inconsistent with their abilities.   They were not all demanding jobs as airline pilots and brain surgeons.   Most boys wanted training in technical and craft skills, while most girls were seeking jobs as telephonists, receptionists, typists and social workers, in offices and libraries.   Many white respondents entertained similar, usually frustrated ambitions, but the blacks were the more likely to have left school with their sights on something better than unskilled jobs in shops, warehouses and factories.   These aspirations may have been 'reasonable', but for the majority they

Table V (in percentages)
Vocational Aspirations on School-Leaving

	WMQ	BMQ	WMU	BMU	WFQ	BFQ	WFU	BFU
Non-manual	22	9	–	2	40	52	24	20
Skilled	61	71	48	76	37	31	26	43
Other	15	11	35	15	13	8	31	26
None	2	9	17	7	10	9	19	11

were unattainable, at least in the short-term, for
their local labour markets offered mainly unskilled
employment.
     It is not the sole reason, but one
explanation for young blacks being the more likely
to leave school without jobs waiting, and taking
longer than whites, on average, to find work when
unemployed, is that they tend to be the more
selective. Likewise part of the explanation for
their higher rate of job-hopping is that blacks are
the more reluctant to settle in 'trash jobs' (9).
Black youth in unskilled occupations express lower
levels of job satisfaction than whites in similar
jobs, and display greater perseverance towards
fulfilling their thwarted ambitions (10). We are
unable to quantify their significance precisely,
but 'attitudes' play some part in young blacks'
exceptionally high levels of unemployment.

RESPONSES

Inner-city blacks appear aspiring only when
comparisons are restricted to locally reared whites.
The former are the more likely to leave school with
qualifications, their sights fixed on non-manual or
skilled jobs. Having caught the 'diploma disease',
many persist in further education (see Table VI),
sometimes adding to their CSEs and '0'-levels,
hoping to bring their chosen careers within reach.
This behaviour seems unrealistically ambitious only
within inner-cities where teachers and careers
officers are accustomed to compliant school-leavers
expressing willingness to consider 'any job that
pays anything above the dole' (11). Non-one is
surprised when young people with white skins, from
middle class backgrounds, persist in education and
refuse to reconcile themselves to lifetimes in
'rubbish jobs'. The lack of 'suitable
opportunities' is defined as the problem, which
is precisely how most young blacks view their
predicaments.

Table VI

	WM	BM	WF	BF
Percentages who had received some further education	29	41	26	51

It can be argued that the proper comparison group, when assessing inner-city blacks' attainments, should be the white population in general rather than just the blacks' neighbours. Blacks with all types and levels of ability and motivation are concentrated in inner-urban, multi-racial districts. Many of today's black school-leavers have talented and ambitious parents, the first generation immigrants, who crossed the world to improve their life-chances, then were obliged to accept under-employment in unskilled occupations. They expect a better deal for their children, who are encouraged to acquire the qualifications and training their parents lacked. Immigrant parents can rarely provide the knowledgeable support that is available in middle class homes, but many are no less keen for their children to reap full advantage of their educational opportunities. In their Birmingham research, Rex and Tomlinson noted that 'even amongst the older generation, there are a considerable number of educated men who are employed as labourers. They, themselves, must experience frustration. But they do this for their children' (12). The cultures in which black youth are reared tend to be status dissenting rather than assenting. The young people are encouraged to 'move ahead' rather than follow in their parents' footsteps, and this is reflected in the former's aspirations. Many who are anti-school are nevertheless pro-qualifications. Instrumental attitudes towards education are common (13). On entering the labour market they are often as perturbed by the quality of the jobs they are invited to consider as the prospect of unemployment. It is Britain's young blacks who are pioneering the vocabulary of 'rubbish jobs', 'shit work' and 'slave labour'. When sent chasing 'trash' depite their credentials, they complain of having been 'let down', 'sold out', and of 'broken promises'. Their parents often agree, then offer the advice that is common in middle class homes: they tell their children to 'try even harder'. Even modest qualifications enhance school-leavers' job prospects, but none carry any guarantee. Within our survey areas, they did not save the majority of their holders, blacks and whites, from unemployment and unskilled jobs.

Black school-leavers' occupational choices are not only 'higher', on average than their white classmates'. Another difference is that the formers' aspirations are not negotiated through a working class culture, passed down the generations, which militates against any desire to join the 'other side', and simultaneously blurs status differences between skilled and other manual jobs. Blacks appear more conscious of a division between all 'status jobs', blue- and white-collar, that require training and skills, and 'slave labour'. They are determined not to be sentenced to life-times in servile, low-paid jobs. Maybe they are responding to the occupational hierarchy's contemporary contours. If so, these responses are intensified by an awareness of their people's slave history; of their exploitation in the Caribbean, and now in Britain, where they remain prisoned in the lowest jobs by the 'normal' operations of prevailing market forces, compounded by racial discrimination that successive governments have failed to counter.

There are further 'qualitative' differences between young blacks' and whites' ambitions. We take it for granted that aspiring whites hope to leave inner-city neighbourhoods. Why would they wish to 'get on' if they were not seeking better homes, surroundings and lifestyles? It is not that blacks would not appreciate better houses and environments. Many are willing to travel outside their immediate areas, for worthwhile jobs. But in the existing social climate many are also equivocal about leaving known people and places, and severing contact with their communities. Would they be accepted elsewhere? Many want better opportunities in education and employment while they remain in Britain's Moss Sides and Brixtons. Does the wider society even understand this type of ambition? Is it structurally capable of meeting these demands?

Their ambitions are 'different', which results in blacks and whites experiencing their disadvantages in different ways, but the main reason for their often divergent reactions is that black youth have a visible explanation for all their difficulties. No matter how strenuously sociol-ogists argue the case, social class barriers remain invisible. It is much easier to see skin pigment-

ation, and to many young blacks the reason why
their aspirations are blocked is as clear as day-
light; they are black people in a white society.
They can see for themselves that their people are
under-employed, while the occupants of 'status jobs'
and expensive houses, plus the police and other
officials, are overwhelmingly white. Any who are
colour-blind find plenty of community spokesmen
prepared to draw their attention to these facts of
life. It is not difficult to convince black youth,
faced with a choice between unemployment and menial
jobs, that they are victims of an unjust society.
Rastafarianism is just one variant of this
cosmology (14). Many young blacks who have not
accepted the 'theology' nevertheless adopt elements
of the culture - the dress, coiffure and pride, and
the more they are drawn into such cultures, the more
discrimination they are likely to encounter in their
efforts to find work, on 'cultural' in addition to
straight-forward racial grounds, as when employers
prohibit 'wraps' in offices and factories.
Simultaneously, the young people's definitions of
their situations make them all the more determined
to cling to their ambitions. They refuse to accept
the roles apparently cast by a society that welcomes
blacks, while they are willing to perform the jobs
no-one else wants. Previous investigators have
noted that 'unemployed, young immigrant workers are
amongst the most alienated and militant elements in
the total working class' (15), and that when they
'succeed educationally, but cannot enter the better
jobs, their energies and intellectual abilities are
almost certain to be directed into radical
politics' (16).
    White school-leavers' interpretations of
their predicaments are also 'politically' significant, but less challenging. The cultural capital
they inherit usually portrays the realities of the
labour market as 'matters of cognition rather than
evaluation' (17), as facts of life to which they
must adjust: '.. the possibility of successful
action to transcend the limits of their situation
is so remote as to be irrelevant' (18). Black
youth are more likely to 'solve' their predicaments
ideologically without surrendering their aspirations.
They 'distance' their 'selves' from the available
unskilled jobs. Few 'opt out'. This type of
withdrawal is easier on a student grant. For
16-year old school-leavers it is not an attractive
option. They have to survive, which may mean
accepting unskilled work, as a temporary measure.

Job-changing then becomes almost a cultural
imperative so that individuals can prove to themselves and to one another that they have not 'given
up'. Many retain their ambitions despite all the
rebuffs. Their number one priority remains a
'status job'. They will accept places on schemes,
courses and projects that promise training, only to
find, in most cases, that these opportunities lead
back to the foot of the labour market, whereupon
their feelings of injustice are amplified. For
many, reconciliation to a lifetime of 'slave labour'
is not second-best. There is more status in
'hustling'; learning to survive on 'casual' earnings, social security, plus support from friends
and families, and unskilled jobs only when
necessary (19). These 'solutions' to their
difficulties sometimes alienate young blacks from
their parents (20), despite the latter's contribution to the pressures to which the young people
are responding. This parent-child conflict can be
over-laboured. It is not the root problem. Joblessness strains family relationships in all ethnic
communities, but most black (and white) respondents
received family support during spells of unemployment.

No-one's interests are served by romanticising
survival strategies bred by limited opportunities.
There are few successful hustlers. It is a role
at which many young people would love to succeed,
and with which they identify vicariously, given
receptive audiences. The reality, however, is
usually a hand-to-mouth existence on social security,
food and lodgings from families, supplemented by
whatever other help and 'earnings' are available.
For the majority, hustling is not a viable long-
term alternative to orthodox employment. Supple-
mentary earnings are usually spasmodic and modest.

URBAN DISORDER

Chronic unemployment, blocked aspirations and
feelings of injustice among young blacks were
'background' ingredients in all the areas that
hosted the more spectacular urban riots in 1981.
Most instant analyses named youth unemployment as
an agent provocateur, but the severity of disorder
was not directly proportionate to levels of joblessness. Clydeside and the North-East offered
nothing dramatic as Brixton. Furthermore, when
they took to the streets, the young people were
not demanding jobs. They made it clear that their

prime hostility was towards the police. Unemployment does not directly and inevitably provoke social unrest. The areas that witnessed the most serious disturbances all had high levels of youth unemployment, plus crime and policing problems, and multi-racial populations. Joblessness, race and crime are the volatile mixture. In isolation they can be contained; together the elements can interact and inflame each other. Britain's ethnic minorities are not attracted by, but they have been funnelled towards disadvantaged areas where above-average unemployment is just one of many scars. Racial discrimination against the minorities, which inflates the areas' unemployment levels, is another illustration, others follow, of how the 'mixture' can create 'tinder boxes' in which any spark, like insensitive policing, is liable to provoke 'trouble'.

In virtually all Britain's inner-cities, whatever their ethnic characters, crime has become endemic, at least among young males. The trend in recorded crime has been upwards, between several plateaux, since the 1950s, and there seems little doubt, in this instance, that official statistics indicate real changes in behaviour. Delinquents are no longer distinguished by their broken homes, or otherwise 'disreputable' family backgrounds. In some neighbourhoods, thefts from shops and cars, plus 'joy-riding', seem to have become normal adolescent recreations (21). And the boundaries of the crimes sanctioned by teenage peer groups appear to have widened. 'People' are no longer secure. 'Mugging' is daring rather than condemned.

Crime can escalate without unemployment. During the 1950s juvenile delinquency and affluence spread simultaneously. But if it is not a direct cause, unemployment places young people 'at risk', on the streets for longer periods, during daytime in addition to evenings (22). It also leaves entire peer groups chronically short of 'bread', and provides a vocabulary of motive. Teachers and youth leaders will explain how, in the absence of legal opportunities, crime is too tempting to be resisted. Young people and their parents offer this 'justification'.

Escalating crime has led to a state of 'war' between the police and local youth in many inner-cities, with the young people winning most battles. Most crime is not cleared up, which places the police under pressure to 'do something'. Local police 'know' who is guilty, and one cost-effective way of 'doing something' is to 'nick' groups or

individuals who are 'hanging about', probably 'up
to no good'. Needless to say, the young people
experience this attention as harassment, and black
youth appear to receive more than their fair share.
Some also regard the police as the front-line force
from a hostile society that is holding them down,
forcing them back. Many of the young people we
interviewed in 1979-80 would have welcomed and
gratefully seized the opportunity to vent their
feelings when disorder flared in 1981. They told
us so. They would have required little encouragement by 'infiltrators' or 'politically motivated
extremists' to take to the streets, to 'break out'
and 'have a go'. Street violence is a language
that the wider society understands. It brings
attention from cabinet ministers, no less. How
else can black youth, and some whites, make the
wider society listen, let alone understand their
frustrations? It will be amazing if the urban
disorder of 1981 is not repeated somewhere, sometime
in the future.

POLICY IMPLICATIONS

How can these situations be defused? One mistake
is to presume that there must be solutions to racial
tensions and young blacks' frustrations, awaiting
discovery once sufficient evidence has been assembled
for fair-minded scrutiny. It is a professional
hazard for politicians to admit that any problems
defy solution, or at least major progress towards,
within a Parliament's lifetime. Hence the
attraction of misleadingly simple diagnoses. If
social scientists make better sense of society, this
is because they are insulated from pressure to offer
remedies. The present analysis has no instant
cures to prescribe; just three points to contribute
to the race relations debate, whose net effect is
to suggest that there may be no solutions, realis-
able even within the medium-term, that will satisfy
all concerned.
        First, young blacks will not acquiesce if
offered equal opportunities with their white
neighbours. Why should they rest content with the
jobs and unemployment rates of the most disadvantaged whites? Few young blacks are enthus-
iastic about the types of amelioration that liberal
whites are currently advocating; more marginal
businesses and jobs, plus schemes and courses which
lead nowhere in particular. The Youth Opportunities
Programme, education in Social and Life Skills, the

Young Workers Scheme, and the Youth Training Scheme
have been invented for other people's children.
How many government ministers and programme
directors are seeking such opportunities for their
own family members? Marketing these opportunities
is more likely to inflame than defuse young blacks'
discontents.

Second, promoting 'positive action' to offer
young blacks parity of opportunity vis-a-vis the
white population in general could stoke as already
visible backlash. We are not suggesting that the
white residents in our survey areas would react
adversely to positive action enabling blacks to
compete on equal terms with their white neighbours.
In 1981 there was little serious antagonism between
black and white working class youth within Britain's
riot areas. Rastafarianism is not essentially
anti-white, but anti-exploitation, though it
happens that whites have been, and are still seen as
the main exploiters. Blacks are aware of class
differences among the white population. Whites can
see, or be persuaded of the justice of anti-discrim-
ination measures that pressure employers to root out
deliberate and unconscious biases in their hiring
practices so that blacks are not repeatedly passed
over while lesser-qualified whites obtain employment.
Measures to remedy black school-leavers' specifically
racial disadvantages may not provoke any backlash,
but our analysis has shown that many of the disadvantages faced by young blacks arise from the
class situations they share with local whites, and
that the blacks are unlikely to be content with
measures that leave these handicaps untouched.
There is a case for widening the life-chances of
all young people in disadvantaged areas, where
opportunities are limited by poor housing, family
poverty, low-achieving schools and depressed labour
markets, but this would involve a 'revolution' in
class relations; a wholesale re-distribution of
privileges from the skilled working class and
white-collar strata. Blacks account for less than
five per cent of the British population. They
could be granted equal opportunity without dissolving
the class structure. Temporary but strenuous
positive action could lead to their re-distribution
through the various socio-economic strata, leaving
the latter more-or-less intact. Action on this
scale, delivering equal opportunity with the white
population in general, would satisfy the black
communities' aspirations, but would whites acquiesce
if their own class disadvantages persisted, while

these barriers were lifted for young blacks? If the ethnic minorities' frustrations were seen to attract special concern and assistance, and if more of the available jobs, particularly the better jobs in inner-cities, were delivered to young blacks, the National Front and kindred organisations could be among the beneficiaries. It is relatively easy to preach racial equality when securely settled in a university. The original advocates of 'positive discrimination' and 'affirmative action' in favour of women, ethnic minorities and the entire working class, envisaged a future of expanding educational and job opportunities, particularly at the more privileged levels. These programmes can become inflammatory rather than ameliorative when opportunities are locked in zero-sum equations.

Third, any solutions to Britain's race relations will be measured in generations rather than years, and will result from ethnic minorities carving their own life-chances. It was once thought possible that, encouraged by 'educative' legislation, the white population might abandon its prejudices, become colour-blind, and allow blacks to disperse throughout society. Is this even an option any longer? Many young blacks are no longer seeking assimilation or 'submersion' into what they regard as an alien society. They are joining their own community organisations and political movements. As yet there is no unity of aims or tactics, but it is these organisations that are taking the fight for justice to central and local government, the police and the white population's interest groups. It might be argued that the black communities have been struggling for advancement ever since large-scale immigration began in the 1950s, impeded by class barriers and racial discrimination, partly masked by a liberal-individualistic ideology, and that pluralism offers no solution, given the ethnic minorities' lack of power. We shall see. Over the generations the cities will not necessarily burn, but if Britain is to become a multi-ethnic, racially equal society, we believe that this will only be through the minorities' own efforts, and rather than a straight law-and-order issue, the unrest of 1981 is better-understood as one stage in this process.

NOTES AND REFERENCES

1. See S. Allen and C. R. Smith, 'Minority Group Experience of the Transition from School to Work', in

P. Brannen, ed., *Entering the World of Work*, HMSO, London (1975); B. Fowler, B. Littlewood and R. Madigan, 'Immigrant School-leavers and the Search for Work', *Sociology*, 11 (1977) pp. 65-85; Commission for Racial Equality, *Looking for Work*, London (1978).

2. For full details of this investigation, which was supported by a grant from the Department of Employment, see K. Roberts, J. Duggan and M. Noble, *Unregistered Youth Unemployment and Outreach Careers Work, Part One, Non-registration*, Department of Employment Research Paper 31, London (1981).

3. Some of these differences are discussed in K. Roberts *et al., op cit.*

4. See Committee of Inquiry into the Education of Children from Ethnic Minority Groups, Interim Report, *West Indian Children in our Schools*, Cmnd 8273, HMSO, London (1981).

5. For similar findings see G. Driver, 'How West Indians do better at School (especially the girls), *New Society* (17 January 1980); M. Fuller, 'Black Girls in a London Comprehensive School', in R. Deem, ed., *Schooling for Women's Work*, Routledge, London (1980).

6. For examples see, Commission for Racial Equality, *op cit*; G. L. Lee and K. J. Wrench, *In Search of a Skill*, Commission for Racial Equality, London (1981).

7. This evidence is presented in full in K. Roberts *et al., op cit.* See also D. Beetham, *Immigrant School-leavers and the Youth Employment Service in Birmingham*, Institute of Race Relations, London (1967).

8. Similar findings are reported in other relevant studies, such as K. Sillitoe, *Young People's Employment Study*, Unpublished Reports 1-4, Office of Population, Censuses and Surveys, London (1980).

9. See also the evidence in P. Figueora, 'School-leavers and the Colour Barrier', *Race* (April 1970) pp. 506-7.

10. K. Sillitoe, *op cit.*

11. Other studies show that teachers and careers officers sometimes label young blacks' aspirations as 'unrealistic'. See Sillitoe, *op. cit.*

12. J. Rex and S. Tomlinson, *Colonial Immigrants in a British City*, Routledge, London (1979) p. 282.

13. M. Stone, *The Education of the Black Child in Britain*, Fontana, London (1981).

14. See E. Cashmore, *Rastaman*, Allen and Unwin, London (1979).

15. J. Rex and S. Tomlinson, *op cit.*, p. 18.

16. *Ibid.*, p. 282.

17. R. M. Blackburn and M. Mann, *The Working Class in the Labour Market*, Macmillan, London (1979) p. 307.

18. *Ibid.*, p. 303.

19. See K. Pryce, *Endless Pressure*, Penguin, Harmondsworth (1979)

20. Community Relations Commission, *Unemployment and Homelessness*, HMSO, London (1974).

21. See H. Parker, *View From the Boys*, David and Charles, New Abbot (1974).

22. See T. Crick, 'Black Youth, Crime and Related Problems', *Youth in Society*, 40 (1980) pp. 20-22.

PART THREE

RACE, CLASS AND EDUCATION IN BRITAIN

              -- A TEACHING BIBLIOGRAPHY

RACE, CLASS AND EDUCATION IN BRITAIN - A BIBLIOGRAPHY

Sally Tomlinson

The arrival of racial and ethnic minority groups and their children brought a new dimension to existing patterns of stratification in Britain, as non-white people began to be incorporated, with varying degrees of success, into a complex, conflict-ridden class society.   The majority of immigrant workers took up lower-paid manual working-class occupations, and many educationalists equated their position with the socially disadvantaged white working class.

However, the arrival of ethnic minorities did coincide with a period of liberal egalitarianism in education, when the education system was committing itself to the rhetoric, if not the practice, of equality of opportunity for all children.   Although there has never been overall national education policy or planning for the incorporation of minority group children, schools originally envisaged their task as 'assimilating' the children into the "British way of life", and while usually focusing on the problems minority children created for schools, did begin to cater for language needs.   More recently schools have begun to recognise the validity of cultural and linguistic pluralism, the necessity to change the school curriculum in a less ethnocentric direction, and the need for improved teacher-training to further the aims of a multi-racial, multi-cultural society.

Migrant workers, in Britain as in the rest of Europe, have been eager for their children to take advantage of an education system which appeared to promise social and economic reward via the acquisition of credentials and skills.   However, over the period of twenty five years, roughly from 1957/82, that minority children have been in the English education system, there has been increasing anxiety, particularly from the West Indian community,

that schools were not equipping children with
credentials or skills to compete with their white
peers for jobs. There were fears that, through the
failure of the education system, minority children
would either remain largely within the working-class,
or worse, form a disadvantaged underclass.

By 1979, concern about the education offered to
racial and ethnic minority groups was so pronounced
that a government committee of enquiry into the
Education of Ethnic Minority Children was set up.
(Committee of Enquiry into the Education of Ethnic
Minority Children, 1981.)

This bibliography begins by documenting books
and articles relating to issues of race and class,
in Britain.   The literature on "Race relations"
occasionally includes one chapter on education,
(e.g. Rose (1969), Abbott (1971), Rex and Tomlinson
(1979)).   The bibliography then moves on to document general literature relating to race and education,
particularly 'readers' which comprise collections of
articles.   There is no over-all study of multi-
racial education in Britain but there have been
several overviews of the literature, (e.g. Taylor
(1974), Tomlinson (1977), Taylor (1981)).   The next
section documents government papers and publications
concerned with race and education, particularly that
produced by the Department of Education and Science,
and the Select Committee on Race Relations and
Immigration (which became a Sub-Committee of the
Home Affairs Committee in 1980).   This section also
includes literature on policies on race and
education, - particularly such crucial issues as
statistical collection, funding, and resources for
minorities, and, an issue of the 1960s, the
dispersal of non-white children from "high
immigrant" schools.

The bibliography then documents some of the
literature in what has become a crucial focus of
concern for minority parents, particularly those of
West Indian origin, - the school performance and
achievement of their children.   Goldman and Taylor
(1966) documented research studies on school
achievement to that date, and Tomlinson (1980)
summarised the major research studies on the
achievement of ethnic minority children to 1980.
A section on language documents literature concerning the teaching of English to non-English speaking
children, the development of the 'mother-tongue'
debate, - as minorities have sought to retain their
own languages, - and the use of West Indian dialect
in schools.

During the 1970's the idea of cultural pluralism became more widely accepted and some schools began to change their practices and curricula in a multi-cultural direction. Literature concerning the development and practice of multi-cultural education and the teaching of race relations is documented and a section concerning teachers and teacher-training for a multi-cultural society follows.

The concluding sections are concerned with literature on the home background of minority group children, with the demand for separate religious schooling for Muslim children, and with home-school relations, followed by literature concerned with minority youth and the school-to-work transition. The relationship of the next generation of ethnic minority people to the British class structure will depend on how far they succeed in entering the labour market on more equal terms than their parents, or whether, if unemployment continues at 1981 levels, they will slip more into an underclass position. It is ultimately by the success or failure of minority youth to obtain employment that the success or failure of the education system will be measured.

The final section of this bibliography includes names, addresses and journals of Institutes and Organizations in Britain concerned with issues in race, class and education.

In this literature compilation articles in weekly journals, notably Education, The Economist, New Society, and The Times Educational Supplement have not been included, as these journals carry articles which are either comment, opinion, or popular versions of research reported elsewhere, but articles from the bi-weekly publication Race Today, which carries a 'black' response, have been noted.

RACE AND CLASS

Books

Abbott, S. (1971) *The Prevention of Racial Discrimination in Britain*, Oxford Univ. Press.

Allen, S. (1971) *New Minorities - Old Conflicts, Asian and West Indian Immigrants in Britain*, Random House, New York.

Banton, M. (1969) *Race Relations*, Tavistock.

Banton, M. (1979) *The Idea of Race*, Tavistock.

Barker, M. (1981) *The New Racism*, Junction Books, London.

Bolt, C. (1971) *Victorian Attitudes to Race*, Routledge and Kegan Paul.

RACE, CLASS AND EDUCATION IN BRITAIN

Commission for Racial Equality (1978) *Five Views of Multi-Racial Britain*, London.

Cross, C. (1978) *Ethnic Minorities in the Inner City*, Commission for Racial Equality, London.

Deakin, N. (1970) *Colour Citizenship and British Society*, Panther. (Abridged edition of Rose, E.J.B. *et al.*).

Foner, N. (1979) *Jamaica Farewell*, Routledge and Kegan Paul.

Hiro, D. (1971) *Black British, White British*, Pelican Books.

(ed.) Husband, C. (1982) *Race in Britain*, Hutchinson University Library Press.

Krausz, E. (1971) *Ethnic Minorities in Britain*, Penguin.

Kuper, L. (1975) *Race, Science and Society*, Allen and Unwin.

(eds.) Miles, R. and Phizacklea, A. (1979) *Racism and Political Action in Britain*, Routledge and Kegal Paul.

Moore, R. (1975) *Racism and Black Resistance in Britain*, Pluto Press.

Mullard, C. (1973) *Black Britain*, Allen and Unwin.

Patterson, S. (1969) *Immigration and Race Relations in Britain*, O.U.P. for I.R.R.

Peach, C. (1968) *West Indian Migration to Britain*, Oxford University Press.

Ratcliffe, P. (1981) *Racism and Re-action*, Routledge and Kegan Paul.

Rex, J. (1971) *Race Relations in Sociological Theory*, Weidenfeld and Nicholson.

Rex, J. (1973) *Race Colonialism and the City*, Routledge and Kegan Paul.

Rex, J. and Tomlinson, S. (1979) *Colonial Immigrants in a British City*, Routledge and Kegan Paul.

Rose, E.J.B. *et al.* (1979) *Colour and Citizenship – a Report on British Race Relations*, Oxford University Press.

Runnymeade Trust and Radical Statistics Race Group (1980) *Britain's Black Population*, Heineman Educational.

Rutter, M. and Madge, N. (1976) *Cycles of Disadvantage*, Heineman.

Smith, D. (1976) *Racial Disadvantage in Britain*, Pelican Books.

Watson, J.L. (1977) *Between Two Cultures*, Blackwell.

Articles

Ben-Tovim, G. and Gabriel, J. (1979) "The Politics of Race in Britain 1962-1979" *Sage Race Relations Abstracts*, Vol. 4, No. 4, pp. 1-56.

Blair, C. (1971) "Immigrant Education and Social Class" *Race Today*, Vol. 3, No. 8, pp. 259-260.

Bourne, J. and Sivanandan, A. (1980) "Cheerleaders and Ombudsmen. The Sociology of Race Relations in Britain" in *Race and Class*, No. 4, pp. 331-352, *Race Relations Abstracts*, Vol. 11.

Bridges, L. (1981) "Keeping the lid on. British urban social policy, 1975-1981" *Race and Class*, Vol. 23, Nos. 2/3, pp. 154-171.

James, A. (1981) "Black - an enquiry into the perjorative associations of an English word" *New Community*, Vol. 9, No. 1, pp. 19-30.

Mullard, C. (1980) *Racism in Society and Schools. History, Policy and Practice* Centre for multi-cultural education: Occasional Paper No. 1, University of London Institute of Education.

Rex, J. (1981) "A Working Paradigm for Race Relations Research" *Ethnic and Racial Studies*, Vol. 4, No. 1, pp. 1-25.

Sivanandan, A. (1976) "Race, Class and the State. The Black Experience in Britain" *Race and Class*, Vol. 17, No. 4, pp. 347-368.

GENERAL: RACE AND EDUCATION

Books

Bhatnager, J. (1970) *Immigrants at School* Cornmarket Press, London.

Bhatnager, J. (1981) *Educating Immigrants* Croom-Helm, London.

Boyle, E.C.G. (1970) *Race Relations and Education* Liverpool University Press.

Burgin, T. and Edsom, P. (1967) *Spring Grove - The Education of Immigrant Children* Oxford University Press.

Craft, M. and Craft, A. (1982) "Multi-cultural Education" in (ed.) Cohen L. *Educational Research and Development in Great Britain* (4th Edition), NFER - Nelson Publishing Company.

Giles, R. (1977) *The West Indian Experience in British Schools* Heineman.

Hawkes, N. (1966) *Immigrant Children in British Schools* Pall Mall Press, I.R.R.

(eds.) James, R. and Jeffcoate, R. (1982) *Multi-Cultural Education*, Harper and Row.

Kirp, D. (1979) *Doing Good by Doing Little, Race and Schooling in Britain* University of California Press.

Laishley, C. and Bolton, F. (1972) *Education for a Multi-racial Society* Fabian Research Series, 303, London.

McNeal, J. and Rogers, M. (1971) *The Multi-Racial School*, Penguin.

Milner, D. (1975) *Children and Race*, Penguin.

(ed.) Parek, Bhikhu (1974) *Colour, Culture and Consciousness - Immigrant Intellectuals in Britain*, Allen and Unwin.

Stoker, D. (1970) *Immigrant Children in Infant Schools* Schools Council Working Paper No. 31, Methuen.

Stone, M. (1981) *The Education of the Black Child in Britain* Fontana.

Taylor, Francine (1974) *Race, School and Community* N.F.E.R.

Slough.

Taylor, M. (1981) *Caught Between - A Review of Research on the Education of Pupils of West Indian Origin*, N.F.E.R. Slough.

Tierney, J. (ed.) (1982) *Race, Immigration and Schooling* Holt-Saunders.

Townsend, E.R.H. and Brittan, E. (1972) *Organization in Multi-racial Schools*, N.F.E.R. Slough.

Townsend, E.R.H. (1971) *Immigrant Pupils in England - the L.E.A. Response*, N.F.E.R. Slough.

Townsend, E.R.H. and Brittan, E. (1973) *Multi-Racial Education Needs and Innovation*, N.F.E.R. Slough.

Verma, G.K. and Bagley, C. (1975) *Race and Education Across Cultures*, Heinemann.

Verma, G.K. and Bagley, C. (1979) *Race, Education and Identity*, Macmillan.

Verma, G.K. and Bagley, C. (1982) *Self-concept Achievement and Multi-Cultural Education*, Macmillan.

Articles

Bagley, C. (1977) "A Comparative Perspective on the Education of Black Children in Britain" *Comparative Education*, Vol. 15, No. 1, pp. 63-81.

Bentley, S. (1976) "Politics, Ethnicity and Education - Some Contemporary Issues" *New Community*, Vol. 5, Autumn, pp. 189-195.

Bolton, E. (1979) "Education in a Multi-Racial Society" *Trends in Education* Vol. 4, pp. 3-7.

Bryne, E.M. (1975) "Inequality in Education - Discriminational Resource Allocation in Schools" *Educational Review*, No. 25, June, pp. 179-191.

Kitwood, R. and Borrill, C. (1980) "The Significance of Schooling for an Ethnic Minority" *Oxford Review of Education*, Vol. 6, No. 3, pp.241-253.

McClean, Martin (1980) "Cultural Autonomy and the Education of Ethnic Minority Groups" *British Journal of Educational Studies* Vol. 28, No. 1, February.

Ohondy, F. (1974) "The Black Explosion in Schools" *Race Today*, February, pp. 44-47.

Street-Porter, R. (1978) 'Race and the Urban Child (Unit 11), and 'Race and Education (Units 12 and 13) of Open University Course E361. 'Education and the Urban Environment'. Block V: Open University Press.

Tomlinson, S. (1977) 'Race and Education in Britain 1960-77: An Overview of the Literature' in 'Race Relations Abstracts', Vol. 2, No. 4, Sage, pp. 1-30.

Watson, K. (1979) "Educational Policies in Multi-Cultural Societies" *Comparative Education* Vol. 15, No. 1, March.

"Who is Educating Who? The Black Education Movement and the Struggle for Power" *Race Today*, Vol. 7, No. 8,

pp. 180-186.
Wilke, Ingeborg (1975) "Schooling of Immigrant Children in
West Germany, Sweden, England - The Educationally
Disadvantaged" *International Review of Education*,
Vol. 2, pp. 357-382.
Wilke, Ingeborg (1975) "Select Bibliography on the Education
of Children of Migrant Workers" *International Review of
Education*, Vol. 21, pp. 383-400.
Worral, K. (1972) "All-black Schools - an Answer to Under-
Performance" *Race Today*, Vol. 4, No. 1, Jan. pp. 7-9.

POLICIES AND PLANNING

Books - Reports

Commission for Racial Equality (1978) *Schools and Ethnic
Minorities*, London.
Committee of Enquiry into the Education of Children from
Ethnic Minority Groups.   Report - *West Indian Children
in our Schools* (The Rampton Report) (1981) HMSO,
London.
Commonwealth Immigrants Advisory Committee (1964) 2nd Report.
Cmnd. 2266, HMSO, London.
Community Relations Commission (1974) *Educational Needs of
Children from Minority Groups*, C.R.C., London.
Community Relations Commission (1976) *Funding Multi-Racial
Education - A National Strategy* Report of a Working
Party convened by the C.R.C.
Department of Education and Science (1963) *English for
Immigrants* Pamphlet No. 43, HMSO, London.
Department of Education and Science (1965) *The Education of
Immigrants* (Circular 7/65), London.
Department of Education and Science (1967-72) Vol. 1,
Statistics in Education, HMSO, London.
Department of Education and Science (1971) *The Education of
Immigrants*, Education Survey 13, HMSO, London.
Department of Education and Science (1972) *The Continuing
Needs of Immigrants*, Education Survey 14, HMSO, London.
Department of Education and Science (1974) *"Educational
Disadvantage and the Needs of Immigrants"*, Cmnd. 5720,
HMSO, London.
Department of Education and Science (1977) *Education in
Schools - A Consultative Document* (Green Paper) HMSO,
London.
Department of Education and Science (1981) Directive of the
Council of the European Community on the Education of
the Children of Immigrant Workers, (Circular 36/81),
London.
Dorn, A. and Troyna, B. (1981) *Multi-Racial Education and the
Politics of Decision-Making* S.S.R.C. Unit of Ethnic
Relations, Aston, Birmingham.

Dorn, A. (1981) *Local Education Authorities and the Implications of Section 71 of the Race Relations Act 1976* C.R.E., London.

Home Affairs Committee (1981) *Racial Disadvantage*, HMSO, London.

Inner London Education Authority (1977) *Multi-Ethnic Education* Joint report of the school sub-committee and the further and higher education sub-committee, London.

Kogan, M. (1975) "Dispersal in the Ealing Local Education Authority System" *Report for the Race Relations Board*, London.

Matthews, A. (1981) *Advisory Approaches in Multi-Cultural Education* Runnymeade Trust, London.

Male, G. (1974) *The Struggle for Power - Who Controls the Schools in England and the U.S.A.* Sage, New York.

Ministry of Education (1963) *English for Immigrants*, HMSO, London.

Litt, E. and Parkinson, M. (1978) *U.S. and U.K. Educational Policy - A Decade of Reform* Praeger Books, New York.

Little, A. and Willey, R. (1981) *Multi-Ethnic Education - The Way Forward* Schools Council, w.p. No. 18, London.

Power J. (1967) *Immigrants in School - A Survey of Administrative Practices* Councils and Education Press, London.

Scarman Report (1981) *The Brixton Disorders. 10th-12th April, 1981.* Report of an Enquiry by Lord Scarman, Cmnd. 8427, HMSO, London.

Select Committee on Race Relations and Immigration (1972-3) *Education* (3 volumes) HMSO, London.

Select Committee on Race Relations and Immigration (1976-7) *The West Indian Community* (3 volumes) HMSO, London.

Tomlinson, S. (1981) "Response of the English Education System to the Children of Immigrant Parentage" in (eds.) C. Bagley-Marrett. *Research in Race and Ethnic Relations* J.A.I. Press, Conneticut.

Troyna, B. (1982) "Ideological and Policy Response to Black Pupils in British Schools" in (ed.) A. Hartnett *The Social Sciences in Educational Studies* Heinemann.

Articles

Killian, L.M. (1979) "School Bussing in Britain" *Harvard Educational Review* Vol. 49, No. 2, pp. 185-206.

Reeves, F. and Chevannes, M. (1981) "The underachievement of Rampton" *Multi-Racial Education*, Vol. 10, No. 1, pp. 35-42.

Stern, V. (1973) "Development in D.E.S. Policy" *New Community* Vol. 3, Winter 1973, pp. 131-134.

Tomlinson, S. (1982) "Inexplicit Policies in Race and Education" *Educational Policy Bulletin*, Vol. 10, No. 1, Spring.

Williams, J. (1981) "Race and Schooling - Some Recent

Contributions" *British Journal of the Sociology of Education*, Vol. 2, No. 2, pp. 221-228.

EDUCATIONAL PERFORMANCE AND ACHIEVEMENT

Books

Bagley, C. (1975) "On the Intellectual Equality of the Races", in (ed.) Verma, G.K. and Bagley, C. *Race and Education Across Cultures*, Heinemann.

Bagley, C., Bart, M. and Wong, J. (1979) "Antecedents of Scholastic Success in West Indian Ten-Year-Olds in London", in (eds.) Verma, G.K. and Bagley, C., *Race Education and Identity*, Macmillan.

Bagley, C. (1982) "Achievement, Behaviour Disorder and Social Circumstances in West Indian Children and Other Minority Groups" in (eds.) Verma, G.K. and Bagley, C. *Self-Esteem, Achievement and Multi-Cultural Education*, Macmillan.

Barnes, J. (1973) *Educational Priority-Curriculum Innovation in London, EPS's*, HMSO, London.

Black Peoples Progressive Association and Redbridge Community Relation Council (1978) *Cause For Concern - West Indian Pupils in Redbridge*, Redbridge.

Coard, B. (1972) *How the West Indian Child is made ESN in the British School System*, New Beacon Books.

Department of Education and Science (1971) *Potential and Progress in a Second Culture* Education Survey, 10, HMSO, London.

Dosanjh, J.S. (1969) *Punjabi Immigrant Children - their Social and Educational Problems in Adjustment. Education Paper No. 10*, Institute of Education, University of Nottingham.

Driver, G. (1979) "Classroom Stress and School Achievement" in (ed.) Khan, V.S. *Minority Families in Britain*, Macmillan.

Driver, G. (1980) *Beyond Underachievement* Commission for Racial Equality, London.

Fuller, M. (1980) "Black Girls in a London Comprehensive School" in (ed.) Deem, R. *Schooling for Womens Work*, Routledge and Kegan Paul.

Ghuman, P. (1975) *The Cultural Context of Thinking - a Comparative Study of Punjabi and English Boys*, N.F.E.R., Slough.

Halsey, A.H. (1972) *Educational Priority - EPA Problems and Policies*, HMSO, London.

Haynes, J. (1971) *Educational Assessment of Immigrant Pupils*, N.F.E.R., Slough.

Hegarty, S. and Lucas, F. (1978) *Able to Learn - the Pursuit of Culture - Fair Assessment*, N.F.E.R., Slough.

Little, A. (1975) "The Educational Achievement of Ethnic

Minority Children in London Schools", in (eds.)
Verma, G.K. and Bagley, C. *Race and Education Across Cultures*, Heinemann.

(ed.) Payne, J. (1974) *Educational Minority - EPA Surveys and Statistics*, Vol. 2, HMSO, London.

Sharpe, S. (1976) *Just Like a Girl*, Penguin.

Stones, E. (1979) "The Colour of Conceptual Learning", in (eds.) Verma, G.K. and Bagley, C. *Race Education and Identity*, Heinemann.

Taylor, M.J. (1981) *Caught Between - A Review of Research into the Education of Pupils of West Indian Origin*, N.F.E.R., Slough.

Tomlinson, S. (1981) *Educational Subnormality: A Study in Decision-Making* Routledge and Kegan Paul.

Vernon, P.E. (1969) *Intelligence and Cultural Environment*, Methuen.

Articles

Ashby, B., Morrison, A. and Butcher, H. (1970) "The Abilities and Attainments of Immigrant Children" *Research in Education*, No. 4.

Bagley, C. (1973) "The Education of Immigrant Children - a Review of Policy and Problems" *British Journal of Social Policy*, Vol. 2, pp. 303-315.

Craft, M. (1980) "The Participation of Ethnic Minorities in Further and Higher Education" *Nuffield Foundation* (unpub.), Oxford.

Driver, G. and Ballard, R. (1979) "Comparing Performance in Multi-Racial Schools - South Asian Pupils at 16 Plus" *New Community*, Vol. 7, No. 2, pp. 143-153.

Essen, J. and Ghodsian, M. (1979) "The Children of Immigrant School Performance", *New Community*, Vol. 7, No. 3, pp. 422-429.

Goldman, R.J. and Taylor, F. (1966) "Coloured Immigrant Children, A Survey of Research Studies and Literature on their Educational Problem and Potential - in Britain", *Educational Research*, Vol. 8, No. 3, pp. 163-183.

Little, A. (1975) "Performance of Children from Ethnic Minority Backgrounds in Primary Schools", *Oxford Review of Education*, Vol. 1, No. 2, pp. 117-135.

Mabey, C. (1981) "Black British Literacy" *Educational Research*, Vol. 23, No. 2, pp. 83-95.

McFie, J. and Thompson, J. (1970) "The Intellectual Abilities of Immigrant Children" *Brit. J. of Educational Psychology*, Vol. 40.

Millins, K. (1981) *Special Access Courses - an evaluation for the C.R.E.* Commission for Racial Equality, London.

Phillips, C.J. (1979) "Educational Under-Achievement in Different Ethnic Groups" *Educational Research*, Vol. 21,

No. 2, pp. 116-129.

Robinson, V. (1980) "The Achievement of Asian Children" *Educational Research*, Vol. 22, No. 2.

Troyna, B. (1978) "Race and Streaming, a Case Study", *Educational Review*, Vol. 30, No. 1, pp. 59-65.

Tomlinson, S. (1978) "West Indian Children and ESN Schooling", *New Community*, Vol. 6, No. 3, pp. 235-242.

Tomlinson, S. (1980) "The Educational Performance of Ethnic Minority Children" *New Community*, Vol. 8, No. 3, pp. 213-234.

Yule, W., Berger, M., Rutter, M. and Yulve, A. (1975) "Children of West Indian Immigrants, Intellectual Performance and Reading Attainment", *J. Child Psychology and Psychiatry*, Vol. 16, pp. 1-17.

LANGUAGE

Books

Brown, D.M. (1979) *Mother-Tongue to English - The Young Child in the Multi-Cultural School*, C.U.P., Cambridge.

Candlin, C. and Derrick, J. (1972) *Language* Community Relations Commission, London.

Campbell-Platt, K. (1978) *Linguistic Minorities in Britain*, Runnymede Trust, London.

Centre for Information in Language Teaching (1976) *Bilingualism and British Education*, London.

Department of Education and Science *A Language for Life* (1975) (The Bullock Report), HMSO, London.

Derrick, J. (1966) *Teaching English to Immigrant Children* N.F.E.R., Slough.

Derrick, J. (1977) *Language Needs of Minority Group Children* N.F.E.R., Slough.

Edwards, V.K. (1979) *The West Indian Language Issue in British Schools*, Routledge and Kegan Paul.

Edwards, V.K. (1980) "Dialect and Reading - a case study of West Indian Children in Britain" in *The Social Psychology of Language* - Institute of Modern Languages, London.

Hestor, H. *et al.* (1977) *English as a Second Language in Multi-Racial Schools*. National Book League, London.

Hornby, P.A. (1977) *Bilingualism - Psychological, Social and Educational Implications* Academic Press, New York.

Khan, V.S. (1978) *Bilingualism and Minority Languages in Britain*, Runnymede Trust, London.

Labov, W. (1973) "The logic of non-standard English" in (ed.) Keddie, N. *Tinker Taylor - the Myth of Cultural Deprivation*, Penguin, Harmondsworth.

Ministry of Education (1963) *English for Immigrants* Pamphlet No. 43, HMSO, London.

Le Page, R.B. (1981) *Caribbean Connections in the Classroom*

Mary Glasgow Language Trust, University of York.

McEwan, E.C., Gipps, C.V. and Sumner, R. (1975) *Language Proficiency in the Multi-Racial Junior School*, N.F.E.R., Slough.

Rosen, H. and Burgess, T. (1980) *Language and Dialects of London School Children* Ward Locks Educational, London.

Schools Council (1967) Working Paper No. 13, *English for the Children of Immigrants*, Evans-Methuen.

Schools Council (1970) Working Paper No. 29 *Teaching English to West Indian Children – The Research Stage of the Project*, Evans-Methuen.

Schools Council (1970) *Scope – an Introductory English Course for Immigrant Children*, Longman, London.

Schools Council (1971) *Scope – Pronunciation for Immigrant Children*, Longman, London.

Stephens, M. (1976) *Linguistic Minorities in Western Europe*, Gomer Press.

Trudgill, P.J. (1978) *Sociolinguistic Patterns in British English*, Arnold, London.

Ward, G.W. (1977) *Deciding What to Teach in English as a Second Language Lesson*, National Association for Multi-Racial Education, Nottingham.

Wilding, J. (1981) *Ethnic Minority Languages in the Classroom*, Leicester Community Relations Council, Leicester.

Articles

Brook, M. (1980) "The Mother-Tongue Issue in Britain – Cultural Diversity or Control?" *British Journal of the Sociology of Education*, Vol. 1, No. 3, pp. 237-256.

Chapman, L. (1980) An Experiment in Mother-tongue Teaching" *Trends in Education*, No. 1.

Cheshire, J. (1981) "Dialect Features and Linguistic Conflict in Schools" *Educational Review*, Vol. 34, No. 1, pp. 54-67.

Edwards, V.K. (1976) "Effects of Dialect on the Comprehension of West Indian Children" *Educational Research*, Vol. 18, No. 2, pp. 83-95.

Edwards, V.K. (1978) "Language Attitudes and Under-performance in West Indian Children" *Educational Review*, Vol. 30, No. 1, pp. 51-58.

Edwards, V.K. (1980) "Black British English – a Bibliographical Essay on the Language of Children of West Indian Origin" *Sage Race Relations Abstracts*, Vol. 5, No. 3/4, pp. 1-26.

Ganguly, S.R. and Ormerod, M.B. (1980) "The Structure and Correlates of Attitudes to English among Pupils of Asian Origin" *Journal of Multi-Lingual and Multi-Cultural Education*, Vol. 1, No. 1, pp. 57-70.

Hestor, H. and Wight, J. (1977) "Language in the Multi-Ethnic Classroom" *Forum*, Vol. 20, No. 1.

Lewis, E.G. (1970) "Immigrants - Their Language and Development" *Trends in Education*, No. 19.

Richmond, J. (1979) "Dialect Features in Mainstream School Writing" *New Approaches in Multi-Racial Education*, Vol. 8, No. 1, pp. 9-15.

Sutcliffe, D. (1976) "Hou dem taak in Bedford Sa" *Multi-Racial School*, Vol. 5, No. 1, pp. 19-24.

Wight, J. (1971) "Dialect in School" *Educational Review*, Vol. 24, No. 1, pp. 47-58.

Wright, J. (1980) "Mother Tongue in British Schools" *The English Magazine*, Vol. 3, Spring.

MULTI-CULTURAL EDUCATION

Books

Afro-Caribbean Education Resource Project (1981) *Images and Reflections - Education and the Afro-Caribbean Child*, Inner London Education Authority, London.

Carby, Hazel V. (1980) *Multi-Cultural Fictions* Centre for Contemporary Cultural Studies, Birmingham race series S.P. No. 58.

(ed.) Code, W. Owen (1978) *World Faiths in Education*, Allen and Unwin.

Childrens Rights Workshop (1975) *Racist and Sexist Images in Childrens Books*, Readers and Writers Publishing Co-op, London. (New Edition 1979).

Elkin, J. (1971) *Books for the Multi-Racial Classroom - India, Pakistan and the West Indies*, Birmingham Public Libraries, Birmingham (2nd Edition 1976).

Goody, J. (1982) "Classroom Interaction in the Multi-Racial School" in (eds.) James, A. and Jeffcoate, *The School in the Multi-Cultural Society*, Harper and Row.

Hicks, D. (1981) *Minorities - a Teachers Resource - Book for the Multi-Ethnic Curriculum*, Heineman Educational Books.

Hicks, D. (1982) "Bias in School Books. Messages from the Ethnocentric Curriculum" in (eds.) James A. and Jeffcoate R. *The School in the Multi-Cultural Society*, Harper and Row.

Klein, G. and Jones, C. (1980) *Assessing Childrens Books for a Multi-Ethnic Society. Practical Guide for Primary and Secondary Schools*. Centre for Urban Educational Studies, London.

Jeffcoate, R. (1979) *Positive Image Towards a Multi-Racial Curriculum*, Writers and Readers Publishing Co-op/Chamelon.

Klein, G. (1982) *Resources for Teaching in Multi-Cultural Britain*, Schools Council Publication, London.

Lynch, J. (1981) "Educational Theory and the Practice of Multi-Cultural Education" in *Teaching in the Multi-Cultural School*, Ward Lock Educational.

Masemann, Vandra L. "Comparative Perspectives on Multi-
    Cultural Education" in (ed.) Bodnar, J. Masemann, Rist,
    R.C. *Multi-Cultural Education - Perspectives for the
    1980s*, Occasional Paper of Dept. of Social Foundations
    and Comparative Education Centre, Buffalo, New York.
Mullard, C. (1982) "Black Kids in White Schools" in (ed.)
    Tierney, J. *Race, Migration and Schooling*, Holt, Saunders.
Proctor, C. (1975) *Racist Textbooks*, National Union of
    Students, London.
Stenhouse, L (1975) "Problems of Research in Teaching about
    Race Relations" in (ed.) Vernon, G.K. and Bagley, C.
    Race and Education Across Cultures, Heinemann.
Schools Council (1981) *Education for a Multi-Racial Society
    Curriculum and Content 5-13*, London.
Verma, G.K. and Bagley, C. (1981) "Social, Personal, and
    Academic Adjustment of Ethnic Minority Pupils in
    British Schools" in (ed.) Bhatnager, J. *Educating
    Immigrants*, Croom-Helm.

Articles

Cole, W. Owen (1981) "Multi Cultural Aspects of Religious
    Education" *Education 3-13*, Vol. 9, No. 2, pp. 9-13.
Dodgeson, P. and Stewart, D. (1981) "Multi-culturalism or
    Anti-Racist Teaching - a Question of Alternatives"
    Multi-Racial Education, Vol. 9, No. 3, pp. 41-51.
Glendenning, F.J. (1971) "Racial Stereotyping in History
    Textbooks" *Race Today*, Vol. 3, No. 2, pp. 52-54.
Gundara, J.S. (1980) "Multi-Cultural Education and the
    Community" *New Approaches in Multi-Cultural Education*,
    Vol. 8, No. 2, pp. 1-3.
Hall, S. (1980) "Teaching Race" *Multi-Racial Education*, Vol.
    9, No. 1, pp. 1-14.
Hicks, D. (1981) "Teaching about Other Peoples: How Biased
    are School Books" *Education 3-13*, Vol. 9, No. 2,
    pp. 14-19.
James, A. (1979) "The Multi-Cultural Curriculum" *New
    Approaches in Multi-Racial Education*, Vol. 8, No. 1,
    pp. 1-5.
Jeffcoate, R. (1976) "Curriculum Planning in a Multi-Racial
    Education" *Educational Research*, Vol. 18, No. 3,
    pp. 192-200.
Jeffcoate, R. (1977) "Childrens Racial Ideas and Feelings"
    English in Education, Vol. 2, No. 1, pp. 32-46.
Jeffcoate, R. (1979) "A Multi-Cultural Curriculum - Beyond
    the Orthodoxy" *Trends in Education*, No. 4, pp. 8-12.
Jeffcoate, R. (1981) "Evaluating the Multi-Cultural
    Curriculum - Pupils Perspectives" *Journal of
    Curriculum Studies*, Vol. 13, No. 1.
McClean, Martin (1980) "Cultural Autonomy and the Education
    of Ethnic Minority Groups" *Brit. J. of Educational*

Studies, Vol. 28, No. 1, Feb. pp. 7-12.

Mullard, C. (1981) "The Social Context and Meaning of Multi-Cultural Education" *Educational Analysis*, Vol. 3, No. 1, pp. 117-140.

Parkinson, J.P. and McDonald, B. (1972) "Teaching Race Neutrally" *Race*, Vol. 13, No. 3, pp. 299-307.

Preiswerk, R. and Perrot, D. (1980) *The Slant of the Pen - Racism in Childrens Books*, World Council of Churches, London.

Phillips-Bell, M. (1981) "Multi-Cultural Education - What is it?" *Multi-Racial Education*, Vol. 10, No. 1, pp. 21-26.

Sikes, P.J. and Sheard, D.J.S. (1978) "Teaching for Better Race Relations" *Cambridge Journal of Education*, Vol. 8, No. 2/3, pp. 165-172.

Townshend, J.R. (1976) "Racism and Sexism in Childrens Books" *New Community*, Vol. 5, Summer, pp. 157-160.

Worral, M. (1978) "Multi-Racial Britain and the Third World. Tensions and Approaches in the Classroom" *The New Era*, Vol. 59, No. 2.

Williams, Jenny (1979) "Perspective on the Multi-Cultural Curriculum" *The Social Science Teacher*, Vol. 8, No. 4, pp. 126-128.

Zec, P. (1980) "Multi-Cultural Education - What Kind of Relativism is Possible" *Journal of Philosophy of Education*, Vol. 14, No. 1, pp. 77-85.

TEACHERS

Books

Bristol National Union of Teachers (1980) *After the Fire - a Report on Education in St. Pauls, Bristol, and Multi-Ethnic Education in Avon, Bristol.*

Chambers, P. (1981) "Teacher Education for a Multi-Cultural Society: Courses at Bradford College" in (ed.) Megarry J. *Education of Minorities*, World Yearbook of Education 1981, Kogar Page.

Cherrington, D. and Giles, R. (1981) "Present Provision in Initial Teacher Training" in (ed.) Craft, M. *Teaching in a Multi-Cultural Society*, Falmer Press, Brighton.

Community Relations Commission/Association of Teachers in Colleges and Departments of Education (1974) (reprinted 1978) *Teacher Education for a Multi-Cultural Society*, London.

Craft, M. (ed.) (1981) *Teaching in a Multi-Cultural Society* Falmer Press, Brighton

Department of Education and Science (1979) *Developments in the B.Ed. Degree*, HMSO, London.

Eggleston, J. (1981) "Present Provision in In-Series Training" in (ed.) Craft, M. *Teaching in a Multi-Cultural Society*, Falmer Press, Brighton.

Gibbes, N. (1980) *West Indian Teachers Speak Out*,
    Lewisham C.R.C. and the Caribbean Teachers
    Association, Lewisham, London.
Giles, R. (1977) *The West Indian Experience in British
    Schools*, Heinemann.
Hill, D. (1976) *Teaching in Multi-Racial Schools*, Methuen.
Hobbs, M. (1976) *Teaching in a Multi-Racial Society*,
    Association of Christian Teachers, London.
(ed.) Lynch, J. (1981) *Teaching in the Multi-Cultural School*,
    Ward Lock Educational.
McNeal, J. and Rogers, M. (1971) *The Multi-Racial School*,
    Penguin, Harmondsworth.
National Union of Teachers (1967) *The Education of Immigrants*,
    London.
National Union of Teachers (1979) *Guidelines for Teachers on
    Racial Stereotypes in Textbooks and Learning Materials*,
    London.
Verma, G.K. and Bagley, C. (1982) "Issues in Multi-Cultural
    Education" in (eds.) Verma, G.K. and Bagley, C.
    Self-Concept, Achievement and Multi-Cultural Education,
    Macmillan.

Articles

Brittan, E. (1976) "Multi-Racial Education.   Teacher Opinion
    on Aspects of School Life. 1. Changes in Curriculum
    and School Organisation" *Education Research*, Vol. 18,
    No. 2, pp. 96-107.
Brittan, E. (1976) "Multi-Racial Education.   Teacher Opinion
    on Aspects of School Life. 2. Pupils and Teachers"
    Educational Research, Vol. 18, No. 3, pp. 182-191.
Centre for Disadvantage (1980) *Enquiry into the Implications
    of Initial and In-Service Education on Educational
    Disadvantage* (unpublished report by Jones and
    Streetporter), Manchester.
Driver, G. (1977) "Cultural Competence, Social Power and
    School Achievement - West Indian Secondary School
    Pupils in the Midlands" *New Community*, Vol. 5, No. 4,
    pp. 353-359.
Green, P. (1981) "Teachers Racial Attitudes and Ethnic
    Minority Children" (unpub.) *Conference Paper*, Cambridge,
    June.
Latham, J. (1982) "Exceptional Children or Exceptional
    Teachers: An Alternative Policy for Teacher Education
    in a Multi-Cultural Society" *Journal of Further and
    Higher Education*, Vol. 6, No. 2.
Maxwell, M. (1969) "Violence in the Toilets - the
    Experiences of a Black School Teacher in Brent Schools"
    Race Today, Jan. pp. 135-139.
Stanton, M. (1970) "Teachers Views on Racial Prejudice"
    English for Immigrants, Vol. 4, pp. 15-19.

Willey, R. (1975) "Teacher Training for a Multi-Cultural
    Society in the U.K." *International Review of
    Education*, Vol. 21, pp. 335-345.
Tomlinson, S. (1980) "Multi-Racial Schooling - Parents and
    Teachers Views" *Education 3-13*, Vol. 9, No. 1, pp. 16-20.

HOME-BACKGROUND AND HOME-SCHOOL RELATIONS

Books

Allen, S. (1971) *New Minorities. Old Conflicts. Asian and
    West Indian Migrants to Britain*, Random House, New York.
Anwar, M. (1979) *The Myth of Return*, Heinemann Educational
    Books.
Dahya, B. (1974) *Urban Ethnicity*, Tavistock, London.
Davison, R.B. (1966) *Black British Immigrants to England*,
    Oxford University Press.
Dench, G. (1975) *The Maltese in London*, Routledge and Kegan
    Paul.
Desai, R. (1963) *Indian Immigrants in Britain*, Oxford
    University Press.
Centre for Information on Language Teaching and Research (1981)
    Teaching Chinese Children - a Teachers Guide, Nuffield
    Foundation, London.
Commission for Racial Equality (1975) *Who Minds - a Study of
    Working Mothers and Child-minders in Ethnic Minority
    Communities*, London.
Cheetham, J. (1972) *Social Work with Immigrants*, Routledge
    and Kegan Paul.
Cheetham, J. *et al.* (1982) *Social and Community Work in a
    Multi-Racial Society*, Harper and Row.
Ellis, J. (1978) *West African Families in Britain*, Routledge
    and Kegan Paul.
Foner, N. (1979) Jamaican Farewell *Jamaican Migrants in
    London*, Routledge and Kegan Paul.
Fitzherbert, K. (1967) *West Indian Children in London*, G. Bell
    and Sons, London.
Helwig, A.W. (1980) *Sikhs in Britain*, Oxford University Press.
Hill, C. (1970) *Immigration and Integration - A Study of the
    Settlement of Coloured Minorities in Britain*, Pergamon
    Press, Oxford.
Hood, J. *et al.* (1970) *The Children of West Indian Immigrants*,
    Institute of Race Relations, London.
James, A. (1974) *Sikh Children in Britain*, Oxford University
    Press.
Jeffery, P. (1976) *Migrants and Refugees - Moslim and
    Christian Pakistani Families in Bristol*, Cambridge
    University Press.
Khan, V.S. (1979) *Minority Families in Britain - Support and
    Stress*, Macmillan.
Khan, V.S. (1982) "The Role of the Culture of Dominance in

Structuring the Experience of Ethnic Minorities" in
(ed.) Husband, C. *Race in Britain*, Hutchinson University
Press.

Krausz, E. (1971) *Ethnic Minorities in Britain*, MacGibbon and
Kee, London.

Lawrence, D. (1974) *Black Migrants. White Natives.* Cambridge
University Press.

Lobo, Edwin de H. (1978) *Children of Immigrants to Britain -
their Health and Social Problems*, Hodder and Stoughton.

Manchester Diocesan Council for Education (1981) *Church,
School, Education and Islam*, Manchester.

Morrish, I. (1971) *The Background of Immigrant Children*,
Allen and Unwin.

Ny Kwee Choo (1968) *The Chinese in London*, Oxford University
Press.

(ed.) Oakley, R. (1968) *New Backgrounds - the Immigrant Child
and the School*, Oxford University Press.

Osborne, B. (1975) *Working Mothers and Child-Minding in the
Central District of Lewisham*, Lewisham Council for
Community Relations, London.

Peach, C. (1968) *West Indian Migration to Britain*, Oxford
University Press.

Pollack, M. (1972) *Todays Three Year Olds in London*,
Heinemann.

Rex. J. and Moore, R. (1967) *Race Community and Conflict -
A Study of Sparkbrook*, Oxford University Press.

Tomlinson, S. (1980) "Ethnic Minority Parents and Education"
in (eds.) Craft, M., Raynor, J. and Cohen, L.
Linking Home and School (3rd edition), Harper and Row.

Watson, J.L. (1977) *Between Two Cultures - Migrants and
Minorities in Britain*, Blackwell, Oxford.

Union of Muslim Organisations of the U.K. and Eire (1978)
*National Muslim Educational Council - Background
Papers*, Union of Muslim Organizations, London.

Articles

Allen, S. (1979) "Pre-School Children. Ethnic Minorities in
Britain" *New Community*, Vol. 7, No. 2, pp. 135-142.

Bagley, C. (1976) "Behavioural Deviance in Ethnic Minority
Children - a Review of Published Studies" *New Community*,
Vol. 5, No. 7, pp. 230-237.

Dahya, B. (1973) "Pakistanis in Britain - Transients or
Settlers" *Race*, Vol. 5, pp. 246-247.

Foner, N. (1975) "The Meaning of Education to Jamaicans at
Home and in School" *New Community*, Vol. 4, pp. 195-202.

George, V. and Millerson, G. (1967) "The Cypriot Community
in London" *Race*, Vol. 8, pp. 277-292.

Ghuman, P.A.S. (1980) "Punjabi Parents and English Education"
Educational Research, Vol. 22, No. 2, pp. 121-130.

Ghuman, P. (1980) "Bhattra Sikhs in Cardiff - Family and

Kinship Organizations" *New Community*, Vol. 8, No. 3, pp. 308-316.

Ghuman, P. and Gallop, R. (1981) "Educational Attitudes of Bengali Families in Cardiff" *Journal of Multilingual and Multi-Cultural Development*, Vol. 2, No. 2.

Gullick, M. (1977) "The Educational Background of Vincentian Immigrants to Britain" *New Community*, Vol. 5, No. 4, pp. 405-410.

Hahlo, K.E. (1980) "Profile of a Gujerati Community in Bolton" *New Community*, Vol. 8, No. 3, pp. 295-307.

Iqubal, M. (1976) "Education and Islam in Britain - A Muslim View" *New Community*, Vol. 5, Autumn, pp. 397-404.

Jones, D. (1979) "The Chinese in Britain - Origins and Development of a Community" *New Community*, Vol. 7, No. 3, pp. 397-402.

Khan, V.S. (1976) "Pakistani Women in Britain" *New Community*, Vol. 5, pp. 99-108.

Khan, V.S. (1981) "Co-operation Between School, Parents and the Communities" *Educational Research Workshop on Education and Migrant Workers*, Dillingen, Holland.

Noor, N.S. and Khalsa, S.S. (1978) *A Survey of Parents Views and Attitudes*, Indian Workers Association, Wolverhampton.

Oakley, R. (1970) "The Cypriots in Britain Today" *Race Today*, No. 2, February, pp. 99-102.

Pryce, K. (1978) "Life-styles of West Indians in Bristol" *New Community*, Vol. 6, No. 3, pp. 207-217.

Rutter, M. *et al.* (1974) "Children of West Indian Immigrants. 1. Rates of Behavioural Deviance and Psychiatric Disorder" *Journal of Child Psychology and Psychiatry*, Vol. 15.

Watson, J.L. (1977) "Chinese Emigrant Ties to the Home Community" *New Community*, Vol. 5, No. 4, pp. 343-352.

Werbner, P. (1981) "Manchester Pakistanis. Life Styles, Ritual, and the Making of Social Distinctions" *New Community*, Vol. 9, No. 2, pp. 216-229.

Wilson, A. (1981) "The Mother in the Inter-Racial Family" *New Community*, Vol. 9, No. 2, pp. 208-215.

YOUTH

Books

Allen, S. and Smith, C. (1975) "Minority Group Experience of the Transition from Education to Work" in (ed.) P. Brannen *Entering the World of Work*, HMSO, London.

All Faiths for One Race (1978) *Talking Blues - The Black Community Speaks About its Relations with the Police*, AFFOR, Birmingham.

Anwar, M. (1976) *Between Two Cultures - A Study of the Relationships Between Generations in the Asian. Community in Britain*, Community Relations Commission,

London.

Ballard, C. (1979) "Conflict, Continuity and Change - Second Generation South Asians" in (eds.) Khan, V.S. *Minority Families in Britain*, Macmillan.

Beetham, D. (1967) *Immigrant School Leavers and the Youth Employment Service*, Institute of Race Relations, London.

Brah, A. (1978) "Age Race and Power Relations - the Case of South Asian Youth in Britain" in (eds.) Day, M. and Marsland, P. *Black Kids. White Kids. What Hope?* National Youth Bureau, Leicester.

Brooks, D. and Singh, K. (1978) *Aspirations Versus Opportunities - Asian and White School-leavers in the Midlands*, Walsall CRC and Leicester CRC.

Cashmore, E. (1979) *Rastaman - the Rastafari Movement in England*, Routledge and Kegan Paul.

Centre for Contemporary Studies (1981) *Nazis in the Playground*, London.

Commission for Racial Equality (1976) *A Second Chance - Further Education in Multi-Racial Areas*, London.

Commission for Racial Equality (1980) *Youth in Multi-Racial Society - The Fire Next Time*, London.

Community Relations Commission (1974) *Unemployment and Homelessness*, London.

Day, M. and Marsland, D. (1978) *Black Kids White Kids - What Hope?* National Youth Bureau, Leicester.

Dickenson, L. *et al.* (1975) *The Immigrant School-Leaver - A Study of Pakistani Pupils in Glasgow*, N.F.E.R. Slough.

Downing, J. (1980) *Now do you know*, World Council of Churches Publication, London.

Garrison, L. (1979) *Black Youth, Rastafarianism and the Identity Crisis*, Afro-Caribbean Education Project, Inner London Education Authority, London.

Hall, S. *et al.* (1978) *Policing the Crisis*, Macmillan, London.

(Hunt Report) (1970) *Young Immigrants and the Youth Service*, HMSO, London.

John, G. (1972) *Race in the Inner City*, Runnymede Trust, London.

John, G. (1978) "Present and Future Policy for Black Youth" in (eds.) Day, M. and Marsland, D. *Black Kids. White Kids. What Hope?* National Youth Bureau, Leicester.

Lee, G. and Wrench, J. (1981) *In Search of a Skill - Ethnic Minority Youth and Apprenticeships*, Commission for Racial Equality, London.

Nottingham Community Relations Commission (1980) *Half a Chance - Young Blacks in Nottingham*, Nottingham CRC.

Pryce, K. (1979) *Endless Pressure*, Penguin, Harmondsworth.

Race and Class Pamphlet No. 6 (1979) *Police Against Black People*, Institute of Race Relations, London.

Scarman Report (1981) *The Brixton Disorders 10th-12th April 1981*, Report of an Enquiry by the Lord Scarman, Cmnd. 8427, HMSO, London.

Taylor, J. (1976) *The Half-Way Generation*, N.F.E.R. Slough.

Troyna, B. (1978) *Rastafarianism, Reggae and Racism*, National
    Association for Multi-Racial Education, Derby.
Troyna, B. and Smith, D. (1982) *Race, School and the Labour
    Market*, National Youth Bureau, Leicester.
Weinreich, P. (1979) "Ethnicity and Adolescent Identity
    Conflicts" in (ed.) Khan, V.S. *Minority Families in
    Britain*, Macmillan.

Articles

Bhatti, F.M. (1978) "Young Pakistanis in Britain - Educational
    Needs and Problems" *New Community*, Vol. 6, No. 3,
    pp. 243-247.
Brah, A. (1978) "South Asian Teenagers in Southall - Their
    Perceptions of Marriage, Family and Ethnic Identity"
    New Community, Vol. 6, No. 3, pp. 197-206.
Campbell, H. (1980) "Rastafari - Culture of Resistance" *Race
    and Class*, Vol. 22, No. 1, pp. 1-22.
Dhondy, F. (1982) "Teaching Young Blacks" in (eds.) James, A.
    and Jeffcoate, R. *Teaching in the Multi-Cultural
    School*, Harper and Row, London.
Figueroa, P.M.E. (1975) "The Employment Prospects of West
    Indian School Leavers" *Social and Economic Studies*,
    Vol. 23, pp. 216-232.
Fowler, R., Littlewood, B. and Madigan, R. (1977) "Immigrant
    School Leavers and the Search for Work" *Sociology*,
    Vol. 11, No. 1, pp. 65-86.
Gaskell, G. and Smith, P. (1981) "'Alienated' Black Youth -
    An Investigation of Conventional Wisdom Explanations"
    New Community, Vol. 9, No. 2, pp. 182-193.
Gilroy, P. (1982) "You can't Fool the Youths, Race and Class
    Formation in the 1980's" *Race and Class*, Vol. 23,
    No. 2/3, pp. 207-222.
Gupta, Y.P. (1977) "Educational Aspirations of Asian
    Immigrant and English School Leavers" *British Journal
    of Sociology*, June 1977, pp. 185-198.
Louden, D. (1978) "Self-esteem and the Laws of Control.
    Some Findings on Immigrant Adolescents in Britain"
    New Community, Vol. 6, No. 3, pp. 218-234.
Moore, D. (1979) "A Second Generation Immigrants View of
    Society" *Trends in Education*, No. 4.
Murdock, G. and Troyna, B. (1981) "Recruiting Racists.
    White Youths and the Radical Right" *Youth in Society*,
    Vol. 60, November.
Office of Population Censuses and Survey *Young Peoples
    Employment Study*, Preliminary Report No. 4, OPCS,
    London.
Peggie, A.C.W. (1979) "Minority Youth Politics in Southall"
    New Community, Vol. 7, No. 2, pp. 170-177.
Sharma, S.M. (1980) "Perceptions of Political Institutions
    Among Asian and English Adolescents in Britain" *New*

Community, Vol. 8, No. 3, pp. 240-247.

Thompson, M. (1974) "The Second Generation - Punjabi or English" *New Community*, Vol. 3, No. 3, pp. 242-248.

Troyna, B. (1979) "Differential Commitments to Ethnic Identity by Black Youths in Britain" *New Community*, Vol. 7, No. 3, pp. 406-414.

The following organizations publish research, materials, and information concerning the education of ethnic minority children in Britain:

Afro-Caribbean Educational Resource Project,
275, Kennington Lane,
London SE11.

All London Teachers against Facism and Racism (ALTARF)
c/o Lambeth Teachers Centre,
Santley Street,
London SW4.

Birmingham Polytechnic,
International Centre for Multi-Cultural Education,
Westbourne Road,
Birmingham B15.
Journal   *Multi-Cultural Education Abstracts*

Department of Multi-Cultural Studies
Bradford College,
Bradford,
West Yorkshire.

Centre for Multi-Cultural Education,
Institute of Education,
Univeristy of London,
26 Bedford Way,
London W1N.

Centre for Urban Educational Studies,
34 Aberdeen Park,
London N.5
Newsheet   *Junction*

Commission for Racial Equality (CRE)   Formerly the Community
10-12 Allington Street   Relations Commission
London
SW1E 5EH
Journal   *New Community*
Paper   *New Equals*
Newsheet   *Education Journal*

RACE, CLASS AND EDUCATION IN BRITAIN

Institute of Race Relations,
247, Pentonville Road,
London N1
Journals   *Race and Class*
              Race Today

Issues in Race and Education,
11 Carleton Gardens,
Brecknock Road,
London N19
Journal   *Issues in Race and Education*

National Association for Multi-Racial Education
86, Station Road,
Mickleover,
Derby
DE3 5FP
Journal   *Multi-Racial Education* (Formerly *New Approaches*
                                in Multi-Racial Education)

National Foundation for Education Research,
The Mere,
Upton Park,
Slough,
Berks.
SL1 2PQ.
Journal   *Educational Research*

National Muslim Educational Council,
c/o Union of Muslim Organizations, 30 Baker Street,
London W1M.

Policy Studies Institute,
1-2 Castle Lane, London SW1E

Runnymede Trust,
62 Chandos Place, London WC2N
Newsheet   *Runnymede Trust Bulletin*

Schools Council, 160 Great Portland Street, London W1N 6LL.

Social Science Research Council, Unit of Ethnic Relations,
University of Aston, St. Peter's College,
Saltley,
Birmingham 5.

West Indian World (Newspaper for West Indians in Britain)
Lenmond Publishing Limited,
85 Harrow Road,
London NW10.

233

AUTHOR INDEX